THE FRAGILE EMPIRE

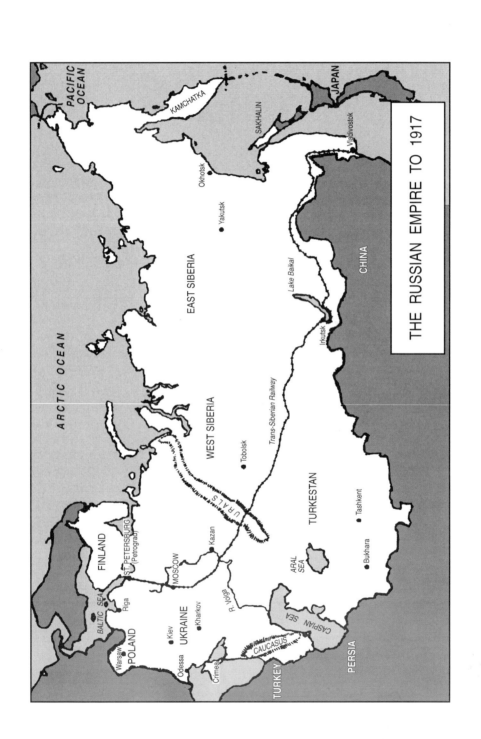

THE RUSSIAN EMPIRE TO 1917

THE FRAGILE EMPIRE
A History of Imperial Russia

Alexander Chubarov

Continuum
New York · London

2001

The Continuum International Publishing Group Inc
370 Lexington Avenue, New York, NY 10017

The Continuum International Publishing Group Ltd
The Tower Building, 11 York Road, London SE1 7NX

Printed in the United States of America

Library of Congress Cataloging-in-Publication Data
Chubarov, Alexander.
   The fragile empire : a history of Imperial Russia / Alexander
Chubarov.
     p. cm.
   Includes bibliographical references and index.
   ISBN 0-8264-1308-0 (pbk)
   1. Russia – History –1689-1801. Russia – History – 1801-1917.
I. Title. II. Title: History of Imperial Russia.
DK127.C5 1999
947 – dc21   99-32919

Grateful acknowledgment is made to Random House, Inc., for permission to reprint "To Chaadayev" from *The Works of Alexander Pushkin*, edited by Avrahm Yarmolinsky. Copyright © 1936 and renewed 1964 by Random House, Inc. Reprinted by permission of Random House, Inc.

Contents

Preface

Perhaps there is no other country in which the past weighs so heavily on the present and the future as it does in Russia. Russian history is never simply the account of vanished epochs but a powerful force molding the country's destiny. With the collapse of the vast and largely unsuccessful communist experiment, which began with the Revolution of 1917, the people of Russia, and in particular its political and cultural elites, are increasingly reexamining the country's prerevolutionary experience. The tsarist past has caught up with Russia's present with a vengeance, as if the seventy-four-year-old Soviet period had never been. Whether in reviving the name St. Petersburg, or reestablishing tsarist state symbols, or resurrecting a national assembly under the old name of the State Duma, or honoring the remains of the last tsarist family by laying them to rest at Peter and Paul Fortress in the former imperial capital, or even debating the restoration of monarchy in Russia, the old regime is still very much with us.

This book reexamines Russia's imperial past from the reign of Peter the Great, the founder of the great empire, until the collapse of tsarism in 1917. Peter the Great's controversial Reform pioneered Russia's process of modernization and "Westernization" and, at the same time, reinforced the oppressive and despotic character of the state, which he inherited from the Muscovite tsars. The Reform sowed the seeds of tensions and contradictions that would, in the end, tear the tsarist empire apart. Yet it also created the conditions for the appearance of new liberalizing and Westernizing trends and reform policies that contributed in subsequent reigns to a gradual emancipation of society from the tight control of the state. By focusing on the key reigns, personalities, and events of the Imperial period, this book ponders the big paradox of Russian history, aptly expressed in the famous phrase of Vasili Klyuchevsky. To the outstanding Russian historian, "the conjunction of despotism and liberty, of civilization and serfdom" appeared to be a puzzle — one that remained unsolved in Russia even into the twentieth century.

The significance of the tsarist experience has been brought into a sharp relief with the dissolution of the Soviet Union. Russia's current reform is the dawn of a new cycle in the series of the attempts at modernization, inaugurated by Peter and continued with varying degree of success and determination by Catherine the Great and Alexander I, Alexander II and Nicholas II. The present attempt is in many respects a continuation of the processes of transformation that were started under the old regime but then aborted under the communists. It seeks to put Russia back on the path of evolution toward a constitutional system of government, an economy based on private ownership, and a civil society more independent from the state. The irony of history is that the tsarist experience, which under the Soviet authorities was portrayed as entirely negative, is now more relevant to Russia's current predicament and incomparably more useful than the seventy-odd-year legacy of the communist project, which seems to have led the country into a historical cul-de-sac.

This book seeks to provide an interpretation of the immediate predecessor of the Soviet empire not in terms of what happened after the collapse of tsarism in 1917, but as it was: as a clearly identifiable stage in the development of the Russian state with its distinctive political, social, economic, and ideological aspects, and in the entirety of its often irreconcilable contradictions and historical paradoxes. Yet so compelling is the relevance of the tsarist past to Russia's current transition that it is difficult to resist the temptation to draw parallels with the present situation.

•

Many thanks to Dr. John Warden, who read a draft of the book and whose comments are much appreciated. I am most grateful for the secretarial assistance of Inna Petrenko. The editorial advice of Frank Oveis of the Continuum Publishing Company has been most helpful.

Finally, the successful completion of this book depended on the willing support of my wife, Marianna, and my son, Eugene.

Introduction

Pre-Petrine Russia

Geopolitical Evolution of the Russian State

The Russian Empire grew out of the Grand Principality of Muscovy, which had come to dominate other Russian principalities due to the success of Moscow grand princes in gathering the fragmented Russian territories into a unified state. Muscovy itself was once a small northeasterly corner of an earlier entity, the Grand Principality of Kiev, also known as the Kievan Rus, which is believed to have been the first Russian state and the cradle of the three branches of the East Slavs: the Great Russians, Ukrainians, and White Russians (or Belorussians).

The Kievan Rus emerged in the ninth century, and its role in the history of Eastern Europe is comparable to that of the Carolingian Empire in Western Europe. It appeared at the time of the active process of state-building over the vast expanse of northern, central, and eastern Europe and, like most other barbarian kingdoms, rose to civilized status by adopting Christianity as its state religion in 988. By that time Christianity had already spread to the territories of the South Slavs and to the Czech and Polish lands inhabited by the West Slavs. Practically at the same time as its adoption by the Kievan Rus, Christianity was adopted in Hungary, Denmark, Norway, and Sweden.

In contrast to central and eastern Europe, however, Kiev's official religion was not the Christianity of the Latin world, but of the Greek world of Byzantium. The main reason for the adoption of the eastern form of Christianity, known also as Orthodox Christianity, was that the Kievan Rus maintained close cultural, economic, and political links with its powerful southern neighbor, the Byzantine Empire, with its center in Constantinople. The conversion to Orthodox Christianity and the subsequent adoption of a written language from Bulgaria, based on Greek and Hebrew alphabets, further strengthened Kiev's southern orientation and led to a gradual cultural separation from its West Slavic neighbors.

The Kievan Rus state expanded to a considerable size and was able to establish links with Western Europe to complement its southern ori-

EVOLUTION OF RUSSIAN STATEHOOD

9th–11th centuries	Kievan Rus
11th–15th centuries	Political Fragmentation of the Russian Lands
1240–1480	Mongol yoke
1462–1682	Muscovite state
1682–1917	Imperial Russia
1917–1991	Soviet Russia
1992–	Russian Federation

entation. By the end of the twelfth century, however, the Kievan Rus had fragmented into smaller feudal principalities. In 1237 the Mongols, led by Batu, a grandson of the great Mongol leader Genghis Khan, were able to exploit this fragmentation, invaded the Russian lands, and established their lordship over them. This severed Russia's links with Western Europe and with the South. Only in 1480 were the Mongols finally expelled from Russia. Their legacy of 240 years was the introduction of a degree of barbarism into Russian life and a relative separation of Russia from the rest of Europe. This legacy lasted for centuries after 1480.

By the late fifteenth century Moscow emerged as the capital of the fledgling centralizing state that had successfully brought under its control formerly disunited Russian lands. In contrast to Western Europe, where flourishing towns and trade links became the cementing force that bound the edifice of national states, the unification of the Russian lands around Moscow proceeded mainly under the pressure of external political factors such as the necessity of achieving national independence from the Mongols. Ultimately, it was the military-political power wielded by the Moscow grand princes, rather than the development of economic ties between Russian principalities, that proved to be a decisive factor in the rebuilding of a Russian unified state and repelling of the Mongols.

The freedom from the Mongol yoke did not bring with it an automatic return of Russia to the mainstream of European civilization. After the final schism of the churches in the early fifteenth century, Muscovy regarded the West with deep suspicion as a world given over to the "Latin heresy." Militarized by its two-century struggle against the Mongols and infused with the messianic zeal of spreading the "true" Christianity, the autocratic Muscovite state began to expand in a determined fashion. By 1600, it had grown twelvefold to become the largest state in Europe.

In the early seventeenth century, having survived "the Time of Troubles" — the devastating period of the dynastic crisis and the Polish-Swedish intervention — Russia proceeded to rebuild its statehood under the leadership of the new dynasty of the Romanovs, established in 1613. By the middle of that century, under the second of Romanov tsars, Alexis, it acquired Siberia in the east, while in the southwest it reestablished its authority over the Ukraine, which sought protection of an Orthodox nation against the Roman Catholic Poles. In the eighteenth century Peter I and Catherine the Great annexed the present-day Baltic states and a substantial share of Poland, thus giving the Russian Empire its basic modern form. To consolidate this development and to assert the rising status of Russia among the European powers, Peter took the Imperial title of old East Rome (Byzantium), thereby claiming for the Muscovite state the mantle of the successor to the Roman Empire. At Peter's command Moscow had to yield its status of the capital city to the new imperial capital of St. Petersburg.

By 1800 Russia had conquered the Crimea, thus gaining access to the Black Sea. By the early nineteenth century it had completed the incorporation of the whole of the Transcaucasian region, including the Azerbaidjanian khanates, Georgia, and Eastern Armenia. During the Napoleonic Wars Finland and Bessarabia were seized. Russia annexed Vladivostok on the Pacific coast by 1860 and the Kazakh lands and central Asia by 1885.

By the second half of the nineteenth century, the Russian Empire's borders had assumed their settled contours. Russia had spread its authority over vast territories, stretching from the Danube's estuary and the Vistula in the west to the Pacific Ocean in the east, from the Eurasian tundra in the north to the borders of Turkey, Iran, Afghanistan, and China in the south. In its territory and population Russia was the biggest world power. Its area totaled 21.3 million square kilometers; its population, according to the general census of 1897, was 128 million (178 million by 1914). In 1917 the Bolsheviks inherited from the tsars the world's largest land mass and one of the most populous countries.

Russia's expansion and, in particular, the incorporation of territories that lagged behind in socioeconomic development or were culturally different conflicted with the country's historic goal of catching up with the advanced countries of the West. Only by straining all its economic, demographic, and military resources could it sustain the status of a great power capable of playing an influential role in the international arena and controlling the numerous nationalities that populated its huge territory. The territorial expansion therefore was a factor that did more to constrain, rather than advance, the economic and sociopolitical development of Russia.

Key Factors of Russian Historical Development

Russian history is commonly perceived, by Russians and foreigners alike, as something basically different from the norms and standards of the West. This popular view of Russia's "otherness" is epitomized in Winston Churchill's famous characterization of Russia as "a riddle wrapped in a mystery inside an enigma."

Historians point to a set of factors that have exercised a profound influence on the course of Russian history for many a century and have contributed to its lasting distinctiveness in comparison with Western societies.

Five factors appear to have been of a particularly profound significance and will be considered here:

- the ecological environment and climate;

- the geopolitical factor;

- the religious factor;

- the distinctive social organization;

- the specific political regime.

Ecological Environment and Climate

The influence of the harsh and inhospitable climate on the life of the people inhabiting the vast expanses of the snowbound Eurasian landmass is recognized by most commentators who have studied characteristics of the Russian historical process. Historians note, for instance, that in central Russia, which constituted the historical core of the Russian state, the annual cycle of agricultural work was unusually short: just 125–130 working-days from mid-April to mid-September. The soil was poor and required careful cultivation, for which the Russian peasant simply did not have enough time. Constrained by time, weather, and primitive agricultural methods, the peasant had to work day and night with little sleep or rest, using the labor of all available members of his family, including children, women, and the elderly. And even in the best of times the soil yielded a harvest that barely covered the basics. By contrast, farmers in Western Europe enjoyed the advantage of a much longer growing season. The winter break in farming in some countries of Western Europe was fairly short (December and January), and therefore the arable land could be cultivated more thoroughly.

This fundamental difference in farming conditions between Russia and Western Europe prevailed throughout the centuries until modern times. Poor crop yields and the dependence of peasant labor on the weather conditioned the extraordinary tenacity of communal institutions in the Russian countryside, which provided a collectivist safety net and a guarantee of survival for the mass of the rural population. Centuries-long experience of life and work in such adverse conditions had taught peasants to devise a whole set of measures to help those members of the community who were on the brink of ruin. Together, as a community, it was easier to find protection from natural calamities, or to meet obligations imposed by the squire and the state. It was advantageous for the village to have common pasture and woodland, a common place for watering the cattle. The village community looked after orphans and childless old people. At regular intervals the land was redistributed among the peasant households in the village to ensure that each family had the amount of land commensurate with its size.

The measures of collectivist relief of this kind survived in the countryside right into the early twentieth century. They outlived the tsarist regime, which collapsed in 1917. Rural egalitarian traditions still existed in the 1920s and up to the start of Stalin's forced collectivization of agriculture at the end of that decade. Stalin's collectivization drive itself, with its imposition of the collective- and state-farm system on peasants, was achieved partly because of the sheer brutality and terror with which it was enforced by the state and partly due to the vestiges of communal traditions and egalitarian attitudes of peasants in the countryside.

Geopolitical Factor

Historians note a number of geopolitical characteristics peculiar to Russia that have been instrumental in shaping its historical development. Three features, in particular, seem to have had a fundamental influence:

1. *The vast, sparsely populated territories* of the Eastern-European Plain and Siberia created favorable conditions for the migration of the peasant population from the historical center of Russia toward its ever-expanding fringes. As a rule, the colonizing Russians did not have to use

force to impose their will on indigenous tribes and ethnic groups in the newly colonized territories of European Russia and Siberia, as there was enough land and living space for all.

The flow of the population to the fringe territories, however, created problems for the state and the ruling classes, which were compelled to tighten control over the movements of the peasant population and to increase its exploitation in order to secure their income. As the state's expenses increased, the grip over the peasants grew tighter, and, eventually, a considerable part of Russian peasantry became bonded to their squires and turned into virtual slaves — or serfs — of their landowning masters or the state.

2. *The lack of natural defensive borders* (such as seas or mountain ranges) exposed Russian territories to foreign invasion both from the east and from the west and greatly threatened the historical existence of the Russian nation. Exploiting this geographical vulnerability, Russia's neighbors, such as Catholic Poland, Sweden, Germany, and even the more distant France (under Napoleon I), launched invasions into Russian territory from the west. Meanwhile, nomads from the Great Steppe were attacking from the east.

The constant threat of military invasion due to the exposed nature of the country's borders put heavy demands on the Russian people, who had to strain their limited economic and human resources, scattered over a vast territory, to maintain their sovereignty. National security interests required the ability to mobilize all available resources of the country in times of military emergency. A poor, sparsely populated agrarian country had to maintain a huge military force in order to protect its extended open borders.

Under these conditions the role and powers of the state swelled out of proportion. A special warrior-class had to be created — one bound by obligations of military service to the state. Means had to be found of rewarding the military class for its services. The only commodity the state had in abundance was land and so land was given to members of the military serving-class with the expectation that, at the state's first behest, landowners would join the Russian military force.

To fulfill the state's obligations, landowners had to be able to count on a stable income from their land, and this necessitated the labor of the peasants. Without a peasant work force, landowners could not provide military services to the state in time of war. The solution to maintaining the country's military security was found in bonding the peasants to their landlords, thus preventing them from leaving their military-obligated masters. Enserfing the peasantry thus ensured that all members of the military class always had a work force on their land and thereby had the means to fulfill their military obligations. In this sense, the appearance of serfdom in Russia can be seen as a desperate measure by the state to maintain the country's military security in extremely difficult economic circumstances.

3. *Russia's half-way geographical location* in the center of the Eurasian landmass, between Europe and Asia, has had a profound effect on the emergence of a distinctive civilization, which was Asiatic in the eyes of the Europeans and too European for the Asians. The Russian state found its fitting symbol in the double-headed eagle of Byzantium, with one of its crowned heads turned to the east and the other, to the west. Adopted as the coat-of-arms of the Muscovite tsars, then of the Russian Empire, and now resurrected as a state attribute of postcommunist Russia, the double-headed eagle symbolizes the dual nature of a great state that extends for thousands of miles across two continents. This state accommodated the traditions and ways of life of its extraordinarily diverse mix of peoples, but at the same time it was also vulnerable to the danger of being torn apart by the incompatibility of the cultures it had brought together into one empire over the course of many centuries.

Russia's geographical location gave birth to an empire whose growth took a direction unfamiliar to Western Europeans. Russia acquired colonies not overseas but along its frontiers, with the result that metropolis and empire became territorially indistinguishable. This type of colonial expansion has left its impact on the imperial mentality of Russians. For most Russians national identity has been inextricably linked with the notion of empire. The English and the French had no doubt where they stood in relation to their colonies for they never identified them with the homeland. By contrast, the Russians, who have always lived among non-Russians, have for centuries equated their national state with an empire.

Religious Factor

If geopolitical characteristics have shaped Russia's "body," along with the temperament, skills, and habits of the Russian people, then the religion — the eastern form of Christianity known as Orthodoxy — has shaped the "soul" of the Russian people and left an indelible mark on their spiritual, cultural, and political traditions.

Both Russia and the West represented predominantly Christian civilizations. However, Christianity had reached them by different channels. Rome had been the West's main mediator of Christianity, while in Russia's case it was the Byzantine Empire that had acted as its Christian "godmother." Byzantium, which was the eastern part of the Roman Empire, saw itself as its heir after the collapse of the Western Empire in 476. Catholicism (the western form of Christianity) reflected the peculiarities of the Roman civilization, while Orthodoxy (the eastern form of Christianity) was imbued with the spirit of the Greek civilization that dominated Byzantium at the time of the implantation of Christianity in Russia.

Central to Orthodox Christian beliefs was the joining together of the earthly order and the heavenly one. The authority of the emperor was the power that linked these two worlds. When exercised properly, the emperor's power was capable of resolving all tensions and contradictions between the imperfect world of mortals and the ideal celestial order. It was able to bring this world in harmony with the next. For this reason, the authority of the "true" orthodox tsar was seen by the Orthodox religion as a guarantee of salvation after death.

In Western Europe, particularly after the sixteenth-century Reformation, the Christian religion motivated individuals to engage in some kind of profitable economic activity. Economic success strengthened the belief of the faithful that they were the "chosen" ones, destined for future individual salvation. In Russia, however, the Orthodox religion promised its people not an economic but a *political* way of *collectivist* salvation. In contrast to Western Christianity, which roused Europeans to seek economic prosperity and encouraged them to develop civil society as a means of protecting their business interests and civil rights, the Russian people were prescribed by their religion to engage in a centuries-long quest for a "true" Christian tsar.

The gradual secularization of these beliefs crystallized into two divergent value systems. In the West, professional success became one of the chief criteria for the evaluation of a person's activity, whereas in Russia, the idea of bringing closer the existing, imperfect world with the divine order resulted in a collectivist movement in search of a better future, in a continual quest for an ideal of social justice. With the collapse of tsarism in 1917, the charismatic power of the communist leader and of the state replaced the divine authority of the emperor as the force that bridged the divide between the earthly order and the radiant collectivist future.

Social Organization

The social structure of pre-Petrine Russia was based on a hierarchy of social estates. In Russia, in contrast to the countries of Western Europe, the system of social estates played a much greater role in determining the nature of the state. Social estates (such as the landed nobility, clergy, merchants, peasants, and townspeople) were large social classes whose position in society was fixed in law and whose obligations or privileges were hereditary. Similar to the countries of Western Europe, the social estate structure in Russia had emerged mainly under the influence of economic relations. However, as in most premodern societies, the Russian government used social estate labels to describe legal, rather than socioeconomic, classes of the population in order to fix people within a rigid, hierarchical social structure. Each person, depending on his or her social estate, had a precise legal status carrying with it particular rights and duties. Compared with Western Europe, the role of the Russian state in molding the social structure was very significant. In order to understand how Russian society worked as a whole, it is important to see the state and the social estates as parts of one integrated system, in which various classes performed specific social functions and shared obligations with respect to one another and to the state.

As the Russian centralized state took shape and grew, certain factors encouraged the emergence and legal codification of a specific system of social organization. Chief among these factors was the vital need for a speedy mobilization of economic and human resources in extremely difficult conditions: the population scattered over a huge territory, Russian regions isolated from one another, market relations at a primitive level, and the constant threat of foreign invasion.

In the West, the lack of spare territories and a high density of population sharpened social contradictions and led to the consolidation of social estates, speeding up the process of the legislative codification of the rights and obligations of social estates and of their individual members. By contrast, during the formation of the Russian centralized state, social tensions were somewhat defused thanks to the "safety valve" of the migration of population to the fringes of the Russian lands. The opposition elements traditionally used the fringe territories as their power bases. The outlying regions often turned into dangerous centers of anti-government revolts, and peasant and Cossack unrest.

In Western Europe, organized migrations of population were one way to ease social conflicts. Sponsored by the church or by the government, these took the form of religious crusades, sea expeditions to discover and colonize new lands, or the enforced exile of the discontented and socially undesirable elements to colonies. By contrast, the main concern of the Russian ruling circles was exactly the opposite: to check the migration of the population to the outskirts of the empire. The need for maximum mobilization of economic and human resources conditioned the active role of the state in the process of the formation and legislative regulation of social estates. The state in Russia played a vital role in ensuring the consensus and rational functioning of the entire social structure.

The solution to the problem of mobilizing the necessary resources was found in the creation of a specific service system. Under this system each stratum of society, or each social estate, had the right to exist only if it performed a certain set of duties and obligations or, to use the contemporary term, *service*.

The linchpin of the service system was CONDITIONAL LAND TENURE. It was *conditional* because the government granted the land, with peasants living on it, to members of the chief serving class — the nobility — on the condition that they perform military or civil service for the state. The main advantage of this system was that it placed substantial military forces at the state's disposal without any cost for their upkeep. The conditional nature of this type of land tenure meant that, in principle, it was not hereditary or even lifelong but depended solely on the landowner giving service to the state. Not only did landowners themselves have to enlist, they were also obligated to bring with them a certain number of their peasants adequately equipped as foot soldiers.

This system of land tenure (known in Russian as the *pomestie* system) took shape toward the end of the fifteenth century when the governments of Ivan III and then Basil III allocated a considerable part of newly conquered lands for distribution to the serving nobility. By the mid-sixteenth century *pomestie* had become the most common type of land tenure in Russian central regions.

By the seventeenth century the *pomestie* system had evolved into an important administrative and economic institution of the state. The state did not have a sufficient number of administrators in the localities; therefore it came to rely on the serving class of the *pomeshchiks* (i.e., *pomestie* landowners) to help collect taxes, recruit for the army and, finally, perform certain police functions. In other words, as Russia's social organization developed, the social estates came to perform specific functions and were given certain obligations and rights connected with the execution of those functions.

Thus, to take the noble estate as an example, its chief legal characteristics were the right to own land and the peasants on it, as well as the obligation to perform services for the state, chief among them, the military service. In the seventeenth and, particularly, in the second half of the eighteenth century, the nobility sought to consolidate its privileged status on the economic basis of the ownership of land and peasants and actively lobbied for the legislative transformation of the conditional land tenure (when manors were given in exchange for state service) into unconditional, hereditary land tenure. The government gradually yielded to the wishes of the service nobility. The decree of 1714 by Peter I conferred hereditary status on the manors of the service nobility. However, the obligation of government service remained in force.

The consolidation of the ruling landed nobility and the strengthening of its economic power went hand in hand with the enserfment of the peasantry. The bonded status of the peasants became gradually fixed in Russia's law codes, starting from the first restrictions of their free movements in the late fifteenth century and reaching the stage of complete bondage, or SERFDOM, by the middle of the seventeenth century.

Serfdom began when peasants were restricted from switching landowners. The law code of 1497 limited for the first time the period during which a peasant could leave one squire and move to another landowner's manor. This period was restricted to just two weeks each year, in late autumn after the end of the harvest season. But even this severely constrained freedom of movement was later taken away from the peasants, leaving them with only one, illegal, way of obtaining personal freedom — by fleeing from their landlords. The state continued to tighten its grip over the person of the peasant by enacting legislation that gradually increased the number of years during which runaway peasants could be chased and by perfecting the system of catching escaped serfs.

Finally, the law code of 1649 removed all time limits on the period during which runaways and their descendants could be hunted down and returned to their former masters. This, in effect, meant the culmination of the enserfment of the peasantry. Under the law code of 1649, a form of a Muscovite "constitution" that became the most important legislation of pre-Petrine Russia, the peasants were bonded to the land and in service to their squires; the small class of townspeople were obligated to perform town duties; and the serving nobility had to perform military and government service.

As a result of the increasing need for legal regimentation of all aspects of public life, the state began to grow and its administrative apparatus considerably expanded. The backbone of the Russian state was formed by central administrative institutions known as *prikazy* (chancelleries). The system of *prikazy* had evolved naturally in the course of the formation and development of the centralized state, growing gradually out of the archaic institutions of the courts of Russia's earlier grand princes.

By the end of the seventeenth century the overall number of administrative *prikazy* reached over eighty, with about forty of them permanently functioning.

Of particular importance were *prikazy* with all-Russian competence. Among these was the *Razriad* — the chancellery that administered matters pertaining to the serving nobility, including the oversight of their service, and that also kept a roll of the nobles. The *Pomestnyi prikaz* ensured the proper functioning of the manor system: it directly oversaw the distribution of the land (together with the peasant households on it) among the serving nobility and formalized transactions involving manorial lands. The Privy *prikaz* was headed personally by the tsar and oversaw the activities of supreme governmental bodies and top civil and military officials. Military matters were controlled by several *prikazy*, each one in charge of a particular branch of the armed forces. The Muscovite administrative system may look archaic now, but, in its day, it was, obviously, capable of ensuring the stability of the Russian system of social estates as well as maintaining vital functions of the state.

The important point to make here is that in pre-Petrine Russia the development of the system of social estates was inextricably linked with the evolution of the administrative apparatus. Indeed, they represent two sides of a single process. The social estates emerged and evolved under the direct intervention of the state, while the administrative institutions and government agencies were created to ensure the smooth operation of the system of social estates. As a result, the social estates and the state became entwined. The close interdependence gave rise to a specific type of the Russian state, a *service state* in which all subjects were bonded either to the place where they lived or to the service they were obligated to perform. All had as their raison d'être service to society. And above all of them reigned the government, with absolute, unrestricted powers. The line between society and the state was difficult to draw: each social estate, stratum, and group performed certain service functions and occupied a clearly defined and legally binding place in a strict hierarchy of power and privilege.

Martin Malia sums up the unique relationship between Russia's social estates and the state in this way: "By the sixteenth century, the service gentry was wholly subordinated to the autocratic tsar, and the peasants were enserfed to support the gentry, while both the peasants and the small class of townsmen paid taxes to the state, and the clergy prayed for the success of the whole. Thus, in Russia the lord-peasant order of traditional Europe was organized to meet the military needs of the monarchy in what is best described as a universal service state."[1]

The landed nobility became the backbone of Russia's social organization. The ascendancy of this ruling group went hand in hand with the imposition of various restrictions on other social classes — on the peasantry most of all, but also on the merchant class and townspeople. The merchants were "tied" in a hierarchy of guilds, following a similar "state-control" pattern. The tight legal regimentation of the social structure constricted economic growth, for it made difficult the development and free play of the market forces. The result of the centuries-long evolution of Russia's distinctive social organization was that social progress became possible only through state regulation of all aspects of socioeconomic development. In contrast to the West, where social progress was achieved through the natural development of economic relations, the Russian state drew its strength and vitality from the use of non-economic methods, such as coercion. Eventually, the state concentrated in its hands the control and distribution of the nation's entire human and material resources. In the words of the Russian historian George Fedotov:

> The entire process of historical development in early Russia took the opposite course to that of Western Europe; it was a development from freedom toward slavery. A slavery dictated not by the whims of rulers, but by a new national goal: the creation of an Empire on the basis of a meager economy. Only extreme all-embracing tension, iron discipline and terrible sacrifices could maintain this beggarly, barbarian, continuously expanding state. ... Consciously or unconsciously, [the Russian people] made the choice between power as a nation and freedom.[2]

In conclusion, it remains to sum up the essential characteristics of Russia's traditional social organization that distinguished it from Western societies.[3] These appear to be the following:

- the "service state" was the specific social organization based on a hierarchy of social estates with legally defined duties in relation to one another and the state;

- the state was not a "superstructure" above society as in the West, but the backbone and the regulator of the entire social structure; the state sometimes even created social groups within it;

- the primary socioeconomic unit was a corporate-collectivist formation based not on the principle of private ownership, as in the West, but on collective or state ownership (e.g., village com-

mune, association of artisans, collective- and state-farms, cooperative, etc.);

- the state, society, and the individual were not separate and autonomous as in the West, but were combined, as it were, in a
collectivist whole;

- the class of service nobility was the spine of Russian statehood (in
pre-Petrine Russia this ruling group was represented by the military landowning class, in Imperial Russia, by the state bureaucracy
recruited from the landowning nobility, and in communist Russia,
by the party-state elite).

This specific type of social organization has proved extremely stable.
It evolved in pre-Petrine Russia and endured for centuries, changing its
forms but not its essence. At times, it went through periods of great
upheavals. Yet after each turbulent period, it reconstituted itself, ensuring the basic continuity and vitality of Russia's historical development
and demonstrating the astonishing durability of social institutions, traditions, and attitudes whose unique combination has marked the Russian
civilization as distinct from Western European civilizations.

Political Regime

Ultimately, it was the power of AUTOCRACY that bound together different social strata and various ethnic groups of a gigantic empire. The
word "autocracy" refers to a regime that concentrates power in the
hands of an absolute ruler ("autocrat"). Russian autocracy rested on
the concept of the traditional "God-given" power of the Russian tsar. Its
sanctity and legitimacy were further enhanced by the idea that Moscow
was the "third Rome." Russian autocracy allowed ideologues to present
the Russian state as the heir to the might of Byzantium (the "second
Rome") and, indeed, of Rome itself. Russian tsars could thus claim
for themselves the supreme status enjoyed by Byzantine and Roman
emperors.

The highly personalized system of rule in Russia had, however, deep,
native roots of its own. The concept of the state in Russia was originally
derived from the role of the head of the extended family in early peasant
society. The father was sovereign of the household, an autocrat in the
broadest sense of the word. He literally owned all the property of the
clan, and all its members bowed obediently to his will. Like the father
of an extended family, the Russian prince emerged as the owner of his

subjects and all the territory in his principality. After the Russian lands had been gathered into one centralized state, the tsars continued to treat its land and people as their property. No Western monarch could apply to himself with greater justification Louis XIV's famous dictum "L'état c'est moi!" than the Russian tsars.

Even in the age of absolutism, Western monarchs could not disregard certain unwritten rules of society. They had to reckon with the interests of powerful social groups like the nobility and the bourgeoisie, and they often faced opposition in the form of a parliament, or municipal councils, or self-governing religious bodies. In contrast, the absolute rule of the tsars met with no opposition from society. The Russian autocrat was a towering figure at the pinnacle of the state pyramid, exercising total power in the country. There were no recognized formal limits on his political authority and no rule of law to curb his arbitrary will. The entire business of government was under his command, including the appointment of senior officials, the imposition of taxes, the issuing of legislation, questions of war and peace, and government expenditure. As for the individual liberties of his subjects, they existed only inasmuch as they were granted by the tsar.

The state, like the Russian autocracy that completely dominates society and treats its subjects as its property, is sometimes referred to as a PATRIMONIAL STATE.[4] It stifles the freedoms of private and public life, inhibits the development of mature civic consciousness in its subjects, and prevents the emergence of organized associations and self-governing bodies that would represent interests of different sections of society. In short, it suppresses all those things that characterize modern forms of political life of the state. While modern predemocratic structures began to evolve in Western Europe in the eighteenth century, and by the middle of the nineteenth century parliamentary democracies and constitutional monarchies had been established throughout almost all of Europe, Russia remained firmly in the grip of autocracy practically right to the very end of tsarism in 1917.

Chapter One

Peter the Great

Peter's Uncertain Legacy

For nearly three centuries Peter the Great's reign (1682–1725) has consistently been seen as one of the focal points of Russian and European history. His reforms left a lasting impression on Russian development and are often regarded as a watershed dividing Russian history into two parts: pre-Petrine and post-Petrine. Indeed, Peter's reforms inaugurated Russia's modern history.

It is difficult to find another period in Russian history as controversial as this. Peter's reign was exceptional as a period of transformation, combining within it and forcefully accentuating all the conflicting tendencies that marked Russian development for years: the seemingly incompatible extremes of a Russia balanced between Europe and Asia, between Muscovite traditional culture and Western civilization, between Eastern despotism and European Enlightenment, and between its status as a European great power and its economy based on serfdom.

In Russia, the political and ideological controversy over Peter's legacy started almost immediately with his death. The history of Russian political and social thought can be seen as the history of the development of contrasting views of the Petrine Reform. This has been particularly true since the time of the "Great Debate" between "Westernizers" and "Slavophiles" in 1840s, which revolved around the issue of the direction that Russia had followed as a result of Peter's transformation. The debate helped crystallize the attitudes of various political currents — conservative, liberal, reactionary, revolutionary, reformist — toward the legacy of Peter the Great. Even more important, the prescriptions and blueprints of Russia's future paths of development were made by these diverse political forces on the basis of their highly controversial and ideologically colored assessments of Peter's reign. Since then, the Petrine Reform has remained as a peculiar touchstone for every Russian ideological and political movement, as the "acid test" of their intentions.

In the present age of Russia's latest attempt at modernization, Peter has once again reemerged as the key figure of Russian history. His Reform continues to dominate Russia's past and, in a vital sense, its future as well. Peter's transformation of Russia contains within it all the essential elements of the age-old Russian dilemma, namely, the problems of continuity and change, of tradition and innovation, and of searching for its own distinct destiny or joining the mainstream of Western civilization. Russian reformers since the time of Peter have all confronted these same dilemmas.

Peter's Motivation

The question of Peter's motivation in launching the Reform is, arguably, the least controversial aspect of his legacy. As any reform program usually implies the existence of some general idea in the mind of the reformer of the aims of the reforms and of the ways to attain them, the question that is often asked is whether young Peter even had such a general blueprint. What we know about the early period of his reign seems to suggest that Peter thirsted for more information, mastered new knowledge and skills, and tested established assumptions by practice. It is highly significant that he befriended people like the Swiss diplomat François Lefort, the experienced general and Scotsman Patrick Gordon, and the scientist, engineer, and Russianized Scotsman James Bruce. In this circle of close companions, some of whom had traveled the extent of Europe to reach Russia, he must have been acutely aware of Russia's backwardness, the need for change, for Europeanization, and at the same time realized that he had almost unlimited resources at his disposal to bring about the desired transformation.

In the early years of his reign, Peter with his circle of like-minded associates, both Russian and Western European, made two trips to the White Sea in the north of Russia (1693–94). There he familiarized himself with shipbuilding. A year later, in 1695, he joined the Azov campaign, which was led by the generals A. Golovin, F. Lefort, and P. Gordon, against the Crimean Tartars and the Turks in the south. The capture of the fortress of Azov in 1696 was Peter's first major military success and a proof that the first steps in the reorganization of the army and the navy had been made in the right direction.

Peter's next important step was quite untypical of a Russian ruler up to that time: he made a long visit to Europe (1697–98), a visit known as the "Great Embassy." Significantly, the aims of the Embassy foreshadowed the main directions of his future Europeanization of Russia. Its main aim was to make closer military and diplomatic alliances with Western powers, against Turkey in particular. It also sought to establish cultural, trade, and technical ties with the West and obtain an informed view about the European way of life. Peter's informal participation in the Embassy gave him an excellent opportunity to learn about various aspects of the life of European states and different sections of Western society — from courtiers to craftspeople. As a result, Peter could form a broad and objective view of the larger world outside Russia and of Russia's place in it.

Throughout almost the whole of the Petrine reign Russia was engaged in the Northern War against Sweden (1700–1721). At that time Sweden was the dominant power in the Baltic, and the early stages of the war had clearly demonstrated that Russia could hope to beat Sweden only if it reorganized its army and created a strong navy. Peter's military reforms were among his most radical and successful ones. He extended conscription for the army, equipped it with modern firearms and artillery, and gave it training manuals acquired from the West. As a result, by the end of his reign Russia had a powerful standing army of two hundred thousand — the largest such force in Europe. The force provided Russia with the military muscle to replace Sweden as the greatest power in northeastern Europe. The war with Sweden ended with the conclusion of the Treaty of Nystadt (1721), which gave Russia access to a strategically important stretch of the Baltic coast. The country had now a much needed access to the sea and sea trade that presented opportunities for economic and cultural exchanges with the countries of Western Europe.

When discussing the pre-Petrine Muscovite state it was noted that by the seventeenth century a certain type of relationship between society and the state had evolved, in which each social class had to perform certain duties and services assigned to it by the state. Russia's traditional political and social structures enabled the state to exercise control over the entire economic and demographic resources of society and mobilize them for the attainment of its strategic objectives. Society on its own lacked any effective levers by which to bring about change. For these reasons, any major reform project could only be implemented by means of administrative intervention by the state.

The reform era of Peter the Great represents a state-driven modernization of this kind. The exigencies of the war with Sweden served only to enhance the state's role as the supreme coordinator of the war effort, bent on pushing through the reform measures necessary for the achievement of the final victory. The Petrine Reform is a classic example of a radical transformation of society directed by the state and implemented from above often against the wishes of broad sections of the population and even in the face of their open resistance. The Reform was conceived of as a broad program of major economic, social, and political changes aimed at modernizing, rationalizing, and Europeanizing Russian society.

Not all historians are convinced of the planned nature of the Petrine Reform. There was much in it, they say, that was not preplanned, that was improvisational or simply an expedient in the conditions of the war with Sweden. Such assessments, however, do not give sufficient credit to Peter's calculated and lifelong ambition to create a rational (or, to use Peter's own expression, "regular") state. The foundations of a rationally governed state were to be laid with the help of an extensive legislative regulation of all aspects of the life of society. A clear example of the purposeful planning by Peter was the construction of the new imperial capital of St. Petersburg. In contrast to the abandoned traditional capital of Moscow, a city that had been built gradually and without a general plan, the founding of St. Petersburg was planned carefully. Peter had drawn up a whole series of decrees that regulated in great detail the location of the city, specified the architecture of its buildings, and laid down the duties of its inhabitants. Having conceived the blueprint of his new capital, he acted vigorously, resorting to unrestrained administrative coercion, to bring his ideal city into life. There is in this an inescapable likeness to the Utopians with their vision of a perfect city, with happy inhabitants whose lives are regulated down to the smallest detail.

Peter's approach to the task of creating a "regular" state was similar to the way he planned the founding of St. Petersburg. He desired to build a state that would rule by carefully thought-through laws that would ensure the effective functioning of the entire administrative mechanism and protect the population from the arbitrariness of officials. To that end, Peter introduced legislation covering practically all aspects of social, economic, and political life, including the definitions of the status of all social estates and classes that made up Russia's social hierarchy, the regulation of industry with special provisions for its priority branches, the regulation of trade, and, finally, the operation of the governmental apparatus and the state bureaucracy. All these measures appear to be part of Peter's comprehensive plan to create a "regular" state that would govern society utilizing progressive legislation adopted by leading Western European powers.

The "Royal Revolutionary"

The most contentious aspect of Peter's legacy, however, is not the question of his motivation in launching Europeanization, but the question of the effects of his Reform on Russia. Were the reforms, for example, revolutionary, signifying a complete break with the Muscovite past? Or were they merely a continuation of changes already set in motion by Peter's predecessors, in particular by his father, Tsar Alexis (reigned 1645–76)?

The extent of Peter's radicalism and innovation can be measured by setting his reforms within the context of the Muscovite past and trying to assess to what degree they represented the continuation of the previous trends and to what extent they signified a break in continuity with the earlier Muscovite Russia. Stephen Lee has grouped Peter's policies in categories according to the degree of their continuity with the previous trends.[1] At one end of the spectrum is a group of policies that represents a clear continuation of the trends and practices of the traditional Muscovite Russia. The best example of the continuity between Peter and his predecessor was the tightening of the control by the state and the nobility over the serfs and the intensification of the economic and social burdens on the Russian masses. This group is represented by such policies as the levying of the soul tax on all males from the "taxpaying" classes (i.e., the entire nonnoble population), the introduction of compulsory military service for most of the Russian male population, and the extension of conscription for construction projects (such as, for instance, the building of St. Petersburg).

At the other end of the spectrum are a few policies that might be called revolutionary in the sense that they signaled a complete change of direction and had no precedents in previous reigns. One obvious example was the creation of a modern navy. Peter was the first tsar not only to establish a powerful navy but also to set up a Russian shipbuilding industry, which transformed Russia from a landlocked military state into one of Europe's largest naval powers. At the close of his reign, Russia had almost fifty major war vessels and a navy of nearly thirty thousand.

The bulk of Peter's innovations occupy the middle ground between examples of clear continuity and totally new departures. These were the policies that had to some extent been anticipated in the past but that were now more fully implemented as a result of more conscious imitation of the West. The word "revolutionary" may still be applied to some of them, but only in the sense of a revolutionary acceleration of past trends rather than of a complete change of direction. This group includes measures such as the creation of a modern army, a radical administrative reform, active efforts to develop the country's industrial capacity, and the promotion of secular culture and education.

Grouping the reforms into categories clarifies the extent of Peter's radicalism and innovation with respect to his predecessors. However, this does not necessarily explain why the radical acceleration of the previous processes and the introduction of entirely new policies happened when they did — in the era of Peter the Great. In order to understand the deeper causes of his Reform, it is necessary to put it into a broader comparative and historical perspective and define its place not simply in relation to Muscovite Russia, but also in the context of European history and contemporary worldwide developments.

The Petrine transformation was launched in the period of early modern history, when the development of economic relations based on the market, new geographical discoveries, pioneering scientific inquiries, the appearance of more efficient means of travel and communication, and new technological innovations were beginning to bind the world into a single civilization. The elements of this new civilization — countries and continents — now actively interacted with one another as parts of a single system. In this new epoch, a nation's economic or social backwardness and its inability to set up an effective system of government posed a real threat to the very sovereignty of the state. Increasingly, the government systems of more advanced countries provided models to be imitated and offered examples of desirable restructuring for their less developed neighbors. The attempt to "catch up" with more developed countries is usually described as MODERNIZATION. Since early modern history, the advanced countries of Western Europe and of the West in general have been the models for modernization. For this reason, the "catching up" phase of development is also referred to as EUROPEANIZATION or WESTERNIZATION.

Concrete modernization attempts may proceed at different paces and with varying intensity. They may have different forms and results. Depending on the speed and effects of reforms, the process of transformation may be represented by two basic types: evolutionary and revolutionary modernizations.[2] These types are the two ends of the spectrum; they encompass between them all the varieties of concrete reform attempts that have taken place in the history of various countries. The evolutionary type of modernization is characterized by a gradual unfolding of the reform process over decades and even centuries. This approach to reform means that traditional institutions and governmental structures are not dissolved outright but are gradually replenished with new content in a process of incremental change.

In contrast, the modernization of society and rationalization of government by revolution mean a certain sharp break with the past. This type of reform results in a fundamental overhaul of the whole system of traditional institutions. To effect a transformation of this kind, an outstanding charismatic leader is usually needed, one whose popularity or authority is sufficient to push through a radical reform program. This type of modernization often results in significant shifts in public consciousness, major changes in the way of life, the mentality, and the attitudes of the people. Contemporaries often view this type of change as the dawn of a new era.

Peter's Reform represents an important new departure in modern world history, for it pioneered the process of modernization and Europeanization that was later to develop on a worldwide scale. Europeanization of Russia was achieved by the deliberate importation of Western values, way of life, legislation, technical terminology, and by the reform of the army, government, and industry, which borrowed heavily from Western models. As a result, by the end of Peter's reign, Russia had acquired a new system of institutions which, while maintaining a certain degree of continuity, demonstrated, at the same time, a radical break with the past. The Petrine transformation was called forth by a combination of major international trends that began to effect developments in Europe and in countries worldwide, and by the operation of the basic tendencies of the Russian historical process. The joint action of these internal and external factors, coupled with the ascendancy to the throne of one of the most charismatic leaders in Russian history, produced a set of circumstances that made the Petrine modernization almost inevitable.

Establishment of Absolutism

The Petrine transformation of the first quarter of the eighteenth century was connected, first of all, with the establishment of a new sociopolitical system in Russia known as absolutism. ABSOLUTISM means a reorganization of a traditional political system on rational foundations. It is a regime that seeks to establish a sound logical base for its absolute and unchecked authority, rather than justifying it by outdated references to tradition or the divine right of kings. The rationalization of the system of government affects all aspects of the life of society including politics, economy, social relations, and culture. The process of rationalization usually begins with an overhaul of the administrative apparatus of the state and its bureaucracy. Administrative reform thus represents a chief element and a driving force of an overall modernization, with bureaucracy playing an increasingly important role in its implementation.

The nature and composition of the ruling elite itself undergo change. The traditional right to ruling status based on noble origins gradually gives way to an elite promoted to high positions on the principle of MERITOCRACY. Thus the rationalization of government leads to the bureaucratization of the elite, its transformation from a privileged class into a professional group of officials and administrators. The conflict of the two principles — high birth versus merit — is only an external manifestation of a more fundamental transition from traditional feudal principles of civil service to its reorganization along more rational lines. This historical tendency was characteristic of European development in general and signified a certain break in continuity with the forms and principles of civil service.

Peter introduced one of the most radical reforms of government in the history of Russia. It followed two main directions. The first was the transformation of the entire system of governmental institutions, which resulted in the replacement of an outdated, patriarchal administrative system of the Muscovite Russia by a more modern and streamlined governmental system. The second was the reorganization of the structure and composition of the administrative apparatus, which led to the emergence of the new bureaucracy and its subsequent consolidation as Russia's new ruling class.

The centerpiece of Peter's administrative reform was the replacement of the Muscovite chancelleries (*prikazy*) by a network of central administrative colleges modeled on the system that existed in Sweden and other parts of Europe. In contrast to the traditional system of *prikazy*, in which all administrative activity had been based on custom and precedent, colleges were modern government departments in which the business of government was conducted on a proper legal basis of norms and regulations. The setting up of the new administrative system reflected Peter's attempt to create an executive apparatus that could ensure proper functioning of a "regular" state. In contrast to the old Muscovite *prikazy*, the new imperial administrative system of colleges was characterized by a higher degree of unification, centralization, and differentiation of administrative functions. The radical overhaul of central institutions of government enabled Peter to overcome resistance to his innovations in the higher echelons of his administration and to forge an executive arm capable of pushing through his bold reform measures.

The process of the rationalization of government involved the restructuring of the traditional hierarchy within the ruling class itself, as well as the reform of the state institutions. The modernizing tsar needed a ruling elite that was efficient and compliant. To some extent, the rise of the new bureaucracy had been prepared by the gradual erosion of the unchallenged privileged status traditionally enjoyed by the top layer of the nobility known as the *boyars*. The elevated status of the *boyars*, in contrast to the lower gentry, the *pomeshchiks,* was based on the claim of high birth, as many of them were the descendants of princes who held principalities in Russia before the establishment of the unified state by the rulers in Moscow. In the first quarter of the eighteenth century this upper echelon of aristocracy still had enormous economic wealth based on their vast landholdings and their ownership of great numbers of peasants. But their position of privilege was increasingly challenged by the elements from the gentry of a less distinguished and ancient lineage whose claims to power rested on their growing economic prosperity and successful political career.

Peter formally overruled the primacy of the old principle of subordination based on pedigree by the introduction, in 1722, of the TABLE OF RANKS, which was directly influenced by similar developments in Prussia and other countries of Europe. The Table of Ranks attempted to combine such parameters as lineage, rank, merit, and years of service to define the status of a civil or military servant in society. It established for all those who owed service to the state a hierarchy of fourteen grades of individual merit. The system applied to military officers as well as to their civilian counterparts. Service, whether in the army or navy or in civil administration, was for life. All entered at the lowest grade and all were given the opportunity to rise to the top. Promotion to the eighth grade carried with it the privileges of nobility, among them the ownership of serfs. Service, in this sense, became a career open to talent.

The Table of Ranks signified greater systematization and unification of the administrative service and thus its rationalization. It helped promote the principle of fitness for government service above considerations of birth and pedigree, and it institutionalized, to some extent, a degree of democratization within the ruling elite, permitting a measure of upward mobility by legalizing the possibility of obtaining noble status through career promotion. The new hierarchy of ranks undermined the position of the big *boyar* aristocracy as a privileged social caste by eroding its power monopoly and expanding the representation of the lower nobility in the high reaches of government. By setting down clear principles of state service and codifying levels of social position and privileges, the Table of Ranks accelerated the process of the transformation of bureaucracy into a social estate in its own right.

At the institutional level, the creation of a Senate in 1711 as a top government agency, replacing the *Boyar* Duma, reflected the waning fortunes of the top *boyar* group. In pre-Petrine Russia the *Boyar* Duma was a supreme consultative body for passing laws and running the administration. Its members were appointed by the tsar and drawn from old, established *boyar* families. In effect, members of the Duma were the very apex of the ruling elite of the Muscovite state, a group of the tsar's top advisers. In the newly created Senate, members were also appointed by the tsar, but in one significant respect the Senate represented a new type of governmental institution. Ability now took priority over high birth, for the modernizing tsar needed capable top administrators who could supervise the effective operation of the new system of administrative colleges, draft necessary legislation, and, in general, spearhead the reform of central government.

The rationalization enforced by Peter in the spheres of civil and military administration was extended further to encompass the cultural and spiritual life of his subjects and even to a minute regimentation of social fashions and dress styles. The middle classes and the nobility were pressed into adopting Western dress and shaving their beards — measures that would have been unthinkable during the reigns of his predecessors. Peter vigorously promoted a new secular culture and Westernized education by giving Russia schools like those found in the advanced countries of the West and by founding the Academy of Sciences to encourage scientific studies.

The Orthodox Church, which occupied a central place in the traditional culture of Russia, was subjected to a particularly radical reorganization. The powerful position of patriarch was abolished. The Holy Synod, consisting of a committee of church officials, all appointed by the tsar, became the governing body of the church. The Synod's work was supervised, on behalf of the tsar, by a layperson, the Ober-Procurator, who ran the church practically as an agency of state. One of the chief reasons for these actions by Peter was to combat the church hierarchy's opposition to his reforms. The government now had effective control over church organizations, their property, and their policies.

The administrative system created as a result of Peter's reforms proved lasting and stable and in all essential aspects survived until the fall of tsarism in 1917, although some of the institutions were assigned different functions or renamed (the Senate, for instance, would evolve into the country's supreme court, and colleges were replaced by ministries in 1801). The Table of Ranks also endured until the collapse of the tsarist regime. The rationalization of the bureaucratic hierarchy strengthened the power of Russian absolutism in that rank, prestige, and even the well-being of civil servants came to depend upon the will and favor of the monarch alone. From the Table of Ranks developed the petrification of the bureaucratic order of Imperial Russia, its gradual consolidation into a new serving class that stood between society and the ruler.

Patterns of Petrine Modernization

Peter's administrative and other reforms represent Russia's first attempt to modernize and catch up with the advanced countries of Western Europe. The reforms display certain characteristics, traces of which can be seen in later periods of major reforms. The Petrine transformation thus set in place patterns that would have a lasting influence on the direction of Russia's development into modern times. Some of the more important of these are the following.

Revolution from Above

Peter was the first Russian ruler who inaugurated the pattern of a revolution from above as the chief response of backward Russia to the challenge of the West. This pattern would be maintained down to the end of the tsarist regime in 1917 and beyond. Alexander II, another renowned tsar-reformer, would epitomize the government's approach to reform in a famous remark made in his address to the nobility in 1856. In his speech, which for the first time made clear his intention to emancipate the serfs, Alexander said it would be preferable to abolish serfdom "from above" than to wait for upheaval from below.

Ironically, many Russian progressives from the oppositionist and revolutionary movements agreed with the tsarist government on this point. The manifest success of the Petrine Reform instilled within the Russian progressive camp a deep conviction that any fundamental change in their country could only be initiated from the top and be carried through by the forcible action of the state. For many this attitude — and the disregard for human sacrifice that it entailed — became an article of faith. This was true, for instance, of the Narodniks — Russian peasant socialists of the nineteenth century — many of whom idolized Peter and his actions and saw in him an ideal patriot. The worship of Peter thus turned into the recognition of the benefits of unrestrained violence.

Even Vladimir Lenin, the Marxist "gravedigger" of Russia's old regime, sought to imitate the brutal methods of Peter's modernization. In 1918, at the head of the fledgling Soviet state and still hoping for a world proletarian revolution, he wrote: "While the revolution in Germany is still slow to break out, our task is to learn state capitalism from the Germans, to do our best to emulate it, not to refrain from dictatorial methods in order to accelerate this emulation even more than Peter accelerated the emulation of Westernism by the barbaric Rus, not to shun barbaric means to fight barbarism."[3] (Here Lenin alludes to the famous dictum of Karl Marx: "Peter the Great smashed Russian barbarism by barbarism.")

Enforced and Violent Nature of Modernization

Force, repression, coercion, and violence became the chief means by which Russia was modernized. Its productive forces were developed by becoming still further enslaved. This paradox is central to an understanding of the Petrine Reform and much else of later developments in Russia.

The apparent incongruity between the progressive aims of the Reform and the barbaric means by which it was implemented were probably best expressed by the outstanding Russian historian Vasili Klyuchevsky, who, at the start of the twentieth century, wrote:

> Peter's reforms were the occasion for a struggle between the despot and the people's inertia. The Tsar hoped to arouse the energies and initiative of a society subdued by serfdom with the menace of his power, and strove... to introduce into Russia the European sciences and education which were essential to social progress. He also wanted the serf, while remaining a serf, to act responsibly and freely. The conjunction of despotism and liberty, of civilization and serfdom, was a paradox which was not resolved in the two centuries after Peter.[4]

The rationalization and modernization initiated by the state unchecked by any kind of control from society inevitably had to be carried through by means of force and administrative coercion. The ideal of an equitable and rational state, which inspired Peter, led in practice to the creation of a police state.

Emergence of "Dual Russia"

The Petrine Reform is often seen as the main cause and the starting point of the irrevocable split of Russian society into two parts. Peter's reforms transformed the upper levels of Russian society while the masses remained largely unaffected by them. Peter had forced the nobility to acquire technical knowledge of Western Europe and to adopt European styles of dress and manners. An increasingly Europeanized education of the upper classes brought with it a familiarity with the philosophies and theories of the Enlightenment. Soon many Russian nobles even preferred to speak the languages of Western Europe (particularly French and German) to Russian. By the nineteenth century their world was European in dress, manners, food, education, attitudes, and language, and was completely alien to the way of life of the Russian popular masses.

Thus a cultural and ideological wall was set up between a secular Westernized elite and the lower classes, who remained bound by tradition and religion. In the words of Tibor Szamuely: "A curious process took place in Russia as a result of the Reform, a process that in a way resembled a foreign conquest *in reverse:* whereas, for instance, in England Norman baron and Saxon peasant gradually grew closer, in time evolving a common nation, a common language, a common culture, in Russia the nobility and the peasantry, already separated by rigid social barriers, rapidly came to inhabit what were to all intents and purposes, different worlds alien and incomprehensible one to the other."[5] This cultural gulf proved to have tragic consequences for Russia. In the nineteenth century many progressively minded members of the Russian educated classes, who sincerely aspired to bridge the cultural divide and atone for the suffering of the masses, joined the Russian revolutionary movement. Their radical blueprints for improving the lot of the common people often reflected their less-than-perfect understanding of the life and mentality of the masses. Utopian and unrealistic, these ideas not only failed to lead the Russian people to the promised luminous future but, tragically, lured the country into a historical cul-de-sac.

One-Sided, "Technocratic" Europeanization

The influence of Western Europe on its eastern neighbor, which became so strong at the time of Peter the Great, had a character entirely of its own. It was discriminating and selective, and showed that Peter's main concern was the acquisition of Western technical knowledge and the importation of modern technological expertise and skills. His chief

ambition was to turn Russia into a great military power capable of holding its own against any combination of its neighbors. Russia had the
size, the population, the abundance of natural resources, and above all,
the unlimited authority of the state. What was needed was European
technology, the "instrumentality" of European civilization and, primarily, Western know-how in military organization and civil administration.
That was all, as far as he was concerned; for the rest, Europe remained
an object of hostility and distrust.

Among the first to notice the one-sided nature of Peter's Westernization was the Russian philosopher Michael Fonvizin, who, in the 1840s,
observed: "If Peter sought to introduce European civilization into Russia, then he was attracted more by its external aspects. The spirit of
this civilization — the spirit of legal freedom and civil rights — was
alien and even repulsive to him, a despot as he was."[6] This view was
echoed later by Klyuchevsky, who wrote about Peter that "In adopting
European technology he remained rather indifferent toward the life and
peoples of Western Europe. That Europe was for him a model factory
and workshop, while he considered the concepts, feelings, social and
political attitudes of the people on whose work this factory relied to
be something alien to Russia. Although he visited the industrial sights
of England many times, he only once looked in on the parliament."[7]
Peter himself expressed his attitude to the West with utmost clarity and
bluntness when on one occasion he told an intimate companion: "We
need Europe for a few decades, later on we must turn our back on it."[8]
As a result of Peter's Westernization, industry and science began to develop rapidly in Russia. Within a short time the country could compete
with its Western neighbors in matters maritime and in the art of building fortifications. A great surge took place in many branches of technical
learning, manufacturing industries sprang up and were improved, trade
expanded. Yet suggestions about how to make the life of society more
humane and democratic remained as before completely neglected and
were unable to reach the hearts and minds of the Russian rulers.

Europeanization as Strengthening the Oppressive Character of the State

The greatest paradox of Peter's Reform was that by shaking up Russian
society, by introducing efficient and up-to-date methods, by equipping
Russia with military and economic might — and achieving all this
mainly by force and administrative coercion — Peter not only preserved

the most salient features of traditional Muscovite society, but actually strengthened and reinvigorated them.

The Petrine paradox was forcefully expressed by the Russian philosopher George Plekhanov: "In his Europeanization of Russia Peter developed to its final, logical conclusion the condition of complete helplessness of the population vis-à-vis the State that is characteristic of Oriental despotism."[9] Some analysts even deny Peter the Europeanizing substance of his innovations. Alexander Kizevetter, for instance, argued: "Far from reducing, Peter increased ever more the burdens, imposed by the State on society. . . . Having considerably modified the external forms of state institutions, Peter left completely untouched the basic principles of the old system of social organization."[10]

The Reform considerably expanded the authority and influence of the Russian government over its own population. The power of the despotic, centralized state was made even more absolute and its arbitrary rule was elevated into the basic principle of government. Society was subjected to yet more rigid regimentation, with the heavy burden of state service made compulsory for all classes of the population. The church was subordinated to the state, and the bondage of peasants was strengthened and made even harsher. In effect, Westernized Russia was in many respects more "Russian" than before.

Barbarian or Transformer?

Any critical assessment of Peter's prodigious labors invariably entails a value judgment about the effects and nature of his transformation. Was it beneficial or destructive to Russia's interests? Did it signify real progress or did it obstruct genuine and urgently needed change? The intellectual and political controversy over Peter's legacy has been raging for nearly two centuries and shows no signs of abating. Its two opposite extremes may be expressed with the help of the following contrasting propositions: (1) "Peter's Reform brought Russians into the fold of the world humanity"; (2) "Peter's aping of Western ways marked the beginning of Russia's descent into barbarity."

Peter was first given credit for being a Great Transformer in the positive sense by a group of Russian nineteenth-century intellectuals known as the "WESTERNIZERS." The Russian philosopher Peter Chaadaev, for example, argued that Peter found Russia as "only a blank page when he came to power, and with a strong hand he wrote on it *Europe* and *Occident*: from that time on we were part of Europe and of the Occident."[11] The Russian historian Sergei Soloviev, too, maintained that "No people have ever equalled the heroic feat performed by the Russians during the first quarter of the eighteenth century."[12] The famous literary critic Vissarion Belinsky compared Peter to a god "who called us back to life, who blew a living soul into the body of ancient Russia, colossal, but sunk in a deadly torpor."[13] The Westernizing intellectuals generally lauded Peter's attempt to Europeanize Russia. But even in their midst there were some whose attitude to Peter was more complex than unequivocal approbation. Some pointed out that, while Peter had introduced Western influences, he had also developed institutions that would impede Russia's future development into a more democratic society along Western lines.

A predominantly negative view of Peter the reformer was developed by the "SLAVOPHILES," who were the intellectual opponents of the "Westernizers." According to the Slavophiles, Peter's reforms had permanently damaged the very fabric of traditional society by introducing alien ideas and institutions. They destroyed the harmonious unity of Russian society by creating a chasm between the government and the people. By implementing the Westernizing reforms, the government had severed itself from its roots in the "Russian Land." One of the chief ideologists of the Slavophiles, Konstantin Aksakov, observed: "The agents of the State, the serving class go over to the side of the State. The populace, the common people proper, continue to live by the old principles. The upheaval is accompanied by violence.... Russia is split in two, into two capitals. On the one hand, the State with its foreign capital of St. Petersburg; and on the other, the Land, the people, with its Russian capital of Moscow."[14]

Yet even the Slavophiles, who generally condemned Peter's reforms, did not completely loose sight of certain positive sides of his transformation. Thus, Ivan Kireevsky regarded highly Peter's efforts to promote enlightenment in Russia and thought that these "...to a great extent justify the extremes to which he went. Love of enlightenment was his passion. He saw it as Russia's sole salvation, and Europe as its only source."[15]

The agonizing ambivalence toward Peter's legacy, which was first so vividly revealed during the protracted and animated debate between Westernizers and Slavophiles a hundred and fifty years ago, has persisted in Russian social and political thought right into the twentieth century. Entirely negative evaluations of Peter's modernization have been arrived at, for example, by such outstanding Russian thinkers as Nicholas Trubestkoy and Nicholas Berdyaev. According to Trubestkoy, Russia, as a result of the Westernization forced upon it by Peter the Great, lost its cultural identity, and yet failed to assimilate properly the Western traditions. It thus ended up in a sort of cultural cul-de-sac: "If before Peter the Great Russia and her culture could be considered almost the most gifted and fertile successor of Byzantium, then after Peter the Great, having taken the road of 'Romano-Germanic' orientation, she found herself at the tail of European culture, in the backyard of civilization."[16]

The philosopher Berdyaev has been probably the strongest critic of Peter in the twentieth century. Berdyaev drew a direct parallel between Peter and the destructive impact of the communist experiment. The Petrine and Bolshevik revolutions, he said, showed "the same barbarity, violence, forcible application of certain principles from above downwards, the same rupture of organic development and repudiation of tradition,... the same desire sharply and radically to change the type of civilization."[17] The resemblance between the radicalism of the Petrine transformation and the Bolshevik methods of social engineering has been noted by the poet Maximilian Voloshin, who in one of his poems has described Peter as "the first Bolshevik."[18]

These negative perceptions contrast with views upholding Peter's claim to greatness. Ivan Il'in, for instance, an outstanding twentieth-century theoretician of Russian monarchism, has called Peter "the greatest of monarchs" and asserted that "Russia needed Peter the Great in order to discover and reveal her great power status ('*velikoderzhavie*')."[19]

Many of Peter's critics and admirers had, of course, their own political axes to grind, which helps to explain to some extent the prevalence of either extremely negative or overwhelmingly positive assessments of what Peter did to Russia. There have always been commentators, however, who tried to bridge the gulf between the two irreconcilable poles of judgment, offering a more balanced and neutral view of Peter's achievement. The nineteenth-century critic Dmitri Pisarev, for example, tried to stay above the fray between the Westernizers and the Slavophiles by contending that "If indeed Peter overset anything, then he overset only what was weak and rotten, what would have collapsed of its own accord. Both the Slavophiles and the Westernizers overestimate the significance of Peter's achievement; the former see him as a corrupter of popular life, the latter, as a sort of a Samson, who destroyed the wall separating Russia from Europe....Peter's work is not at all as pregnant with historic consequences as it seems to his enthusiastic admirers and hardened opponents."[20]

The prominent historian Sergei Platonov, too, denied Peter the title

of a royal revolutionary, arguing that there was no radical break in political, economic, or social development under Peter: "Was his activity
traditional, or did it represent a sharp and sudden revolution in the
life of the Muscovite state, for which the country was entirely unprepared? The answer is quite clear. Peter's reforms were not a revolution,
either in their substance or their results. Peter was not a 'Royal Revolutionary,' as he is sometimes called."[21] In Platonov's opinion, Peter's
reforms merely accelerated processes begun under his predecessors; for
this reason they could not be regarded as a particularly exceptional
contribution to Russian development. This view, interestingly enough,
is corroborated in an observation made much earlier, in the eighteenth
century, by no less a figure than Catherine the Great herself, who was
one of Peter's most celebrated successors and admirers. She believed that
"the reform, undertaken by Peter the Great, had been started by Tsar
Alexis. The latter had already set about changing attire and many other
customs."[22]

Many analysts now adopt the line that Peter acted as a catalyst of Europeanization, which had started before his time, by speeding up policies
already slowly taking shape. Under him Russia was undergoing, in the
main, a process of forced and greatly accelerated evolution rather than
of true revolution. Peter did not place his imprint on a "blank sheet," as
Chaadaev claimed; he simply introduced changes that were within the
context of Muscovite developments.

At the same time, many critics agree with the view of Klyuchevsky
that the pace of his changes must have appeared revolutionary at
the time:

> Started and carried through by the sovereign, the people's usual
> leader, the reforms were undertaken in conditions of upheaval, al-
> most of revolution, not because of their objects but because of
> their methods, and by the impressions they made on the nerves and
> imaginations of the people. Perhaps it was more of a shock than
> a revolution, but the shock was the unforeseen and unintended
> consequence of the reform.[23]

In other words, Peter acted with such vigor and energy and enforced
his changes at such a pace and volume that his actions certainly seemed
revolutionary to those who felt their immediate effects.

The number of contrasting views of Peter can be multiplied infinitely.
The important thing to understand is that behind the controversy over
the nature of Peter's Reform there is always present, explicitly or im-
plicitly, another fundamental argument: about the nature of pre-Petrine

Russia. The controversy over Peter is a debate about the Russian nation itself, about its roots, destiny, and place in a wider world. If Peter had inherited from the Muscovite tsars a nation of barbarians, then his methods were justified and he deserves to be called a Great Transformer. If, however, Peter tried to impose his changes on a civilization he did not understand and could not appreciate, then Peter, automatically, becomes a tyrant and a barbarian. The stakes are so high because this debate touches the centrality of what Russia was and is. For this reason, Peter's legacy is likely to remain for some time an issue not easily amenable to dispassionate, nonpartisan inquiry.

Chapter Two

Catherine the Great

Enlightened Absolutism or Enlightened Despotism?

Catherine's reign (1762–96) was one of the most remarkable in Russian history. It has often been seen as an important complement to Peter's period, as an age in which the absolutism established by her great predecessor was tempered by Enlightenment. In the eloquent phrase of a contemporary poet, Michael Kheraskov:

> Peter gave Russians a body,
> Catherine gave them a soul.[1]

This sentiment would be reiterated by many, including the famous literary critic Vissarion Belinsky, who, in 1841, remarked: "Peter had awakened Russia from apathetic sleep, but it was Catherine who breathed life into her."[2]

Indeed, Peter's approach to the task of Europeanization was one of hard-headed pragmatism. The major Western influences that stimulated his reform efforts were the scientific movement and the rationalism of the late seventeenth century. He used Western ideas and techniques to create a powerful empire and to augment the autocratic prerogative of the tsar. In contrast, Catherine's emphasis was more on the intellectual. She was more receptive to the somewhat more refined arguments of the eighteenth-century *philosophes* and political thinkers. Despite this distinction in the sort of Western influences affecting the two reigns, there was more than a little continuity between them and between the problems that the two great rulers had to contend with.

Prior to her appearance on the Russian scene, Catherine was an obscure German princess known by the name of Sophia Augusta. Born in 1729, she came to Russia when she was about fifteen years old to marry the heir of the Russian throne. With her conversion to Orthodoxy she took the name of Catherine. In 1762 she secured the Russian throne through a coup d'état against her husband, Peter III.

By the time of her accession to the throne Catherine was well versed in the contemporary achievements of European philosophical, political, and economic thought. She corresponded with Voltaire and most of the other great men of the age, and her letters show her to be well-informed and lively if not profound. She also had some definite ideas of her own about what needed to be done to ensure the well-being of the state. By absorbing contemporary political theories and adding her own understanding of Russia's problems to them, Catherine had arrived at a political program that informed her domestic policies to the end of her reign. The ideological base of this program was the principles of the Enlightenment. For this reason, the period in Russian history associated with Catherine's reign is often referred to as "ENLIGHTENED ABSOLUTISM."

The eighteenth century is famous as the age of European absolute monarchy. The term "enlightened absolutism" is usually applied to the several decades of European history that preceded the French revolution of 1789. The monarchs regarded as "enlightened" were principally Frederick the Great of Prussia, Joseph II of Austria, Charles III of Spain, and Catherine the Great of Russia. These sovereigns are believed to have used their absolute prerogatives to implement reforms based on the ideas of the Enlightenment.

By that time, European political thought had come to a new understanding of the role of the monarch and his relationship with his subjects. Increasingly the monarch was seen as a first servant of the state, as a caring head of society. Not all analysts are convinced, however, that the concept of "enlightened absolutism" is applicable to Catherine's Russia. Some prefer to speak of "ENLIGHTENED DESPOTISM" instead. The question that is often asked is whether indeed Catherine was an enlightened despot.

For many commentators the ideals of the Enlightenment espoused by Catherine appear to be incompatible with the reality of serfdom in Russia in the second half of the eighteenth century. They suspect that all her talk about Enlightenment and the liberal phraseology of her correspondence with Voltaire were nothing but a smoke screen that the empress used to conceal her vanity, her lust for power, and her own rather reactionary views. However, in recent decades this rather unflattering perception of Catherine has been yielding ground to a more positive view, according to which Catherine did, indeed, sincerely aspire to imprint an enlightened stamp on her autocratic rule and even partially succeeded.

Catherine as Enlightened Lawmaker

It is useful to consider some of the ideas that influenced her policies and look at the ways in which she tried to implement them. As far back as the seventeenth century, Western thinkers — the English political theorist Thomas Hobbes (1588–1679), in particular — had formulated the theory of the social contract. According to this theory, the state was created by people who agreed among themselves to transfer part of their rights to the state in return for its protection. But if the state was created in this way, then it followed that it was possible to improve and perfect the state for the sake of the common good with the help of rational and useful laws.

The ideas of the social-contract approach were further developed by French political theorists of the eighteenth century, in particular by Charles-Louis Montesquieu (1689–1755), the author of *The Spirit of the Laws* (1748), which was highly regarded by Catherine the Great. Montesquieu believed that there were three forms of government: monarchy, republic, and tyranny. For a monarch not to turn into a tyrant, laws were needed that would define rights and obligations both of the monarch and his subjects. The monarch was a wise and enlightened lawmaker who gradually perfected the laws on the basis of accurate knowledge of the country's historical and cultural traditions.

Montesquieu is also credited with elaborating the all-important concept of the separation of powers, whereby the executive, legislative, and judicial branches of government are independent of each other, and each has the power to act as a check and balance over the others' actions. He held the separation of powers to be a basic constitutional need if the political liberties of citizens were to be protected from tyrannical governments.

The ideas formulated by Montesquieu were absorbed by Catherine and formed the basis of her theoretical outlook. They combined with the empress's own views about the national interests and needs of Russia. First of all, Catherine saw herself as the heir and successor of Peter the Great, with whom she strove all her life to compete for glory. She saw Peter's main achievements as the Europeanization of Russia and its transformation into a powerful empire with a leading role in world politics. Catherine was convinced that the success of the Petrine Reform was the best proof that Russia belonged to European civilization.

Peter's idea of a "regular" state was also akin to her philosophical outlook. She, however, disapproved of borrowing uncritically from the West and of the haste and brutality with which Peter carried out his transformation. She made gradualism into one of the most important guiding principles of her reign.

One early example of Catherine considering ambitious change based on the Enlightenment was the calling, in 1767, of the LEGISLATIVE COMMISSION — a temporary consultative body created to revise Russia's laws. This unique and unprecedented effort in Russian history involved a cross section of the Russian population in a state-sponsored and state-organized national debate on all essential economic, social, and legal issues of the day. The membership of the Commission consisted of 572 deputies elected by all classes of the 30 million-strong population of Russia. The serfs were excluded, but the peasantry was represented, although their deputies were not elected to the Commission but appointed by the empress.

Catherine requested that the Commission draft memoranda with suggestions for improvement and change. She herself set the tone for the Commission in a keynote *Instruction* that she wrote personally. The *Instruction* borrowed many of the ideas of the Enlightenment and was applauded throughout the continent for its liberal spirit. Catherine startled people's representatives by the bold language of the *Instruction,* which contained references to universal freedom and liberty and even included statements like this: "Contrary to the flatterers who daily keep telling the monarchs that peoples were created for them, We believe and take pride in saying that We were created for our people."[3] And she clearly tried to impress the lawmakers of the Commission with more humane ideas, such as opposition to capital punishment and torture.

Deliberations in the Commission took more than a year, but produced no immediate results. Commission delegates proved poorly prepared for lawmaking activities. Many of them had a low level of education and culture and lacked parliamentary experience and legal learning. To most of them, the question of universal freedom and liberty raised by the empress in the *Instruction* was, apparently, of little interest. They were much more concerned about protecting the privileges of the group or class they represented. The nobility, especially, fiercely opposed even the slightest suggestion of other classes encroaching on the sphere of its economic interests, particularly, agricultural production. They did not want to hear about any weakening of serfdom, let alone its abolition. The delegates from the peasantry differed sharply from the representatives of the nobility over the issue of serfdom. Some other social estates, such as townspeople and the merchant class, in particular, sought for themselves some of the privileges enjoyed by the nobility, chief among them the right to buy land and peasants whose labor they could use in their factories.

Bitter confrontations took place among the delegates, and in December 1768, using the start of hostilities against Turkey as the pretext, the empress dissolved the Commission. Although it failed to provide a new enlightened code of laws, the Commission did give the empress a clearer picture of conditions in her adopted country. Catherine's attempt to effect legislative change in cooperation with representatives of different social groups led her to the realization of the deep-seated conservatism of broad sections of her subjects. She concluded that it was impossible to introduce genuinely radical reforms. The failure of the Commission discredited the whole idea of representative legislative assemblies for many years to come.

The Golden Age of Nobility

Though the Commission failed to produce immediate results, it did present the basic grievances of the population to Catherine. The quarrels that surfaced among the delegates reflected the main tensions and contradictions of Russian society. Arguably, the most important of these was the conflict between the nobility and the peasantry.

The eighteenth century, particularly its second half, was the "golden age" of the nobility. The nobles had three main objectives: the ending of compulsory service, full rights of ownership of landed property, and the final enserfment of the peasantry. They achieved all of these, but the resulting dislocation of the Russian social system had dire consequences for the country's future.

The exclusive rights were won by the nobility over a period of about fifty years. In 1731 the *pomeschik* (the owner of a *pomestie,* or manor granted for state service) became the full proprietor of his estate. In 1736 the compulsory lifelong service of the nobility was cut down to a term of twenty-five years. The right to hold serfs became the exclusive privilege of the hereditary noblemen. In 1762 compulsory service for the nobility was abolished and "every member of the Russian well-born nobility" was granted "his freedom and liberty." In other words, one of the two main classes of Russian society had been officially emancipated.

The exclusive privileges of the landowning nobility were finally codified and reinforced by Catherine's CHARTER OF THE NOBILITY in 1785. This confirmed the nobility's hereditary status and its exemptions from compulsory service, taxation, loss of rank or estates, and from corporal punishment. It also formally invested it with corporate organizations, namely, provincial and district assemblies of nobility.

The official emancipation of nobility from compulsory service to the state was one of the great turning points of Russian history. As has been explained by Tibor Szamuely: "Hardly anyone realized at the time that by triumphantly asserting their independence of the State the nobility were encompassing their own eventual and inexorable downfall. They sought to emulate the privileged position of the Western European aristocracy — but their title to land and serfs was based not on ancient feudal rights secured in law, but solely on their unremitting military service to the State."[4] The point is that nobility's lifelong state service had been the original justification for the introduction of serfdom. Having wriggled out of its state obligations, the traditional serving class of nobility thus emancipated itself from the very condition of its original status of privilege. As a result, the generally accepted basis for its authority was gone, and in the eyes of the peasantry the nobility's privileges and property rights (such as the right to land and serfs) became illegal. The peasant masses felt that the next logical step should be their own emancipation and endowment with the land they had tilled since time immemorial. In reality the landed proprietors, far from alleviating the condition of the peasants, established a despotic and extortionate rule over their peasantry in which serfdom was indeed indistinguishable from slavery.

Russia's "Peculiar Institution"

At the end of Catherine's reign Russia had a population of 36 million, the largest of any state in Europe. It had increased threefold in the seventy years since the death of Peter the Great, partly through territorial acquisition but in the main by natural increase. Of these 36 million, it is estimated that 34 million were peasants. There were two main groups of peasants — landlords' serfs and state peasants. Landlords' serfs, who belonged to individual members of the nobility and lived on private estates, were the bigger group — nearly 20 million; the remainder, state peasants, belonged to the government, but their existence was not far removed from the strict condition of serfdom.

Agricultural methods almost everywhere were still primitive. Though the land belonged, in law, to landlords or the state, peasants usually controlled the way it was farmed. Usually, open fields were divided among peasant households in the village in the traditional pattern of long, narrow strips of arable land, scattered throughout the village. Each household received strips from different parts of the arable land. In this way the village commune ensured that each household had a fair share of good and bad land. The strips were tilled with a light, wooden plough (*sokha*) that only scratched the surface of the soil. On the majority of estates the serfs might number anywhere from a hundred to a thousand. But this age was noted for its scores of fabulously rich serf-owners who possessed tens and even hundreds of thousands of serfs.

Serf dues were of two types: rent (*obrok*) and labor (*barshchina*). *Obrok,* which commonly consisted of both cash and kind, was the rule in the less fertile areas of the north; *barshchina* was the norm in the black-earth areas and was most often fixed at three days of labor a week. But it was here, where soils were fertile and farming was profitable, that the landowners had grown most exacting. Many of them required their serfs to labor on the demesne lands set aside for the landlord's own use as much as six days in the week, leaving the peasant with just one day to look after the strips of land that sustained his family.

In addition to the *obrok* and *barshchina* forms of feudal dues, peasants also had to pay state taxes. The main direct monetary tax was the poll tax, introduced by Peter the Great and levied on all males from the "tax-paying" classes. Compulsory army recruitment was another type of direct taxation levied not on property but on human beings. Army recruits from the peasantry had to serve for life (their service was reduced to twenty-five years in 1793). The death rate in the army (mainly from disease) was high and few soldiers lived long enough to return to civilian life.

Russia's peasant population was held in the condition of economic slavery by means of coercion, arbitrary punishment, and sheer brutality. In the words of Richard D. Charques: "The everyday conditions of existence for the peasantry steadily became more brutalized in the golden age of the nobility. The discipline of serfdom was maintained more than all else by corporal punishment; never was the practice of flogging in Russia so extensive, never was the knout considered so sovereign a remedy for peasant failings."[5] Although serfdom was not exactly slavery, the absence of any civil and political rights and the lack of any legal protection against landlords or government officials meant that in reality the serfs were often treated as chattel. The trade in serfs flourished, continuing throughout Catherine's reign, both in private sales and public auctions. Human beings were openly offered for sale in the newspapers as may be seen from the following advertisements:

> To be sold: a barber, and in addition to that four bedsteads, an eiderdown and other domestic chattels.

> To be sold: banqueting tablecloths and also two trained girls and a peasant.

To be sold: a girl of sixteen of good behavior and a second-hand slightly used carriage.[6]

Did Catherine make an attempt to face the problem of serfdom? Hardly. In fact, she extended serfdom to the Ukraine, where the land was distributed among the nobility, many of them the special recipients of her bounty. However well-intentioned she might have been, Catherine faced the same dilemma that confronted any ruler who wanted to reform Russia's "Peculiar Institution" of serfdom: the entire class of the nobility depended for their livelihood on the ownership of people. The whole society was organized in such a way that it seemed impossible to deprive the nobility of their sustenance without bringing the state to the ground. Catherine's victorious wars and her brilliant court, the spread of Western culture, with its improvements in the standards of living of the upper classes — all were provided at the expense of the serfs. The "Peculiar Institution" was getting worse all the time.

This was the situation that led to the greatest of Russian peasant rebellions — the PUGACHEV REVOLT of 1773. Pugachev was a Don Cossack, a former convict and deserter from the Russian army. He raised the revolt in the provinces east of the Volga and was soon leader of an army of serfs, laborers from the mines and factories of the Urals, and Cossacks. The rebels wanted the division of the landlords' estates among the peasants. In Pugachev's own words: "We shall behead every noble in the land and take over the land for ourselves." Pugachev led his army into the valley of the Volga and sacked several important towns. Nobles and landlords were tortured and killed, buildings set on fire, estates plundered. Only with great difficulty were the troublesome areas brought under control. Pugachev was caught and brought in an iron cage to Moscow, where he was tried and executed in 1775.

Pugachev's rebellion had sent a powerful signal to the ruling classes about the magnitude of discontent among the peasants. His ghost continued to haunt the autocracy, while the spirit of his revolt would inspire those later revolutionary activists who believed in the innately anti-authoritarian and insurrectionary nature of the Russian masses.

Absolute Monarchy or Arbitrary Autocracy?

Catherine's thirty-four-year-long reign represented the second attempt in the eighteenth century to modernize Russia's economy and its social structure. Like her great predecessor, Peter I, Catherine had set out to transform the country without touching the foundations of serfdom, and, like him, she achieved considerable success. In her reign the economic resources of the country increased substantially. As a result of the wars with Turkey and the partitioning of Poland, Russia acquired eleven new provinces. The population of the empire doubled, and state revenues increased fourfold. By the end of her reign, the transformation of Russia into a great power, begun by her predecessor, was complete.

In addition, Catherine attempted something that Peter would have never thought of doing. She rendered signal service to Russia by her brave attempt to implant in its inhospitable climate the ideas and the liberal spirit of the Enlightenment. In her excellent summation of Catherine's legacy Isabel de Madariaga observes:

> Her greatness lies not so much in her territorial acquisitions but in the new relationship between rulers and ruled which she fostered. Starting with the Legislative Commission the idea of national debate became conceivable.... Instruments of public control were multiplied and penetrated deeper into society, new concepts of justice and legality were put before an untutored public.... The elite of Russian society basked in a new-found sense of freedom and self-respect, and the area of private as distinct from state activity expanded immeasurably. Learning thrived, and the court itself acted as the source of literary, artistic and musical patronage.... [F]or a brief period, at the end of the eighteenth century, Russia and Western Europe converged: the spatial abyss and the lag in time were reduced. After Catherine's death their ways diverged again. ... With the advance of the nineteenth century, Russia and the West moved further and further apart; the tempo of Russian development slowed down, while that of European growth accelerated.... Those who remembered Catherine's rule looked back on it then as a time when autocracy had been "cleaned from the stains of tyranny," when a despotism had been turned into a monarchy.[7]

Catherine tried hard, particularly in the early years of her reign, to foster enlightenment in her adopted country and to purge Russia of some of its more barbaric traditions. Well-educated and intelligent, she came closer than her predecessors to the understanding of the evil of serfdom. She was perhaps the first Russian monarch who was personally in favor of abolishing archaic social relations. Yet the obstacles she encountered were too powerful even for an autocratic ruler to overcome. Her humane and philanthropic ideas did not find much support in Russian semifeudal society. The ruling nobility was firmly against any reform of the country's social structure. Many of its members were probably even unable to conceive of a condition for their servants other than serfdom. The harsh conditions of Russian life and the need to safeguard her place on the throne set limits to Catherine's ability to implement change. After the Pugachev revolt and the French Revolution the empress herself gave up any plans for reform. Her enlightened absolutism, based on false premises and unreal expectations, failed to accelerate Russia's advance along the road of European progress.

Catherine's efforts were lauded and acclaimed by contemporary European powers that warmly welcomed Russia into the charmed circle of enlightened monarchies. But in reality Russian absolute monarchy (in the European sense) still retained many characteristics of a feudal society. In the eighteenth century there was no longer any Western monarch who possessed the degree of power wielded by the Russian tsar. Western monarchs could not disregard the unwritten rules of society, which since ancient times had come to be expressed in the description of the monarch as "first among equals."

Western "absolutism," even at its height, was never truly absolute. The monarch's authority was limited by the power of the church, by strongly established privileged classes, by provincial autonomies and local charters, by powerful economic interests, and by accepted traditional customs and rights such as those of petition or of nonpolitical association. The rights of the individual may have been an unrecognized abstraction, but the rights and the effective powers of the various social groups constituted a formidable force that put limits on the power of the monarch.

Not even after the granting of the Charter of the Nobility did anything faintly resembling such a system make its appearance in Russia. The nobility could be deprived of their newfound privileges at the stroke of a pen — as Paul I, Catherine's son and successor, was to show. Their privileges, their possessions, and even their continuing existence as a class became in the long run more dependent on the state than ever before. The gentry continued to live, as before, in the conviction that the government would provide them with an appointment and guarantee their livelihood. The Russian autocrat remained a towering figure at the pinnacle of the pyramid of state, exercising total power in the country. The absolute rule of the tsar met with no opposition from society. True, there were spontaneous popular revolts like that led by Pugachev, but their leaders themselves often harbored autocratic aspirations and would have assumed the throne if the opportunity arose. (Pugachev, for one, claimed to be Peter III, deposed and murdered by Catherine in 1762 with the help of the guards and officers loyal to her.)

In order to bring out more clearly the difference between Russian and European absolutism, it is helpful to introduce a distinction between ABSOLUTE AND ARBITRARY government. In reality the fundamentals of the Russian monarchy had more in common with the principles of arbitrary autocracy than with those of eighteenth-century absolutism. Under arbitrary governments all subjects are serfs or slaves of the supreme power, for everything in reality belongs to the ruler. The ruler has unlimited powers over not only the property, but also the lives of his subjects. The only law is the arbitrary will of the monarch.

Beneath the veneer of Catherine's enlightened absolutism was the bedrock of arbitrary autocracy. To quote the Russian historian Michael Bogoslovsky: "[T]he whole social structure of the State, from top to bottom, was marked by the brand of bondage. All social classes were enslaved. The Russian imperial court modelled upon Western lines, dazzling foreigners by its splendor and brilliance, the principal medium for the introduction of European society — was in actual fact nothing but a vast serf-holding estate."[8]

However, some very important modifications to the age-old set up of Russian society had developed by the end of the eighteenth century. The traditional organization of the Russian "service state," in which the land, the peasants, and the government service of the gentry had represented interconnected elements of an integrated system, was destabilized. The original consensus of the service state was being eroded by the growth of social polarization and by the deepening of divisions between the main social groups. Some of the main elements of the old system were changed. Particularly significant was the evolution of the ruling gentry class, which in a comparatively short period of time had obtained a new legal status. Having achieved its own emancipation from the obligation of government service, the gentry were strongly against liberating their serfs.

On the whole, this second attempt since Peter the Great to mobilize the remaining resources of the autocratic-serfdom system was barely sufficient to enable Russia to make its entry into the nineteenth century. The potential of the traditional system had been exhausted. Serfdom was now clearly the chief obstacle to the process of modernization of the country. Its perpetuation led to the ever-widening gap in levels of development between Russia and the leading countries of Western Europe. With every new generation the possibility of a crisis loomed larger and larger.

Chapter Three

Alexander I

Civic Awakening

The start of the nineteenth century in Russia marked the birth of a movement that had as its aim the emancipation of society from the strangling grip of the autocratic regime. The rise of the movement had been stimulated by already existing "pockets of freedom," which were either sanctified in traditions or appeared as consequences of certain policies introduced by the government. Indeed, the tsarist government itself was responsible for the emergence of the elements of freedom and for the appearance of an ever-growing number of freethinking individuals among its subjects. Peter's Reform had given some of the earliest and most powerful impulses to the emergence of these liberalizing trends. He had encouraged them by, for instance, taking the decision to "cut out" a window on Europe and introducing Western customs and education into the everyday life of the nobility. His successors developed them by, for example, allowing public opinion to discuss issues concerned with state institutions and the condition of lower estates, as happened during the work of Catherine's Legislative Commission.

In the nineteenth century the autocratic government would continue to contribute by its policies to the process of a gradual emancipation of society from the tight control of the state. On the government's initiative, the personal bonding of peasants to landowners would be abolished, an independent judiciary would be introduced, and local government bodies, comprised of representatives of all major social classes, would be set up. By sanctioning these developments, the autocratic regime was itself an agent of change, an active party in the process of civic emancipation. There were other players also involved in this process, represented by social forces that were actively pressing for change. However, most of these forces had themselves appeared as a result of the government's policies.

Peter the Great's Reform, in particular, had generated numerous sources of future social conflicts. It enforced complete subordination of the individual to the state, yet it also gave rise to an ideological uncertainty over the nature of this state. From the time of the Petrine Reform the government combined within itself two conflicting and incompatible elements: the sacred inviolability of the supreme autocratic authority, on the one hand, and the spirit of the European Enlightenment, on the other. The Enlightenment introduced into Russian society not just Western standards of education but, more importantly, the European spirit of freedom. It also provided an ideological base for the appearance of the INTELLIGENTSIA — a community of people independent from the state and in opposition to it. This group within Russia's educated elite upheld the pro-Western trend for enlightenment and liberalization and actively opposed the conservative tradition of autocratic government.

The tsarist government, by its own legislation, had helped to create the conditions for the emergence of the freethinking stratum of intelligentsia. Of particular importance was the publication in 1785 of the Charter of the Nobility, which officially recognized the existence of a privileged estate in the structure of the autocratic empire based on serfdom. The "noble gentle dignity" of this estate was proclaimed to be inviolable and hereditary. The gentry, according to this document, could not be deprived of its noble status, life, or property without a trial. Members of the noble estate could only be tried by someone of equally noble origin. They could not be subjected to corporal punishment. The decree freed members of the nobility from mandatory state service and thus created preconditions for transforming their manors into centers of culture and education and for the formation of intelligentsia. However, it also sowed the seeds of future discord between the freethinking gentry and government bureaucracy that began gradually to supplant the gentry as a new "serving class" of the state.

From the time of the publication of the Charter of the Nobility until the era of the "Great Reforms" of the 1860s, the process of the gradual emancipation of society would develop within the limits of this "freedom for the few," which the autocracy had granted to the nobility in the last quarter of the eighteenth century. Even then, the gains of the nobility remained insecure; they could always be taken away from them at the will of the tsar. The arbitrary and willful style of government of Catherine's son and successor Paul (1796–1801) was a clear proof of that. By the end of his short reign Paul had virtually annulled most of the articles of the Charter of the Nobility, including the gentry's exemption from corporal punishment and their right to make collective representations to the tsar. Paul restricted the gentry's freedom from compulsory service and the right of assembly. Practically all that was left of the Charter was the right of the nobles not to be deprived of their status except by the power of the tsar.

Still, some of the important new trends introduced into Russian life during Catherine's reign had survived the harsh reign of her son. The ideas of the Enlightenment, which taught that the rule of individuals should be replaced by the rule of law as the main condition for the establishment of civil society, began to shape the new mentality of the intelligentsia of noble origin.

It is not surprising, then, that Russia's first intellectual rebel appeared during the reign of Catherine the Great. This was ALEXANDER RADISHCHEV (1749–1802). Radishchev was a member of the nobility who had been educated abroad. In an eloquent little book with the innocent title of *A Journey from St. Petersburg to Moscow* (1790), Radishchev vividly portrayed the injustices of serfdom and criticized Russia's autocratic government. Radishchev described such scandals of serfdom as the practice of forced marriages between serfs, auction sales of serfs, and the pressing of serfs into the army even when they were the sole support of their families. He was the first Russian writer to focus attention on the inequity of an empire based upon such an institution as serfdom and to condemn this institution clearly and publicly.

Radishchev incurred Catherine's deep displeasure. Having read his book, she is reported to have exclaimed in horror: "Worse than Pugachev!" Radishchev was sentenced to death for producing such an indictment of Russian society, but the sentence was later commuted to penal servitude for life in Siberia. He languished in exile throughout the reign of Catherine's son Paul until the accession of her grandson Alexander in 1801. Alexander not only granted Radishchev his royal forgiveness but even involved him in the work of a commission on the codification of laws. This sudden turnabout in Radishchev's fate became possible thanks to a new spiritual and intellectual climate that marked the early years of Alexander's reign. A relative relaxation of the autocratic regime under Alexander I has earned his reign (1801–25) the name of the ERA OF LIBERALISM.

Speransky's Plan of Government Reform

In considering who would inherit the Russian throne after her, Catherine the Great hoped to bypass her unloved son Paul and make her grandson Alexander (b. 1777) her immediate successor. Her plan did not work out quite as she intended. But because she had such high hopes for her grandson, she took special interest in Alexander's education. Catherine invited the Swiss tutor LaHarpe to introduce her grandson to some of the achievements of European social and political thought, in which she herself had always had such a keen interest. The democratically minded LaHarpe, who, strangely enough for a tutor of a future autocratic ruler, was an advocate of a republican form of government, became a major influence on Alexander's childhood, implanting in his royal pupil a respect for the ideas of the Enlightenment. (It is worth noting that LaHarpe was the cousin of the French revolutionary leader Marat.) Raised on the milk of the Enlightenment, Alexander became the first tsar to address seriously the twin problems of serfdom and autocracy and to draw plans for a complete transformation of the Russian social and political system.

The young emperor was supported in these activities by a small group of earnest young aristocrats and officials. The leading part in this close circle of reform-minded men was played by MICHAEL SPERANSKY (1772–1839) — a man of low origin who rose to the highest reaches of the Russian government to become probably the most brilliant Russian statesman of the nineteenth century. In the course of several years Speransky had risen to the position of the tsar's closest adviser. Alexander entrusted him with the preparation of memoranda containing a detailed analysis of Russian society and a program of far-reaching reforms. These papers, which were made public only many decades after Speransky's death, were written with maximum frankness and fairness, for they were intended for the consideration of the tsar alone. Speransky's analysis, made by a man who uniquely combined an extensive practical knowledge of administration and government with personal understanding of the life of the people, gave the most authoritative and truthful picture of the Russian social and political system at the beginning of the nineteenth century.

Speransky told Alexander the unpalatable truth about the Russian political system, describing its chief defects, such as the complete neglect of the principle of separation of powers and the unlimited prerogatives of the supreme autocrat. Without mincing words, he branded such a system as despotic and saw it as a main reason why Russia's population was deprived of civil and political rights:

> The fundamental principle of Russian government is the autocratic ruler who combines within his person all legislative and executive powers, and who disposes unconditionally of all the nation's resources. There are no physical limits to this principle. . . .

When the powers of the sovereign authority are unlimited, when the forces of the State are combined within the sovereign authority to such an extent that no rights are left over for the subjects — then such a State exists in slavery and its government is despotic.[1]

According to Speransky, a state founded on the autocratic principle, whatever superficial constitution it may have, or whatever may be asserted in its Charter of the Nobility, cannot be law-based, because its so-called "codes" and "laws" are nothing but the arbitrary decisions of the tsar and his government, which they can revoke or change any time they please. In such a state all subjects and all social classes, regardless of their relationship to one another, exist in slavery to the autocratic authority, which is in complete possession of the political and civil liberties of its subjects:

> I wish someone could point out to me the difference between the peasants' subservience to their landowners and the nobility's subservience to the Sovereign, or could show that the Sovereign's powers over the landowners are not identical with those the landowners wield over their peasants.
>
> In short: instead of all the pretentious divisions of the free Russian people into the absolutely free classes of nobility, merchants, etc., I can find only two conditions existing in Russia: the Sovereign's slaves, and the landowners' slaves. The first can be termed free only with regards to the second, but actually there are no truly free men in Russia, except beggars and philosophers.[2]

The significance of Speransky's analysis is that it clearly shows that, despite the Petrine Reform and Catherine's "enlightened absolutism," the basic, essential features of Russia's sociopolitical system were still practically unchanged in the nineteenth century from what they had been three hundred years before, during the reign of Ivan the Terrible (1547–84). The state was still omnipotent, exercising unlimited control over the lives and property of all its subjects. If anything, as a result of the Petrine Reform and of the final enserfment of the peasantry, it had become even stronger. And, towering above everything else, was the unchallenged authority of the supreme ruler. No laws, institutions, or liberties could exist outside the autocrat's sovereign will.

Speransky's analysis showed, in the clearest way possible, the urgent need to lay down firm fundamental laws and establish institutions that would put an end to arbitrary rule and set limits to autocratic govern-

SPERANSKY'S PLAN OF GOVERNMENT REFORM[3]

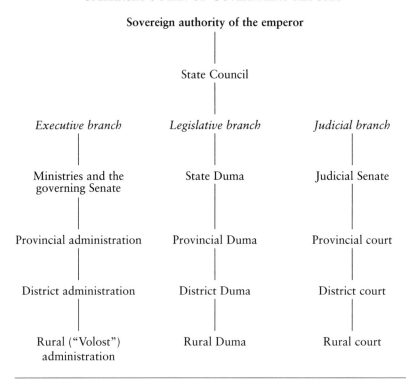

Sovereign authority of the emperor

State Council

Executive branch	*Legislative branch*	*Judicial branch*
Ministries and the governing Senate	State Duma	Judicial Senate
Provincial administration	Provincial Duma	Provincial court
District administration	District Duma	District court
Rural ("Volost") administration	Rural Duma	Rural court

ment. A convinced monarchist himself, Speransky sought to transform the Russian autocracy into a powerful constitutional monarchy, in which there would be a place for the separation of powers, local self-government, civil rights for all sectors of the population, and a national legislative assembly.

Speransky's reform plans envisaged the setting up of a State Council that would act, effectively, as an upper house of a Russian parliament; the reorganization of ministries with the intention of making them genuinely responsible for their spheres of competence; and the restructuring of the judiciary. The first phase of government reform was to be followed up by elections of deputies to a State Duma (a lower house of parliament), after which Russia's transformation into a parliamentary monarchy would be complete.

The implementation of his plans began on 1 January 1810 when the State Council was set up. A few months later the reorganization of ministries was launched, but it bogged down immediately in bureaucratic morass. Speransky's brilliant blueprint, thought through to the last technical detail, underestimated the effect the reorganization plan might have on some powerful vested interests. The proposed changes — affecting the fundamental questions of rank, finance, and power — encountered fierce opposition in the courtly circles. Only the emperor had the authority to push through the reform and shelter Speransky from his critics. However, Speransky's conservative opponents from among the nobility and government bureaucracy persuaded the emperor to shelve the projects and dismiss the would-be reformer from the Court. Speransky fell from power and went into exile.

After the fall of Speransky, Russian domestic policy took a largely conservative turn. The liberal hopes of the early period of Alexander's reign faded and vanished. The emperor increasingly came to be associated with reactionary policies and the tightening of police powers of the state. Besides, Russia's involvement in Napoleonic wars proved to be a powerful distraction, taking Alexander's mind off Russian realities. The success in defeating Napoleon in 1812 and the triumphant entry of the Russian tsar and his army into Paris in the spring of 1814 made Russia the most powerful and respected country on the continent. The glory of victory proved an excellent justification for the preservation of the status quo.

In the late period of his reign Alexander gave up plans to reform the empire's social and political system. Yet the ideas and the principles of government reform elaborated by his "enlightened bureaucrat" Speransky would continue to provide guidance to Russian reform-minded officials for many decades to come. Sixty years later, his ideas would be used to implement a liberal judicial reform. A century later, during the Revolution of 1905, his legacy would be reexamined again and would inform important constitutional changes that gave Russians civil liberties and an elected Duma.

The Decembrists

In the first decade of the nineteenth century, when Speransky developed his plans for constitutional change, Russian society at large did not yet display any deep political interest in the ideas of reform. It was the war of 1812 with Napoleon that reawakened active public consciousness and instilled the awareness that Russia had a distinctive political system, different from that of other leading European countries. The postwar era produced Russia's first revolutionaries — members of the Decembrist conspiracy. Considered to be the first in a series of revolutionary plotters out to overturn Russia's social and political system, the

Decembrists had been educated in the ideas of the Enlightenment and drew their inspiration from the political systems of Western Europe.

Many of the plotters were aristocratic officers in elite guards regiments who had served in Western Europe during the Napoleonic wars, where they became acutely aware of the backwardness of Russia, based on autocracy and serfdom. Several of the plotters were even members of the tsar's court and military entourage. All of them were disillusioned and frustrated with Alexander I, who had apparently lost his early interest in domestic reform. Their disaffection with the regime and their burning desire to serve the noble cause of freeing their country from "the yoke of tyranny" were powerfully captured in poetic form by Alexander Pushkin (1799–1837), Russia's greatest poet and a contemporary, sympathizer, and personal friend of some of the conspirators. The poem ("To Chaadaev") was written in 1818 and deserves to be quoted in full for the insight it provides into the spiritual world, hopes, aspirations, and motivation of the liberal-minded members of the Russian educated society:

> Not long we basked in the illusion
> Of love, of hope, of quiet fame;
> Like morning mists, a dream's delusion,
> Youth's pastimes vanished as they came.
> But still, with strong desires burning,
> Beneath oppression's fateful hand,
> The summons of the fatherland
> We are impatiently discerning;
> In hope, in torment, we are turning
> Toward freedom, waiting her command—
> Thus anguished do young lovers stand
> Who wait the promised tryst with yearning.
> While freedom kindles us, my friend,
> While honor calls us and we hear it,
> Come: to our country let us tend
> The noble promptings of the spirit.
> Comrade, believe: joy's star will leap
> Upon our sight, a radiant token;
> Russia will rouse from her long sleep;
> And where autocracy lies, broken,
> Our names shall yet be graven deep.[4]

Inspired by the lofty goal of overthrowing Russia's age-old despotism, the aristocratic revolutionaries set out to form their first organization, the Union of Salvation, which was established in St. Petersburg in 1816.

Over the next nine years, several branches were set up in other parts of Russia. By the early 1820s the movement developed at two centers: St. Petersburg and the Ukraine. In St. Petersburg the plotters formed the Northern Society, while in the Ukraine, where a substantial part of the Russian army was quartered, the officers involved in the conspiracy established the Southern Society.

The leaders of the two Societies — Nikita Muraviov and Colonel Paul Pestel — worked out clear and detailed reform programs. Muraviov in his "Constitution" proposed to establish CONSTITUTIONAL MONARCHY in Russia. According to his plan, the tsar would remain head of the executive, while the supreme legislative power would be transferred to a People's Assembly, a parliament elected on the basis of a high property qualification. Serfdom would be abolished outright and each freed peasant would be given a plot of land.

Pestel's "Russian Pravda" (Russian law) was more radical. Russia was to be transformed into a REPUBLIC. All branches of government — both a legislative People's Assembly and an executive State Duma — would be formed on the basis of universal franchise without any property qualifications. Serfdom would be abolished and a public land fund would be created out of land previously owned by the crown and the church and partially confiscated from the nobility. From this fund each peasant would receive land sufficient to meet basic needs.

Pestel also advanced the idea of a TEMPORARY DICTATORSHIP that would be needed to maintain order and defend the revolution. In this view he was a pupil of the French Jacobins and a forerunner of Vladimir Lenin, who, in the twentieth century, would put into effect the system of dictatorship known as "the dictatorship of the proletariat." The substantive difference, however, was that in Pestel's project it was to be a dictatorship of the liberal-minded aristocracy.

The members of these secret organizations of nobility regarded conspiracy and an armed coup as the only method of struggle open to them. They saw their chance in December 1825 when news came of Alexander I's death. The line of succession was in doubt. As Alexander had no children, he was to be succeeded by one of his two brothers: Grand Duke Constantine or Grand Duke Nicholas. The plotters in St. Petersburg decided to stage a demonstration for the candidacy of Constantine against his younger brother, Nicholas.

On 14 December (hence the name DECEMBRISTS) members of the Northern Society led some army units into the Senate Square in St. Petersburg trying to prevent Nicholas from taking the oath of allegiance as the new tsar. The plotters had succeeded in convincing their

soldiers that the oath required of them was illegal, that they must uphold the rights of Emperor Constantine and demand a constitution. It
was said that the simple peasant recruits thought *konstitutsia* (Russian
for "constitution") was the name of Constantine's wife. The misappre-
hension of a single word speaks volumes about the tragic divide that
separated the noble conspirators from the illiterate masses.

On 29 December in the Ukraine the Southern Society made its move
by attempting to incite the Chernigov regiment to mutiny. Both revolts
were ruthlessly crushed by the authorities. Arrests and investigations
were immediately started, and 120 men were brought to trial, among
them many members of leading noble families in Russia. Although the
sentences were lightened by Nicholas, five ringleaders were hanged,
among them Paul Pestel, and thirty-one were condemned to hard labor
in Siberia; the remainder were exiled to Siberia or committed to prison
for various periods of time.

The crushing of the Decembrist conspiracy opened a rift between the
ruling groups and progressive elements of Russian society that would
never be healed again. Many members of Russia's intellectual elite had
deep sympathy for the cause of the Decembrists. Their collective feelings
were powerfully expressed by Alexander Pushkin in a poem written in
1827, soon after the conspirators had been sentenced. It encapsulates the
vision of the Decembrists as the Titans in the struggle against autocracy
and the belief in the righteousness of their cause and in its ultimate
triumph:

> In deep Siberian mines retain
> A proud and patient resignation;
> Your grievous toil is not in vain
> Nor yet your thought's high aspiration.
>
> Grief's constant sister, hope is nigh,
> Shines out in dungeons black and dreary
> To cheer the weak, revive the weary;
> The hour will come for which you sigh,
>
> When love and friendship reaching through
> Will penetrate the bars of anguish,
> The convict warrens where you languish,
> As my free voice now reaches you.
>
> Each hateful manacle and chain
> Will fall; your dungeons break asunder;

> Outside waits freedom's joyous wonder
> As comrades give you swords again.[5]

The Decembrist revolt is justly regarded as the beginning of the nineteenth-century revolutionary movement in Russia. Decembrism as a movement was a significant symptom of the social and political situation in Russian in the first quarter of the nineteenth century. At the same time, it contained within it the seeds of different political and ideological trends that would develop more fully in the future: from conservative and liberal to ultra-revolutionary. The ideological freedom and diversity of Decembrism were the secret of its perennial appeal. The Decembrists were revered as martyrs, and the ideals and example of these aristocratic revolutionaries continued to inspire later generations of reformers, radicals, and revolutionaries alike.

Alexander I's reign, during the first quarter of the nineteenth century, contained within it different alternatives for Russia's future. Presided over by a half-hearted ruler, the government vacillated between reform and stagnation, opting finally for the latter. The reawakened public movement contained both a moderate trend in favor of the transformation of tsarist autocracy into a constitutional monarchy, and a revolutionary strand advocating a violent overthrow of the existing order and its replacement by a new one. In the life of the Russian society of that era all of those trends were closely connected, as were the individuals who represented them. The advocates of change in government circles, like Michael Speransky, and in secret societies, like Paul Pestel, belonged to the same ruling class of the nobility and shared the same ideology based on the ideas of the Enlightenment. The impossibility of voicing their ideas openly in public and thus forming a broad reformist coalition led to a split between enlightened government officials, who elaborated their plans in the secrecy of government privy committees, and progressively minded members of the gentry, who saw their only chance of effecting political change in the clandestine activities of underground movements.

The crushing of the Decembrists was a national tragedy that removed from active public life a whole generation of the country's most talented, educated, and honest people. Russia's evolution along the Western European path to a constitutional, law-governed state was delayed considerably. The gulf between the government and society began to widen, turning more and more into an irreconcilable ideological confrontation and leading to the growing alienation of the "thinking minority" from the state.

Chapter Four

Nicholas I

The Triumph of Reaction

The reign of Nicholas I (1825–55) has been described as "the apogee of absolutism." Nicholas's first important act as tsar — crushing the Decembrist rebellion — determined the course of domestic policy throughout his thirty-year reign. Nicholas became an enemy of serious political and social reform. Russian society was put into a deep freeze, while in the foreign arena, Nicholas used Russian power to combat revolutions in other parts of Europe.

The most important influence on Nicholas's early years was his service in the army during and after the Napoleonic wars. He came to see military behavior, with its harsh discipline, as an ideal for himself and the rest of society. As emperor he made the rigid army-like regimentation of the state system and the life of his subjects his priority. The experience of advanced European countries — particularly England, which many others at the time considered to be exemplary — seemed to Nicholas to be unsuitable for the specific conditions of Russia. After a trip to England in 1817 and a visit to parliament, Nicholas observed: "If some evil genius, to our misfortune, transferred to us all these clubs and meetings which produce more noise than substance, I would ask God to repeat the miracle of the confusion of languages or, even better, to deny the gift of speech to those who put it to such use."[1]

To maintain the status quo in Russia, Nicholas relied on the twin pillars of the police and the government bureaucracy. One of his first acts on coming to power was the establishment in 1826 of the Third Section of the Imperial Chancellery, designed to prevent revolution by controlling the actions, thoughts, and behavior of Russians. The Third Section oversaw the most efficient secret police in pre-1917 Russia. The country was covered by a comprehensive network of police spies and informers. Another principal task of the Third Section was the enforcement of Russia's rigid censorship laws. The oppressive atmosphere of harsh military discipline and an all-pervading fear of Nicholas's reign was later vividly conveyed by the satirist Saltykov-Shchedrin, who in one sentence captured the spirit of that grim era: "A desert landscape, with a jail in the middle; above it, in place of the sky, hung a grey soldier's greatcoat. "

The police state of Nicholas I leaned on the government bureaucracy to implement its reactionary policies. After its emancipation from compulsory service in 1762, the nobility's willingness to serve as either civil or military officials of the government had declined. From that time on it became possible to distinguish between those nobles who worked as government officials and those who did not. Under Nicholas, the number and importance of the state bureaucracy was growing rapidly. Whether they were of noble rank or not, most officials were dependent on government salaries for a livelihood and were, therefore, more susceptible to discipline. The government relied increasingly on the state bureaucracy as a new "service class" for the routine execution of its decisions. "By the middle of the century," wrote Vasili Klyuchevsky, "Russia was governed by neither aristocracy nor democracy, but by the bureaucracy, i.e., by a crowd of individuals of heterogeneous origin, acting outside society and lacking any definite social complexion, and joined together only by the table of ranks."[2]

Russia was now under the complete and undivided rule of the colossal administrative apparatus comprised of hosts of venal and corrupt officials. The Russian government was transformed into a police-bureaucratic dictatorship without deep roots in Russian society at large.[3]

The rise of the state bureaucracy went hand in hand with the decline of the nobility. A number of factors combined to undermine the position of this old privileged social estate. Ever since they had won exemption from compulsory service, the nobles had become less necessary to the autocracy as they had lost their vital political status as the serving military class of Russian society. The nobility's economic position had gravely deteriorated as well, as a result of several causes, chief among which were inefficient farming methods, a lack of capital with which to modernize, and the consequent inability to compete in the world market for grain exports. To make matters worse, most nobles despised mercantile habits of mind, and few had the inclination or entrepreneurial skills to run their estates like businesses. By the end of Nicholas's reign two-thirds of landowners' serfs were mortgaged.[4] Increasingly the nobility came to depend on income from state employment, either as military officers or government officials.

The decline of the nobility meant that the bureaucratic state now directly confronted the millions of enslaved peasants. The peasant problem had now become central to every aspect of Russian life. Although over the first half of the nineteenth century Russia had become a more urbanized society, it kept its basically rural character, with the peasantry still making up 84 percent of the population. There was no middle class to speak of, and the intelligentsia was only just emerging. Russia was now the only major country of Europe that had preserved an extensive system of serfdom. The pressing need for peasant emancipation was borne in upon everyone with ever-growing clarity.

From a legal point of view there was nothing to prevent the government from emancipating the peasants by a stroke of the pen. But this would have meant a complete transformation of Russian society, a perilous leap into the unknown fraught with unfathomable consequences. What would be the effect of emancipation on peasants and on their productivity, the backbone of the state economy? Could it not provoke revolutionary outbreaks if the peasants were led to expect too much? What would be the possible effect upon the landowning nobility, the class whose services had chiefly sustained autocracy? Could the nobility be persuaded to give some of its land to the emancipated peasants?

Russia's rulers must also have been aware that the emancipation of the peasants without land would create huge problems, as it had done in the Baltic region at the beginning of the nineteenth century. The emancipation of the Baltic serfs, enacted by Alexander I between 1811 and 1819, may have been an experiment in preparation for a larger emancipation. The effect of that experiment on the peasants was largely negative: freed but with no land, they soon sank into poverty. The reform in the Baltic provinces had made it clear that a larger emancipation would have to tackle the difficult problem of provision of adequate land for newly freed peasants. Obviously, Nicholas's elder brother was not ready to come to grips with this problem and he abandoned plans of a larger emancipation.

These and similar concerns may help explain why every monarch from Catherine the Great to Nicholas I, although personally favoring the abolition of serfdom, hesitated and retreated from taking the fateful step.

The "Great Debate"

Having turned away from radical reform, the government of Nicholas I endeavored to maintain political order and social stability by police repression and by promulgating the official doctrine of "ORTHODOXY —

AUTOCRACY — RUSSIAN NATIONALITY." The doctrine's first component proclaimed the essential role that the official Orthodox Church and its teachings occupied in Russian life — in spite of the fact that Orthodoxy enforced by police and other compulsive measures could hardly cement together peoples of many faiths collected into one empire. The church itself was firmly under control of the state so that even sermons were vetted by the police. The second component proclaimed that Russia needed an absolute monarch as the central element in its political system. The tsar was not merely an absolute ruler but one whose authority was derived from God. The final component proclaimed the special character and value of the Russian people. In practice this principle was translated into the enforced policy of Russification, which could only damage ethnic relations in a multinational state. It contributed nothing to improving the lot of ethnic Russians.

Despite the reactionary and militaristic nature of Nicholas's rule and the rigor of censorship enforced by the Third Section of his Chancery, some remarkably vigorous intellectual activity did take place during his reign resulting in the emergence of oppositionist ideologies and attitudes that sharply contrasted with the patriarchal-conservative view of Russian society promulgated by the three-pronged official doctrine. One of the most significant manifestations of this activity took shape in a debate centered on the legacy of Peter the Great and the desirability of following the West or retaining Russia's special traditions and characteristics.

The debate was prompted by a general feeling spreading among the educated classes that before starting to draw up concrete programs of reform it was necessary to air broader issues of Russia's destiny, chart possible paths of its future development, and identify the peculiarities and moving forces of Russian history. These issues became dominant in Russian literature and in social and political journalism. They animated drawing room discussions and sparked lively debates in small circles of like-minded friends. By the late 1830s a number of distinctive strands of social thought had emerged. Each offered its own interpretation of Russia's past and future. Representatives of the strands of political thought became known as Slavophiles, Westernizers, and Radicals.

The SLAVOPHILES, led by writers like Alexei Khomiakov (1804–60), Konstantin Aksakov (1817–60), and Ivan Kireevsky (1806–56), were the first group to challenge the westernizing orientation of Russian culture since the time of Peter the Great and to uphold the supremacy of Russia's own peculiar cultural and social traditions.[5] In their view, Russia had for a long time been following a completely different path from that of Western Europe. European history was predicated on state despotism and the constant struggle between egoistic individuals and antagonistic social groups aggravated by the growth of laissez-faire capitalism. By contrast, Russian society was founded on the collectivist principle of the commune, all members of which were united by common interests. The next important element of Russian life was the Orthodox religion, which by its precepts had strengthened even more the original ability of Russians to sacrifice their individual interests for the sake of collectivist good, and had taught them to help the weak and bear patiently the hardships of life. As for the state, it had traditionally looked after its people, defended the nation from aggressive neighbors, maintained order and stability, but had not interfered in the spiritual, private, or communal life of the people.

All this was changed, in the Slavophiles' view, by the reforms of Peter the Great. As a result of the transformation he inspired, the original harmonious structure of Russian society and the cooperative spirit of Russian life were destroyed. In their opinion, it was Peter who introduced serfdom, which split the Russian nation into masters and slaves. Peter also attempted to inculcate Western morals, manners, and culture in the governing class, thus separating it completely from the popular masses. In contrast, the common people retained what was best in the old Russia, namely, communal traditions and the Orthodox faith. Peter was also responsible for creating a despotic state that treated the population merely as building material for the establishment of a grand empire.

Having condemned Peter for importing Western ideas and institutions, Slavophiles called for the revival of Russia's old ways of social and state life. The principal objective of any reform program, in their view, was the reestablishment and revitalization of the spiritual unity of the Russian nation. To achieve this, it was necessary, above all, to abolish serfdom, which like an impenetrable wall separated the peasants from the rest of society. The political regime of autocracy was to be cleansed of the repulsive traits of despotism, but preserved. The lost link between the state and the people would be restored by the infusion of wide *glasnost,* i.e., openness, in public life, and by the revival of some traditional institutions, such as, for instance, *zemsky sobor* (Assembly of the Land) — a popular assembly in medieval Russia.

In contrast to the Slavophiles, the WESTERNIZERS were a diverse group united by their rejection of the view that Russia was unique.[6] They firmly believed that Russia advanced along the European path of development, which was the only possible way for a civilized country to go. Russia had taken this path later than most European countries —

at the beginning of the eighteenth century — as a result of Peter the Great's Reform. Naturally, its level of development lagged behind that of the advanced countries of Western Europe. But Russia's progress in the "Western" direction would continue and would lead to the same changes as other European countries had already gone through, namely, the replacement of serf labor by free labor and the transformation of the despotic system of government into a constitutional one. The main task of the educated classes was to instill in Russian society an awareness of the inevitability of change and to work to impress this idea on the authorities. The state and society in close collaboration would prepare and implement judicious and consistent reforms that should enable Russia to close the gap with Western Europe.

The RADICALS, represented by thinkers like Alexander Herzen (1812–70) and Vissarion Belinsky (1811–48), shared the main ideas of the Westernizers, but the early stages of the "Great Debate" had revealed serious theoretical differences between representatives of the Radicals and the Westernizers, and the division between the two intellectual trends would continue to grow. The more radically minded intellectuals were, at the same time, not inclined to idealize contemporary Europe, although they agreed with the Westernizers that Russia was following a common path with other European nations that would inevitably lead to the abolition of serfdom and the introduction of a constitutional system of government. What they found particularly objectionable was the prospect of the importation to Russia of the European bourgeois system. In their view, Russia should not simply strive to catch up with the advanced countries of the West by borrowing their institutions uncritically, but should, together with them, make a bold leap toward a totally new and in principle different system of life — SOCIALISM. The Radicals were also inclined to more direct, revolutionary methods of social change than the Westernizers, who considered reforms introduced from above to be the only acceptable way forward for Russia.

Despite their different visions of Russia's past and future, and their sometimes mutually incompatible views, representatives of the three different trends within the intellectual opposition were, in effect, pushing in the same direction. All were unanimous in their judgment that any reform had to start by resolving Russia's two cardinal issues. The abolition of serfdom and the reform of the autocratic system of government were the twin objectives that progressives of all persuasions set out to achieve. The opposition's activities were strictly legal, but they were wide-ranging and diverse, and produced a much greater impact on society than the conspiratorial Decembrist movement.

Through the medium of university lectures, journalistic and literary work, and salon debates, the opposition was gnawing away at the old foundations of society, raising grave moral concerns about serfdom, instilling widespread condemnation of the autocratic-serfdom system, and mobilizing public opinion in support of reform. The results of this "quiet work," to use Herzen's phrase, would bear fruit in the next reign. Through schools, clubs, salons, and personal friendships, the reformist ideas aired and developed in the 1830s and 1840s would spread from educated society to reach the key decision-makers in the government who in the 1850s and 1860s were to spearhead Alexander II's reforms. The great liberal modernization of Alexander II's era had been intellectually prepared by the "Great Debate."

It is impossible to overestimate the impact of Westernizer-Slavophile controversy on the future intellectual and political history of Russia. Many of the later disputes and divisions between different factions, schools of thought, and political parties in Russia can be analyzed in terms of those who saw Western orientation as a single solution to Russian problems and those who professed their belief in Russia's own distinct path of development. Indeed, the debate about the correlation between national and "adopted" elements within Russian civilization is still alive and readily detectable in the intellectual discussions and political confrontations within Russia in the last decade of the twentieth century.

Alexander Herzen and Peasant Socialism

The "Great Debate" of the 1840s produced many outstanding intellectuals whose opinions and theories would instruct and inspire future generations of Russian progressives. Among them Alexander Herzen occupies a special place as a social thinker whose ideas to a large extent formed the ideological core of the Russian revolutionary tradition. He is often described as the founder of Russian socialism, but his views and experience strongly influenced the development of Russian liberalism as well. During the "Great Debate" he rose to the position of one of the leaders of the Radical wing of the intellectual opposition.

Herzen was the son of a rich landowner, but early in life he came to realize the inequity of serfdom. At the age of fourteen, during the coronation of Nicholas I, which followed shortly after the execution of the Decembrists, he vowed vengeance for the executed and pledged to devote his life to the struggle "against this throne, this altar, these cannons" (meaning the cannons that fired at the mutinous regiments in the Senate Square, on Nicholas's order, on the day of the Decembrist revolt). In the early 1830s Herzen became familiar with socialist theories of the French philosophers Saint-Simon (1760–1825) and Charles Fourier (1772–1837). What particularly attracted Herzen in socialism was the idea of a brotherhood of people — liberated individuals — united in a free community for the sake of lofty and noble goals of goodness and justice.

In the 1840s Herzen became a leading member of the radical wing of Westernizers. He left Russia in 1847 and spent the remainder of his life in exile in the West. There he set up Russia's first free press by establishing a newspaper, *The Bell* (*Kolokol*), which he published in London from 1857 to 1867 and which, though forbidden, was widely read in Russia — even by the tsar. *The Bell* campaigned on such issues as the emancipation of peasants (this included granting them land), the abolition of corporal punishment, freedom of speech, greater public accountability, and opposition to bureaucratic arbitrariness and corruption. Herzen's newspaper set a benchmark of free speech for Russian progressive journalism for decades to come.

Following the failure of the Revolution of 1848 in France, Herzen came to question whether Western Europe was breaking a path that Russia should follow. The spectacle of the shooting down of the Paris workers and the ruthless suppression of the desperate revolt of the French proletariat shocked him to his foundations. The more he saw of the West, the more critical he became of European capitalist progress and bourgeois civilization, which now appeared to him as an outwardly civilized but inwardly inhumane world. He came to the conviction that personal freedom, divorced from the collectivist foundation of society, was not enough for the realization of the ideals of truth and justice.

Under the influence of his European experience his views changed. The youthful extremism of his early Westernism began to give way to ideas more in tune with the Slavophile way of thinking, while the ideas that he had learned from the French socialists were transformed into a Russian brand of socialism founded on the peasant commune. Through a fusion of the three elements of Westernism, Slavophilism, and socialism, Herzen founded the uniquely Russian philosophy of "peasant socialism," which became known as NARODNICHESTVO (sometimes translated into English as "POPULISM"). This philosophical theory was to provide the ideological basis of the nineteenth-century revolutionary movement in Russia until the appearance of Karl Marx's proletarian socialism.

Village Commune

Herzen became convinced that a political revolution was not enough to alter radically the basic conditions of the life of society. What was needed was a transformation of social conditions and, above all, of the relations of ownership. The Western European experience seemed to provide overwhelming evidence that it was precisely the problem of property rights that became the chief obstacle impeding the evolution of humanity because it split society into two unequal and antagonistic parts: the propertied minority and the dispossessed majority. Disillusioned with bourgeois civilization, Herzen turned to Russia's traditional institutions in search of the foundations of a better society for the future. He found them in the VILLAGE COMMUNE (in Russian, *obshchina* or *mir*).

The communes, owing to their democratic traditions, periodic redistribution of land, and collective use of pasture and grazing grounds, appeared to him to provide ready-made building-blocks of the economic and administrative foundations of the society of the future. In his view, this unique institution gave the Russian people a great advantage over the Western nations in their advance toward socialism, since the special properties of the commune made the Russian peasant an instinctive socialist. Herzen transformed the *obshchina* into the cornerstone of Russian peasant socialism:

> Our people's life is based on the village community, with division of the fields, with communistic landownership, with elected administration and equal responsibility for each worker.... The natural unaffectedness of our rural life, the precarious and unestablished nature of economic and legal concepts, the vagueness of property rights, the absence of a bourgeoisie, our own extraordinary adaptability: all these represent a position superior to nations that are fully constituted and tired.... The only thing that is conservative on our shifting, unsettled soil is the village commune — that is, the only thing deserving preservation.... I believe, with all my heart and mind, that it is our door on which history is knocking.
>
> The word *Socialism* is unknown to our people, but its meaning is close to the hearts of Russians who have lived for ages in the village commune.... I boldly repeat that the mere fact of communal landownership and partition of the fields justifies the assumption that our untilled black earth is *more capable* of germinating the seed brought from Western fields... [i.e., socialism].[7]

Herzen realized that the primitive socialist properties of village life were nothing more than "raw material" for the society of the future. Two crucial conditions had to be met before the village commune would be able to develop its innate socialist potential to the full. First, it had to be liberated from the oppressive control of the authorities, and, second, it needed to adopt advanced technical methods from the West and use them to modernize its economic activity. Only then would it be able to translate socialist ideals into life and to satisfy most fully the material and cultural needs of its members.

His theory, based on a belief in the inbred socialist tendencies of the Russian people, allowed Herzen to adopt the European concept of socialism to Russian conditions and to show for the first time that backward Russia was actually more prepared for the introduction of socialism than industrialized Europe. The communal organization seemed to provide an ideal form of harmonizing personal interests with the collectivist character of production. It would provide the basis for an egalitarian society and would open for Russia a new, noncapitalist path of development, thus enabling it to avoid the evils of capitalism. Herzen's vision of a regenerated Russia, free of exploitation and inequalities in wealth, inspired a whole cohort of new revolutionaries — NARODNIKS (or "POPULISTS"), many of whom indulged in a most extravagant idealization of the commune.

However, in their glorification of the commune, Herzen and his followers often lost sight of the reality that was somewhat less exciting. As later studies of the commune were to show, its origins did not go back into the hoary mists of antiquity but dated back to approximately the sixteenth and seventeenth centuries, when the *obshchina* began to evolve as an institution that formed part and parcel of the Russian service state. Far from being an example of spontaneous socialism of the Russian peasants, it was created with the active encouragement of the state, if not on its direct initiative. The state charged the commune with the collective responsibility for the orderly payment of taxes by the peasants. To cope with this task, the commune gradually gained wide-ranging powers: it distributed the tax obligation among its members, enforced payment, administered punishments to recalcitrant peasants, and prevented members from escaping. Most importantly, it provided the means to pay tax by assigning each male member a plot of land roughly commensurate with the size of his family. As the size of peasant households (constituting the commune) changed with time, the land was periodically reapportioned among its members in order to spread the tax burden fairly.

The state-sponsored nature of the village community has been best summed up by Tibor Szamuely, who points out that in reality the *ob-shchina* "represented the basic administrative unit of the country, the vital cog on which, in the final analysis, the Russian economic and financial system turned. The village community could lead an existence and play a part independent of the landowner, even though it was composed entirely of his bond slaves, because its principal function was service to the state, the common master of lord and serf alike.... The *obshchina* was the agency through which the state could mobilize the energies and resources of the peasant serfs toward the solution of its tasks."[8] The commune thus existed with the full blessing of the state and acted as a collective guarantor for the payment of taxes.

The communal ownership of the land and the repartitioning of the land among members of the community — the features that particularly fired the imagination of Russian peasant socialists — were the properties of the *obshchina* that stood in the way of agricultural progress and perpetuated the poverty of its members. One of the leading Russian historians of the twentieth century, V. Diakin, explains why:

> It was the commune, and not the individual peasant or peasant family, that had control of the arable lands. The lands under the plough were divided up periodically according to the number of "souls," working males. The striving after a just distribution degenerated into petty levelling. A peasant household would be given a whole number of strips in different places, low-lying and on the hill, on sandy soil and on clay, close to the village and further away. This number sometimes amounted to dozens, while the width of the strips was measured with a yardstick or even the traditional peasant's bast shoe. On such strips only a common rotation of crops was possible: sow the same as everyone else, and at the same time as everyone else. Otherwise the animals let onto the field will trample your strip. It makes no sense to fertilize or improve the soil — at redistribution somebody else might be given it. The commune stands in the way of agricultural progress. It prevents people dying from hunger, but it leaves no room for the more enterprising and resourceful to get ahead.[9]

The equality of members of the commune was equality in poverty. The primitive egalitarianism of the *obshchina* cultivated the type of collectivism that suppressed the individual, and fostered a formal equality that enforced the equal misery and slavery of its members. This aspect of the commune was not lost on Nicholas Ogarev, Herzen's closest friend and lifelong ideological companion. He had spent several years on his estate and had acquired a genuine love and compassion for his peasants, whose life he could observe on a daily basis. He, however, did not idealize their way of life:

> Our *obshchina* represents the equality of servitude....The commune is an expression of the envy of all against one, of the community against the individual. In the West the idea of equality presumes the equal well-being of all, but the equality of the commune requires that all be equally miserable. As a result...the peasant (or rather, the Russian in general) is unable to comprehend the possibility of a man not belonging to something, of a man simply existing by himself.[10]

Thus the actual workings of the communal system bore little resemblance to the idyllic image of harmonious cooperation and dignified egalitarianism conjured up by Herzen and his followers. The commune perpetuated equality in poverty, deprived the peasants of incentives to improve their farming methods, and hindered technical progress. The great distance between the ideals of the Narodniks and the reality would have dramatic and even tragic consequences for the nineteenth-century revolutionary movement.

Chapter Five

Alexander II

Competition with the West

The age of Nicholas I represented in many ways the pinnacle of achievement for the Russian monarchy. Never in its whole history was it as powerful both at home and abroad. Nicholas I managed to maintain the status quo within the country by doing everything in his power to freeze its social and political development for the three decades of his reign. However, he turned away from reform at a time when the rest of Europe was undergoing rapid transformation under the influence of the developing capitalism. While capitalism was only slowly beginning to affect Russia, it was revolutionizing Great Britain, Belgium, and France. The great industrial revolution spreading across the continent of Europe stopped short of the Russian borders. In agriculture, the institution of serfdom and the inability of most landowners to modernize their estates blocked any major change. The empire of the tsars failed to keep pace with other European countries. By the middle of the nineteenth century it appeared to many "a colossus on feet of clay."

Russian backwardness was dramatically revealed at the close of Nicholas's reign during the CRIMEAN WAR (1853–56), in which an isolated Russia was opposed by the British, French, Turks, and Piedmontese. The war showed Russia to be militarily inferior to the more industrialized countries of Western Europe. The Russians' weapons and military equipment proved obsolete. Their infantry's small arms were no match for modern Western European rifles, which could open fire at four times the distance of Russia's antiquated handguns. The Black Sea fleet, composed of wooden sailing vessels, could not compete with the steam-propelled warships of the allies. In addition, the country's transportation system failed to serve adequately the needs of the war. Unlike their stand in 1812 against Napoleon, in the Crimea the Russians were unable to defend their own territory against outside invasion.

Russia's defeats in the Crimean War seriously undermined its military prestige and dealt a severe blow to national self-esteem. They even provided grounds for talks about Nicholas having deliberately taken his own life. The catastrophe of the war underlined the pressing need for fundamental reforms. It sounded a painful alarm call and was one of the causes of the series of important internal reforms that were carried out by Nicholas's heir, Alexander II (1855–81).

The Crimean War and the subsequent reforms of Alexander II underscored with absolute clarity, for the second time since Peter's reign, the significance of COMPETITION WITH THE WEST as one of the key factors in Russian history. The past three centuries of Russian history, ever since the days of Peter the Great, have been punctuated by reforms induced by the Russian government's efforts to catch up with and overtake its Western rivals. Dominic Lieven presents Russian modern and contemporary history in terms of three great cycles of modernization, all of them triggered by competition with the West. Each of the three cycles was initiated from above, by the state, and each was designed to achieve parity or better in the competition with the leading Western Great powers.[1]

The first of these cycles lasted from the 1690s to the 1850s and is described by Lieven as "catching up with Louis XIV." Its aim was to make Russia the equal of the other great European absolute monarchies that dominated the continent in the eighteenth century. The best-known figure associated with this cycle is Peter the Great, who by defeating the Swedes made Russia a European great power. But the attempt to catch up with Russia's European neighbors would achieve full success only later in the eighteenth century, during the reign of Catherine the Great. By the end of the century Russia had secured the position as one of the continent's three or four greatest military powers and was universally recognized abroad as the equal of Habsburg Austria or Bourbon France.

Alexander I's defeat of Napoleon further increased his country's prestige, and in the first half of the nineteenth century Russia was generally perceived to be the continent's leading military power. However, it was during that time — under the impact of the industrial revolution — that the factors that determined a country's power were undergoing fundamental change. Capitalism was transforming agrarian societies of the leading European states, revolutionizing their industrial bases, and increasing the size of urban populations. The persistence of traditional institutions — serfdom, in particular — now seemed to place Russia behind other countries of the continent. By the close of Nicholas's reign the picture of a powerful Russia, dominating the international order, had disappeared. As Russia fell behind the rate of development of other nations, so its foreign policy became less successful, declining from the tremendous triumph over Napoleon to the disaster of the Crimean War.

The Crimean War had demonstrated Russia's military and economic weaknesses to the Russian government in a shocking and humiliating fashion. Russia's ruling circles were compelled to accept the fact that in the second half of the nineteenth century it was no longer possible to retain serfdom and manage without a rationally organized legal system, local self-government, or a modern army, and at the same time, continue to aspire to the status of a leading European power. As a result, the government initiated the second great cycle of modernization, which lasted from the 1850s to the 1970s. Lieven describes this as "Russia's attempt to remain a great power in the smokestack era." The renewed process of catching up with the West, begun by the imperial regime and interrupted by the First World War and the revolution, was completed under the communist government. Stalin's industrialization and the routing of Nazi Germany in 1945 marked the Soviet Union's achievement of great-power status in the industrial era.

By the 1970s the Soviet Union had achieved seemingly assured superpower status through military parity with the United States. Not since the days of Nicholas I had Russian power been rated so highly at home or abroad. Realities were, however, as deceptive in the Brezhnev era (1964–82) as they had been in the reign of Nicholas I. The factors of power in the world were changing quickly. In Nicholas's day it had been the spread of the industrial revolution in Western Europe that had jeopardized Russia's status as a great power. Under Brezhnev it was the revolution of the microchip and the computer. Gorbachev (1985–91) initiated the third great cycle of modernization from above in order to help Russia catch up with its Western competitors in the new era of the scientific and technical revolution.

This description of Russia's development over the last three centuries in terms of the three cycles of modernization shows clearly the place and the significance of Alexander II's "Great Reforms" in the context of Russian modern and contemporary history. It also helps to illustrate some striking parallels between Alexander's era of the "Great Reforms" and the era of Gorbachev's *perestroika* 130 years later. In both periods a new generation of young, reforming politicians launched sweeping changes from above after a prolonged era of political oppression and economic stagnation. The results, however, were expressly different: in one case, the reformed system survived for another sixty years; in the other case, it collapsed.

Peasant Emancipation

As a young man, Alexander had not shown himself to be more liberal than his father, Nicholas I. However, many analysts agree that he had had the advantage of a more enlightened and humanitarian upbringing under the tutorship of excellent teachers and mentors, including the Russian poet Vasili Zhukovsky. Being the heir apparent of the Russian emperor, Alexander prepared himself very seriously for his future vocation. For almost twenty years from the day he came of age to the day he ascended to the throne, he was very actively engaged in the running of the state. His father introduced him into top governmental agencies such as the Senate and Synod, the committee of ministers, and even the State Council. He frequently deputized for Nicholas in the tsar's absence. In 1848 Alexander carried out a variety of diplomatic tasks at the courts of Vienna and Berlin, and in other European capitals. Thus he gained extensive experience in the affairs of state — military, diplomatic, and legal.

His accession to the throne on 19 February 1855 came at a very difficult time for Russia. The situation on both the foreign and domestic fronts looked extremely grave. The obvious failures of the Russian army in the Crimea were demoralizing for the entire nation. Therefore, the first task facing the new ruler was to end the Crimean campaign as quickly as possible on terms that were more or less acceptable. Indeed, this soon took place.

The defeats of the Crimean War led to a critical reexamination of Russian institutions. Serfdom was blamed for the backwardness of Russia's military industry as well as the ignorance and poor health of the army's rank and file, who were conscripted serfs. Moreover, the labor of serfs could no longer be considered economically efficient. It was clear that serfdom had become a drag on Russia's economy. In addition, the works of a series of liberal-minded writers, philosophers, historians, and literary critics, starting with Alexander Radishchev's inflammatory book, put the moral case against serfdom. Their work aroused moral concerns of the educated classes over the condition of millions in Russia — fellow Christians — who were exploited and treated like slaves. By the end of Nicholas's reign educated members of the nobility accepted that serfdom was morally indefensible.

The discussion circles that appeared in the 1840s and 1850s had brought together the more enlightened representatives of educated society and progressive members of the bureaucracy, thus providing a forum for the exchange of ideas, knowledge, and practical experience necessary for the success of the impending reform. After Alexander's accession, liberal-minded intellectuals, including prominent Westernizers and Slavophiles, were brought into government departments to help reform-minded civil servants draw up plans for Russia's transformation. All this partly helped overcome the alienation of the intellectual elite from the officialdom that was typical of Nicholas's era.

The expectations of the progressives were heightened when Alexander's accession brought with it an amnesty for the Decembrists still in exile. The first years of his reign were also marked by some easing of censorship and a revival of social and political journalism. Filled with hope, Alexander Herzen from his far-away exile in London addressed his imperial namesake in an open letter published in his magazine *The Bell*:

> Your Majesty, your reign begins under a strikingly happy constellation. You have no bloodstains on you, your conscience is untroubled. . . . You did not need to announce your accession to the people with executions. There is scarcely a single example in the chronicle of your house of such a clean beginning. To be sure, my pennant is not yours: I am an incorrigible socialist, you an autocratic emperor; yet our banners might have one thing in common, namely . . . — a love of the people. . . . And in the name of that I am willing to make a great sacrifice. What long years of persecution, prison, exile, tedious wandering from country to country could not achieve, I am willing to do for love of the people. I am prepared to wait, to efface myself, to talk of something else, if only I have alive within me the hope that You will do something for Russia.[2]

Herzen's appeal would not be wasted. Indeed, Alexander II's reign proved to be one of the most consistent attempts to shake up the entire structure of the Russian Empire. His reforms encompassed all of the three chief spheres of the country's life: socioeconomic relations (the peasant emancipation and the land settlement); the political sphere (the introduction of local self-government, the judicial and military reforms); education and culture (the school and university reforms and the new censorship regulations). The extent and effectiveness of the reformist policies in these various spheres may have been different, but their combined liberalizing impulse propelled Russia in the right direction, helping it overcome economic backwardness, familiarizing its educated classes with European political culture, introducing elements of legality and of the rule of law into the political system, and giving society greater independence along the lines of local self-administration.

The "architects" of Alexander's Reform were young, liberal-minded government officials, such as the Miliutin brothers, S. Zarudny, and many others. The new tsar himself took the lead in preparing the most crucial reform of all: the emancipation of the serfs. He first made his intentions clear in an address to the nobility in Moscow in 1856 in which he tried to forestall the inevitable dissatisfaction of the landowners with the impending loss of their "christened property" by pointing out that it would be preferable to abolish serfdom "from above" than wait for the upheaval from below. He said: "[T]he existing system of serf-owning cannot remain unchanged. It is better to begin abolishing serfdom from above than to wait for it to begin to abolish itself from below. I ask you, gentlemen, to think of ways of doing this. Pass on my words to the nobles for consideration."[3]

Two years later committees composed of members of the landed nobility were established in all provinces with the express purpose of studying the issue of emancipation, but also in order to make the squires feel involved in the process of the preparation of a reform that was to transform so radically their traditional ways. The government's decision to invite representatives of the nobility to contribute to the drafting of reform legislation was designed to check the growth of the gentry's spontaneous discontent and transform its displeasure with the proposed emancipation into a constructive work for the benefit of the reform. An Editing Commission, set up in 1859, examined the individual plans prepared by the committees of the nobility at the local level and produced an overall plan that was quickly adopted by the government.

On 19 February 1861 the Imperial Order on the Emancipation of the Peasants from Serfdom was decreed. From the political, legal, and moral points of view, a peaceful emancipation of 23 million peasants from the condition of serfdom was an event unprecedented in world history. This tremendous work could be compared only with the abolition of slavery in the United States, which followed four years later. In the Russian case, however, the emancipation was carried out on an infinitely larger scale, and was achieved without civil war and without devastation or armed coercion. It revealed a great paradox: only an autocrat could achieve a "peaceful" transformation like this; in a democracy, which must compromise on such issues to satisfy pressure groups, such bold actions are much more difficult!

The essential features of the complex legislation were as follows. First, the serfs were given their technical, legal liberty: that is, they were no longer the private property of their masters and were free to trade, marry, litigate, and acquire property. Second, the serfs were freed with allotments of land, assigned to them from their previous owner's estate, for their own use. However, they were to pay a series of "redemption payments" to the government for these land-allotments (the government paid the landowners for the loss of some of their land at once). The high level of the redemption dues, set at 6 percent interest over a period of forty-nine years, meant that the peasants were forced to pay a price for their land that was far in excess of its current market value, and represented a "hidden" compensation to the nobility for the loss of their servile labor.

In addition, the landlords were able to cut off for themselves over one-fifth, or even two-fifths, of the land the peasants farmed before the emancipation. They retained possession of the best parts of the peasants' allotments, including woods, meadows, watering places, and grazing grounds, without which the peasants could not engage in independent farming.

Another crucial feature of the legislation was the fact that the land that the peasants received was granted not on an individual but on a collective basis — to the village commune. The *obshchina* retained extensive powers over its members, both of an economic and of a quasi-judicial nature. Taxes, redemption payments, and other dues were communally collected and paid; the land was periodically redivided among the members in the commune, as before; no peasant was free to leave the commune without the permission of the village elders; and the commune retained judicial powers to banish its wayward members to exile in Siberia. The retention of the *obshchina* as an official institution meant that although the peasant had been freed from his bondage to the serf-owner, he remained in bondage to the commune.

In addition, peasants were still subject to corporal punishment, military conscription, payment of the poll-tax, and certain other obligations from which other social classes were exempt. In other words, the peasantry did not receive equal status with the other classes in Russian society. It remained a separate "caste" with its own internal structures, procedures, laws, and economic arrangements. Bound to the commune, without individual land tenure, subjected to heavy taxes and periodic redistribution of land to enforce complete egalitarianism, the peasantry remained a rebellious and impoverished neofeudal mass with a poorly developed sense of private property and law. For decades it would continue to dream of a new partition of land.

The emancipation reform cannot be appraised on a simple "positive or negative" scale. On the one hand, the abolition of serfdom led to irreversible changes in all spheres of Russian life giving a powerful impulse to the development of new socioeconomic relations. It accelerated the process of the cleavage of the peasantry, with more enterprising peasants increasing their wealth and leaving the patriarchal commune while others grew destitute and turned into dispossessed proletarians. As a result, mines and factories in rapidly developing industrial regions gained a steady flow of cheap wage labor. As the natural economy disintegrated, the Russian internal market's capacity increased. All this taken together gave a powerful boost to the growth of industrial production. By the early 1880s the industrial revolution in Russia had arrived. Alongside the older, traditional branches of industry, new ones were created: coal-mining, oil-extracting, machine-building; the country was covered by a network of railways. The new social classes of bourgeoisie and industrial proletariat were rapidly developing. All strata of society were experiencing change.

On the other hand, the reform had conserved some of the elements and relations of the old serfdom system. The pressure of circumstances had impelled the authorities to implement the abolition of serfdom and thus undermine the landowners' economy. But at the same time the government sought to maintain this traditional economy by compensating the former serf-owners' losses as much as it could. This compensation had to be shouldered entirely by the peasants who were being freed. No wonder that the peasants were bitterly disappointed by the emancipation settlement. The feeling grew among them that they were being deceived by greedy landowners and that the true intentions of the tsar were being thwarted. They resented not receiving all the land they formerly tilled, they objected to the burdens, and they felt constrained by the commune, which was often under the undue influence of a village elder or priest or a rich peasant (derogatively referred to as a *kulak*, "fist"). The contradictory nature of the peasant reform aggravated the traits of backwardness in village life and in the final analysis led to a deeper crisis.

This is how Nicholas Berdyaev assessed the situation in postreform Russia:

> The peasants were liberated and given land. . . . But the peasants, in spite of the fact that they possessed the larger part of the land, remained unorganized and discontented. The level of agricultural skill was low and at a primitive stage, and the peasants had not sufficient land for their subsistence. A class regime still remained, and the peasant, as a man, continued to be humiliated. Russia was still an aristocratic country, and feudalism was not entirely

superseded until the actual revolution of 1917. The great mag-
nates who possessed immense estates still remained. Manners and
morals were feudal. Notwithstanding the immense significance of
the reform, everyone was discontented.[4]

The retention of the commune was arguably the chief stumbling-
block that hindered the modernization of the agrarian sector and
prevented capitalist development in rural areas. The practice of periodic equalization of landholdings between peasant households made it
difficult for successful peasants to accumulate land and become small
entrepreneurial farmers. In addition, the 1861 Act slowed capitalist development in urban areas by making it difficult for destitute peasants to
leave their land and become full-time wage-workers. Lack of capital investment, periodic reallocation of land, primitive agricultural methods,
the crippling financial burden of redemption payments, and the imped-
iments to labor mobility imposed by the village commune ensured that
the agrarian sector of the Russian economy more or less stagnated for
the next forty years.

Post-1861 Liberal Reforms

As much of Russian life had been constructed around the institution
of serfdom, its abolition inevitably required other reforms. The emancipation of serfs necessitated liberalizing changes in areas including local
government, the judicial system, and the military.

Administrative Reform

The Emancipation Proclamation was followed by the publication on
1 January 1864 of regulations about the *zemstvos,* organs of district and provincial government. The new law granted all classes of
the population in the provinces and districts the opportunity to elect
the bodies that would decide practically all questions concerning the
administration of the local economy.

Zemstvos had never been intended as genuinely democratic institutions: elections into these new bodies were indirect, and landowners
were overrepresented (they held about three-quarters of the available
positions). Nevertheless, for the first time, elected representatives of all
classes — landowners, the village communities, and the townspeople —
had a forum in which they worked together.

The work of *zemstvos* was restricted to local, district, and provincial administration. They dealt with local education, welfare, health, agriculture, road and industrial construction, and many other aspects of local government. Unfortunately the funds at the disposal of the *zemstvos* were often insufficient and their taxing power restricted. Moreover, they were carefully watched by police and government officials, for the Russian government was too jealous of its own powers to permit them an independent role. Yet despite their modest powers and the fact that in practice they were dominated by the landowning nobility, the new bodies contributed much to the betterment of conditions of the population by setting up schools, bringing doctors and agronomists to help rural communities, funding the building of roads, etc. Thus the *zemstvos* had an important effect on Russian life.

Six years later, in 1870, the municipal reform in the towns was introduced along lines similar to the *zemstvos* reform. The municipal reform set up city and town Dumas (councils), thus granting the right of internal self-administration to all classes of the population in towns and cities.

The administrative reform signified a small but portentous step toward representative forms of government. However, the most important achievement of the newly created bodies of local self-administration may have been to provide a framework for the emerging civil society and to serve as a training ground for political leaders. Some members of the gentry used the success of local self-government to argue for a national representative assembly. *Zemstvos* became a base for "gentry liberalism," encouraging groups within the gentry to call for a limited, constitutional monarchy. In the revolutionary 1880s their work was interrupted, but later they gained increased prestige.

Legal Reform

The abolition of serfdom led to the reorganization of the judiciary. Out of the whole package of Alexander's liberalizing measures, the legal reform was arguably the most consistent and progressive, upholding the idea of the supremacy of the law and of respect for it. The basis for the restructuring of the administration of justice was laid by the Judicial Statutes, enacted in 1864. The courts were completely separated from other departments of state and became open and independent with the participation of juries drawn from the local population. Justices of the peace were now to be elected by the population. The adversarial trial system was introduced for the first time, as was an independent bar and the right to counsel.

The reformed judicial system went a long way toward meeting the standards of impartial justice and ensuring equality of all Russians before the law. However, an important exception was made for the peasantry. Cases between peasants were decided by a system of special courts. Separating peasants from the regular judicial system kept up the old distinction between free citizens and serfs.

The new courts provided a forum and another opportunity for the public voicing of nonconformist and critical opinion. The reform led to the development of a large class of lawyers. Many members of the newly established legal profession later played a prominent part in antigovernment politics.

Military Reform

The emancipation meant changes in the military, since the old military system had conscripted men from the serf population only and had required them to serve for twenty-five years.

In 1874 a military statute was adopted that put in effect a system of conscription that imposed compulsory military service on the entire male population for a period of between six months and six years depending on the individual's education. A system of education for all soldiers and officers was instituted. This helped make army service more humane and civilized. Russian military successes in the war with Turkey in 1877–78 were in large measure attributable to the military reform.

Education

The early years of Alexander's reign introduced liberal trends in education. A statute of 1863 had given the universities elected boards of professors and rectors and thus self-administration. The close supervision placed over the universities, which had prevailed in the era of Nicholas I, was now lifted, opening the way for the formation of numerous circles and associations and thus to greater public activity.

Major changes were begun, too, in the field of female education: many courses for women appeared, providing an education that followed university curricula. General primary education began to develop. Following the institution of the *zemstvos*, numerous elementary schools were established on their initiative in European Russia. By 1880 such schools had more than a million students.

The liberalizing trends in education led to the flowering of Russian science and culture in the decades that followed.

Relaxation of Censorship

Under Alexander II censorship rules were also revised. In 1865 edicts were issued easing rigid censorship regulations for a significant number of books and periodicals (with the exception of newspapers of mass circulation). The abolition at the end of Alexander's reign of the Third Section of the Imperial Chancellery, which had originally been set up by his father to enforce thought control, also helped ease the constraints of censorship. As a result, progressive journalism flourished, presenting the Russian educated public with a truthful and critical picture of the country's social and political problems.

Results of the "Great Reforms"

The "Great Reform" laws of 1861–65 altered the structure of the empire fundamentally, but it would take years before their practical effect was fully felt. Officials learned only gradually to work within the new system; their minds and the mentality of the masses had to be adjusted to radically changed circumstances. Yet these progressive changes initiated by Alexander II's government were all symptomatic of the transition that Russia was slowly undergoing from a semifeudal to something approaching a modern capitalist society.

However, in trying to balance the interests of nobles and peasants, while retaining its own powers intact, the Russian government could satisfy neither of these major classes of traditional Russian society. The reforms accelerated the process of the economic decline of the nobility, which lost the basic privilege of serf-ownership and thus a guaranteed income gained through the exploitation of serf labor. The payments nobles received in return for the land the government forced them to sell meant little in the long run: a substantial part of what they received went to repay old debts. Many nobles found it hard to adapt and to learn businesslike habits of mind. Some preferred to sell more of their land than to economize. By 1911 nobles owned only half of the land that was theirs in 1862. The reforms had created a rift between government and the nobility, which believed that its interests had been ignored.

As for peasants, the immediate benefit of the reform was that they received their personal freedom. However, the land settlement went against the traditional belief of peasants that the land should belong to those who farmed it. The minimal allotment of land that the former serf-owners were obliged to provide to their peasants, so that they could feed themselves, had to be redeemed by whole decades of hard labor. Most peasants were dismayed by the prospect of paying for land they had always believed to be theirs by right. Moreover, the prices for land were fixed at a level well above its free market value. In effect, the government made former serfs pay for their personal freedom as well as for their land. Most important of all, the land settlement sold peasants less land than they had used before the reform. This created the problem of land shortage, which was compounded by the rapid growth of village population during the next half-century. Their deep dissatisfaction with the land settlement notwithstanding, the peasants must have felt they had gained something through the reform, for their disturbances, which had continued for so long under serfdom, greatly diminished in scale and number in the forty years after 1862.

The paradoxical nature of Alexander's "controlled liberalization" was that alongside the new institutions remnants of the old regime survived — most notably of course the autocracy. The emperor believed that with the abolition of serfdom the problem of slavery and the barbaric dependence of certain classes of people on others had been resolved. He did not accept that his social and economic reforms should be accompanied by radical reforms of the political system, that the monarchy itself should change. Although progressively minded members of the nobility urged him to "crown his reforms with a constitution" and to permit the establishing of parliamentary or semi-parliamentary institutions, the reforming tsar resolutely refused to listen to such pleas.

Only in the last year of his life was the tsar persuaded by the newly appointed progressively inclined minister of the interior MICHAEL LORIS-MELIKOV (1825–88) to take up the idea of political reform. Loris-Melikov realized that the intransigence of the authorities alienated and radicalized the liberal circles of educated society, making them view the revolutionaries as their possible allies. The establishment of a nationally elected body of representatives was the most important concession that the government could make in order to win the liberal opposition over to its side. According to Loris-Melikov's plan, this national body was to take the form of a preliminary committee of the State Council. The committee would be comprised of elected representatives of provincial *zemstvos* and towns and would examine draft bills before they were passed for approval to the State Council. Moreover, ten or fifteen of these public representatives would also participate in the legislative work of the State Council itself.

In February 1881 these proposals were discussed by a special conference of senior officials presided over by Alexander. Although the notion of public representatives in the State Council was rejected, the idea of having elected representatives in a preliminary committee was approved. On the morning of 1 March 1881, the very day on which he met his tragic death at the hands of terrorist revolutionaries, Alexander II signed the government announcement about the convocation of a preliminary committee and, speaking to the members of the royal family, declared that he had made "the first step towards the constitution." The tragedy of Alexander's murder was that his heir, Alexander III, rejected Loris-Melikov's scheme, and the idea of a nationally elected representative institution, which would have signified an epoch-making advance for Russia, was abandoned for a quarter of a century.

In spite of all the positive changes that Alexander II's reforms had brought to Russia, the country remained in essence as before an auto-cratic monarchy with no place for either a constitution or parliament. As before, the landowners, the nobles, and their children enjoyed many privileges, while the rights (both civil and property) of the other estates were still restricted. The peasants, in particular, despite the fact that they were now free, remained socially segregated from the rest of the population.

Alexander's biggest failing was his refusal to combine the abolition of serfdom in the socioeconomic sphere with *political* emancipation of his subjects. He had abolished the slavish dependence of the peasantry on landed nobility, but he did little to eliminate the slavish dependence of both peasantry and gentry on the Sovereign. By preserving the control of the commune and the state over the person of the peasant, by denying the gentry and other classes a role in government at an all-Russia level, the autocracy absolved them from civic and political responsibility and delayed the "coming of age" of Russian society.

The "Great Reforms" had raised the expectations of the progres-sives, belonging to different sections of the population. Frustrated with the government's refusal to change the political structure of tsarism and deeply disappointed with the emancipation settlement, more and more members of the educated classes were becoming attracted by the pros-pect of popular revolution as the only means to bring down the existing political system and give the mass of the Russian population real land and liberty. These two demands (land and liberty) became the rally-ing cry of the Russian revolutionary Narodnichestvo — the ideological movement that became a major focus of opposition to the policies of Alexander II.

Chapter Six

The Revolutionary Movement

Origins of the Intelligentsia
and Its *Raznochintsy* Element

By no means had the radically minded intellectuals been satisfied by the reform of 1861. Many believed that it left the peasantry as exploited and as unfree as before. Far from hailing Alexander as a great reformer, they accused him of being the swindler tsar who had left the peasants to complete ruination by not providing them with enough land. They saw that the legal freedom conceded to the peasants meant little while they remained in grinding poverty. In their view, the tsar had betrayed the hopes of the people by not granting ex-serfs equal economic and civil rights with the other social classes. The radicals argued that revolution was now the only way to achieve genuine emancipation and a fair land settlement. A large part of the educated society was consumed by revolutionary attitudes.

In part, this dissension was due to some relaxation of censorship and the freer intellectual atmosphere permitted under Alexander II. But even more important were significant changes in the social composition of the educated society: it was losing fast its exclusive "noble" origin. Educational reforms had opened the prospect of higher education to representatives of all social estates, contributing to the blurring of the borderlines between noble and nonnoble classes. Children of peasants, townsfolk, clergy, and impoverished gentry could now enter universities, become educated, and then go to join the ranks of this peculiarly Russian phenomenon known as the INTELLIGENTSIA. They acquired new social identity and often lost links with their original social milieu.

In mid-nineteenth-century Russia the members of the intelligentsia formed a small and underprivileged group that enjoyed neither the material wealth of the nobility nor the political influence of the bureaucracy. They were brain wage-workers who relied for their living on their education and intellect. Some became journalists, or writers. Others were members of the professions, such as lawyers, doctors, and teachers. The ever-increasing numbers of educated young people earned a living in government employment as veterinarians, agronomists, or statisticians. In the milieu of this "thinking minority" some of the more radical attitudes began to take root leading to the appearance of dissidents and revolutionaries.

Some historians interpret mid-nineteenth-century Russian radicalism in terms of different generations, one more radical than the next. In this view, members of the generation of the 1840s were the "NOBLE FATHERS." On the whole, the radicals of this generation, represented by such thinkers as Alexander Herzen, were "idealists" who were reluctant to use violence and who pinned their hopes on reform from above.

In contrast to their more "idealistic" forerunners, the new radicals of the generation of the 1860s were more influenced by modern science and materialism. They advocated revolutionary remedies for Russia's problems and were more willing to use extreme, violent means to achieve their ends. They are usually referred to as the "PLEBEIAN SONS" since most ardent radicals of the new generation came from the milieu of the *raznochintsy.*

The word RAZNOCHINTSY (*lit.* "men of mixed ranks") appeared at a time when old class labels, used to describe Russia's important social strata, could no longer grasp a complex and changing reality. *Raznochintsy* were educated members of Russian society drawn from the small townsfolk, the clergy, the merchants, and the peasantry, as distinct from those drawn from the nobility. The emergence of this borderline social group, made up of people of various social estates, was a clear indication of the process of erosion that was beginning to affect the traditional social structure.

Being part of the educated elite, *raznochintsy* did not hold high rank (*chin*) in the Table of Ranks, and so they did not fully belong to the ruling group. Unlike the gentry or merchants, they did not have the right to own land, or to engage in trade and crafts. They had to survive on the income from their intellectual labor, which was not valued very highly. Their wages were between three and fourteen roubles a month at the time when the subsistence level was ten roubles a month. For these reasons, *raznochintsy,* unlike the agitators of Western Europe, were often indigent and not essentially "bourgeois." Nor were these city- and university-bred men and women close to the soil and the people living on it, for their education and urban lifestyle set them apart from the illiterate rural population.

Most members of the intelligentsia came from these *raznochintsy* groups, which belonged neither to the propertied classes nor to the popular masses. By the 1860s the social concept of *raznochintsy* had become wider and was now applied to a social movement. Anyone who chose to stand outside the traditional social structure became a member of *raznochintsy*. He could be a former member of the landed gentry who had severed ties with his own social class, or the son of a cleric who decided against following in the footsteps of his father, or a shopkeeper who gave up his trade, or even the son of a general or civil servant. Having joined the ranks of *raznochintsy*, former landowners renounced the entire class of landowners as a matter of principle, former seminarians turned into the most virulent opponents of the church, former shopkeepers became sworn enemies of the bourgeoisie, while the sons of generals and civil servants denounced militarism and bureaucracy. From the 1860s onwards *raznochintsy* provided most of the leaders for the Russian revolutionary movement.

In the conditions of political indifference and social inertness of an overwhelming majority of the peasantry, the intelligentsia, drawn from the nobility and from the mixed ranks of the *raznochintsy*, began to play an increasingly important role in shaping Russia's future. As a group that had a virtual monopoly on European education and culture inside Russia, it was the only channel through which new ideologies could reach the illiterate masses. It is hardly possible to evaluate the course and results of the Russian revolutionary movement without an understanding of certain key characteristics that defined not just the social but also the intellectual and psychological makeup of the members of this group.

Intellectual and Psychological Makeup of the Intelligentsia

The intelligentsia was distinguished primarily by a STRONG SOCIAL CONSCIOUSNESS — one that had been aroused by a feeling of guilt that the whole of their life and culture was founded upon the exploitation of fellow Christians who were forced to live and work in conditions of an unjustified and unnatural enslavement. Many members of the intelligentsia felt they were forever in debt to these people and that they had to pay this debt by devoting their entire lives to righting this injustice. A GUILT COMPLEX played an immense part in the psychology of the intelligentsia. Out of guilt came a desire to atone for past "sins" and a readiness to sacrifice for the sake of the people. The Russian thinker Sergei Bulgakov coined the phrase "social penitence" to describe this peculiar frame of mind of the members of the Russian intelligentsia.[1] They were penitents who sought to make amends not to God, but to the popular masses, the Russian *narod*. Atonement for serfdom became the intelligentsia's collective mission.

The next important characteristic of the intelligentsia was an essentially "ANTI-BOURGEOIS" mentality. Typically found among the *raznochintsy* (because of their pervasive indigence), this mentality was also characteristic of the intelligentsia of noble origin, for their members were brought up in a privileged environment far removed from the pressures of earning a living and from similar concerns of a more seamy, "bourgeois" side of existence. To some extent, this helps to explain why, ideologically, members of the intelligentsia were inclined to socialism. They tended to treat wealth with contempt. The fair redistribution of wealth and not its creation was by far their main concern. As one Russian thinker has observed, their "love for the poor turned into love of poverty."[2]

A mood of total ALIENATION FROM THE STATE was another defining feature of the Russian intelligentsia. By denying the members of the intelligentsia the possibility of influencing the life of society and by subjecting them to harsh police persecution, the autocracy fostered in their milieu the feeling of a deep-seated hostility toward the state and its representatives. It drove the educated minority to embrace radical ideological systems, including various forms of Russian socialism. In its final and most absolute form this alienation found expression in anarchism as a complete negation of the state and public order.

The revolt from obedience to the state and from established values had also forged the main moral philosophy of the Russian intelligentsia, which became known as NIHILISM. Its name (from the Latin *nihil,* "nothing") implied a moral revolt against the existing order, a total negation of the surrounding world. Nihilism evolved in the postreform decade of the 1860s as a hallmark of the new generation of radicals. Its main objective was personal liberation — from family and social prejudices, from blind obedience to authorities, from the burden of centuries-old traditions in all spheres of life. Nihilists were required to develop their intellects by mastering the natural sciences, in search of some free, rational, and practical occupation, in order to build their lives and those close to them on rational, mutually beneficial foundations. This new moral attitude played a key role in shaping the mindset and ways of behavior of the intelligentsia as a whole.

Nihilists repudiated the established order and its standards. They waged an uncompromising struggle against the hypocrisy and dissimulation of the old, received ways of private and public life. However, this positive and healthy side of nihilism was often outweighed by its negativist attitude toward all traditions, a cult of totally destructive criticism, and a rejection of absolute spiritual values. Its maximalism often translated into impatience, intolerance, ideological obsession, and fanaticism.

Nihilists extended their total rejection of current beliefs from morals to religion. ATHEISM AND ANTI-RELIGIOUSNESS have often been singled out as cornerstones of the intellectual makeup of the Russian radicals. The rejection of religion was connected with their belief in the omnipotence of modern science and in boundless human progress. For them science was a force capable of resolving all issues — even those that traditionally belonged to the sphere of religion. They attributed all ills in society not to the frailty of the human condition, but to some extraneous maladjustments of the social mechanism, which could be put right by means of social reforms based on "scientifically correct," materialistic doctrines. Their atheism and their trust in science and progress were themselves akin to a naive religious faith. A Russian thinker once observed that "socialism was Christianity without God."[3] The young radicals fused socialism, materialism, and atheism into a kind of militant, secular religion, which they embraced unquestioningly and dogmatically.

In the materialistic philosophy of the intelligentsia the place of God was taken by the "People," first the peasant and later the proletarian masses. The intelligentsia indulged in a lavish IDEALIZATION OF THE POPULAR MASSES, based on a belief in their innate socialist qualities. "The people" (in Russian *narod,* hence the name of the movement: Narodnichestvo, "worship of the people") and traditional institutions such as the village commune were transformed in the minds of radical intellectuals into a highly colored icon that bore little resemblance to actual peasants and their way of life. Members of the intelligentsia combined the deification of the masses with a conviction that they had a mission to save the people from suffering and show it the way to absolute and everlasting happiness on earth. The peculiar fusion of anti-religiousness with the near-religious worship of the people and with a messianic zeal to act as its deliverer has been captured in Simeon Frank's paradoxical definition of the intelligentsia as "a militant monastic order of the Nihilist religion of earthly welfare."[4]

Nihilism as a wholesale negation of all existing religious, moral, spiritual, aesthetic, and other values meant that the intelligentsia refused to recognize any absolute values or standards of judgment. These were replaced by a single moral criterion: "the interests of the people." The great cause of the liberation of the people and the establishment of a kingdom of justice on earth sanctified everything done in its name. This was the reasoning behind what is usually described as the intelligentsia's UTILITARIAN MORALITY: whatever advanced the achievement of social justice was good; whatever impeded it in any way was bad.

This approach, which treated as moral any action believed to be advancing the cause of social justice, found its complete expression in the IDEA OF THE END JUSTIFYING THE MEANS. The revolutionary groups and radical intelligentsia as a whole were quick to embrace this maxim unquestioningly and even enthusiastically. Steeling themselves for an uncompromising struggle against tyranny, they often saw violent, terrorist acts as the only option open to them to achieve their objectives. Readiness to sacrifice oneself, to give up one's life, served only to amplify the inclination toward extreme measures: anything was permitted to those who were prepared to die for the cause and constantly risked their lives for it.

This led some members of the intelligentsia to a romantic idealization of revolutionary struggle and of heroic "revolutionary" acts. "REVOLUTIONISM" became an obsession with many of the new radicals, particularly among the younger rebels, many of whom were students. For them the term "revolutionary" carried only the noblest of connotations. They turned terrorism into a cult and saw it as a preserve of exceptional men and women — intrepid "revolutionary fighters." Blinded by their admiration of heroic acts, the young radicals completely overlooked the destructive side of revolution. To them, it was a most potent *creative* force that, by destroying the old order right down to its foundations, made the task of the historic transformation so much simpler. All that was required were strong nerves and muscles, courage and determination. All this the young radicals had in abundance.

The above characteristics of the Russian intelligentsia allow it to be distinguished from other sections of the educated classes in Russia as a community of people united by their adherence to certain sociopolitical and moral principles such as a revolt from obedience to the state, antireligiousness, nihilism, materialism, socialism, etc. Some of these traits are already discernible in Herzen's generation of radicals. They are easily recognizable in the intellectual makeup of the younger generation of the 1860s. And they would fully develop and become hallmarks of the subsequent generations of the Russian intelligentsia right into the early twentieth century, determining to a great extent the nature and direction of the Russian revolutionary movement and of the Russian Revolution.

Nicholas Chernyshevsky

If Alexander Herzen is often considered to be the main representative of the generation of the "noble fathers," Nicholas Chernyshevsky (1828–89) epitomizes the type of radical from the new generation of the "plebeian sons." The son of a priest and a typical member of the *raznochintsy,* Chernyshevsky began his career as a journalist and literary critic whose writings were to make him the main spokesperson and ideologue of the younger generation of the radically minded intellectuals. Dissatisfied with the conditions of the Emancipation Act of 1861, they found in him their leader and source of inspiration.

Chernyshevsky is believed to have been one of the main organizers of the "manifestos campaign" following the publication of the Emancipation Act of 1861. The campaign was started by radicals in St. Petersburg, Moscow, and other cities, who circulated political broadsheets and leaflets in which the peasant reform was subjected to severe criticism. These propaganda documents threatened a popular insurrection if the demands of more radical and consistent reforms were not met. The authorities responded by making a whole series of arrests. Many revolutionaries, including Chernyshevsky, were found guilty of sedition and sentenced to hard labor.

Chernyshevsky's writings extolled the active position of a free individual who felt part of a human collective. Like Herzen before him, he believed that the village commune could become the best form for the realization of the collectivist instincts of the individual. The fact that it had survived for so long seemed in itself sufficient proof that the socialist ideal could, indeed, be translated into life. At the same time, Chernyshevsky's approach to this antiquated institution of Russian life was more realistic. He saw it, mainly, as a means of combining the personal interest of the worker with a collectivist form of production. The commune was a transitional form toward a collectivist type of economy which would replace capitalism and would combine "the owner, the boss, and the worker in one person." He gave some stirring descriptions of cooperative associations of workers of the future in his celebrated novel *What Is to Be Done?* Chernyshevsky wrote this novel in prison in 1863 while undergoing interrogation on charges of high treason and sedition. As it was a work of fiction, the book passed the censor without being given a second thought. It was promptly published in a magazine that Chernyshevsky had edited before his arrest. The fictional form had been chosen as the only way available to Chernyshevsky to present his description of the Socialists, the revolutionaries — the "NEW MEN," as he called them, dedicated to changing the existing order.

The book created an instantaneous sensation. For the first time the young generation of intelligentsia was given an inspiring model of dedicated, self-sacrificing heroes determined to create a revolution for the benefit of the masses. Endowed with exceptional intellectual and physical qualities, Chernyshevsky's "New Men" were to constitute an educated and politically engaged elite, the heroes who were to lead the Russian people toward a kingdom of justice on earth. They were still

> few in number, but through them the life of all mankind expands; without them it would have been stifled. They are few in number, but they put others in a position to breathe, others who without these few would have been suffocated. Great is the number of good and honest people, but such men are rare. They are like the bouquet in fine wine, its strength and its aroma. They are the best among the best, they are the movers of the movers, they are the salt of the salt of the earth.[5]

Chernyshevsky's message was not lost on the young generation of intellectuals. They took it as a call for a new revolutionary elite — dedicated and disciplined — that would alone be able to lead the Russian people toward the promised land of justice and equality. Chernyshevsky's heroes — and especially his favorite, the superman Rakhmetov, who steeled his character for the liberation struggle by sleeping on planks studded with nails — became the ideal prototypes upon whom generations of young radicals consciously modeled themselves.

The book became an inspiration for hundreds of thousands of men and women and converted many to the cause of the revolutionary struggle. In the words of Tibor Szamuely: "Within a few short years the New Men had stepped out of the pages of the novel into real life: acquiring flesh and blood, they established secret societies, distributed leaflets, threw bombs, went to the people, trudged to Siberia, ascended the scaffold. They became the men and women of the Russian revolutionary movement."[6]

One of the novel's future readers would be a seventeen-year-old schoolboy in the little town of Simbirsk, Vladimir Ulianov, better known by his pseudonym of Lenin. Years later, in conversation with a fellow revolutionary, Lenin described the profound impression made upon him by *What Is to Be Done?*

Hundreds of people became revolutionaries under its influence....
My brother, for example, was captivated by him [Chernyshevsky],
and so was I. *He completely transformed my outlook....* I spent
not days but several weeks reading it. Only then did I understand
its depth. This novel provides inspiration for a lifetime....[7]

When in 1902 Lenin produced his most important book, in which for
the first time he laid down the organizational principles of the Bolshevik Party, he published it under the same title as Chernyshevsky's
novel. Indeed, much of what he said there about the new type of dedicated professional revolutionary reads almost like a more levelheaded
and systematic representation of Chernyshevsky's New Men.

Trends within Revolutionary Narodnichestvo

The ideas of Herzen and Chernyshevsky had to a large extent prepared
for the appearance in the late 1860s and early 1870s of the ideology of
revolutionary Narodnichestvo. They had sown the seeds of the movement that found its full expression in the works of Michael Bakunin
(1814–76), Peter Lavrov (1823–1900), Peter Tkachev (1844–86), and
other prominent Narodniks. The theoreticians of Narodnichestvo were
firmly convinced that humankind in its development would inevitably
reach socialism, and Russia, in their opinion, had an obvious advantage
in this quest over many other countries. The basic difference between
Russia and Western Europe was the survival of the commune. They believed that the commune had preserved the socialist ideal of collective
ownership, which had long ago disappeared in the rest of Europe. The
commune distributed the peasants' basic productive resource — land —
on egalitarian principles, thus ensuring a basic equality of wealth. The
optimism of the Narodniks stemmed from the conviction that the village commune represented an embryo of socialism and was therefore
a guarantee of a relatively smooth and painless transition to a new
social order.

Russia's prospects looked particularly attractive to the Narodniks because they hoped that the germs of socialism inherent in the village
commune would enable their country to sidestep capitalism and thus
avoid the proletarianization of the peasantry and the formation of the
exploiting class of bourgeoisie. In order to restructure society on socialist foundations it was necessary to release the innate socialist potential
of the commune by freeing it from socioeconomic and political pres-

sures. This was to be achieved by transferring all land to peasants, lifting the crippling burden of taxation, and removing administrative-police controls.

The leading ideologists of Narodnichestvo agreed on these general theoretical propositions, but they differed over how to implement them into life. BAKUNIN, a daring revolutionary and an "apostle" of anarchism, pinned his hopes on a spontaneous peasant uprising. In his opinion, the peasants were ready for revolution; all they needed was a push, which should be provided by the revolutionary intelligentsia. The intelligentsia should not try to dictate its program to the people but work to reignite in Russian village communes the dormant spirit of freedom, making villagers realize the need to unite in the struggle for their liberation.

The emphasis on infusing the masses with revolutionary ardor rather than on a carefully planned organization of revolution was a weakness in Bakunin's approach. Despite this, his ideas were extremely popular among the most radicalized young people who yearned for practical action and wished to make revolution immediately. The adherents of Bakunin's ideas represented the INSURRECTIONIST tendency in revolutionary Narodnichestvo.

LAVROV, who was a professor of mathematics in military educational institutions and had the rank of a colonel of the Russian army, also supported the idea of the peasant insurrection and considered the intellectual-revolutionaries to be the force that would be able to stir up the masses to revolution. But in contrast to Bakunin, he believed that the intelligentsia needed time to find common language with the peasantry and convince it of the necessity of revolution. He advocated a prolonged period of intensive propaganda of the ideas of revolutionary Narodnichestvo among the peasantry. Lavrov's supporters represented, accordingly, the PROPAGANDIST trend. His views about the necessity of establishing a broadly based, popular party, which would deliberately plan and carry through the socialist revolution, would inform the activities of the next generations of Russian radicals.

Finally, there was the CONSPIRATORIAL trend, which reflected the attitude of the segment of the intelligentsia that was skeptical of the people's power to make the revolution and pinned its hopes on forming a conspiracy with the aim of overthrowing the tsarist government and accomplishing socialist transformations. The main theoretician of this trend was TKACHEV, who believed that the popular masses and the intelligentsia were too far apart and that the gulf between them could not be bridged. In the conditions of the autocratic-bureaucratic system, it was impossible, he argued, to incite peasants to revolution. The intelligentsia could rely only on its own efforts to free the peasant commune. It should form a conspiracy, stage an armed coup, seize government power, and then implement the necessary transformations from above.

Some analysts have argued that the basic points of Tkachev's program — the decisive role of a centralized and disciplined conspiratorial party; the necessity for a seizure of political power by a minority revolutionary organization; and the establishment of a strong minority dictatorship that would introduce socialism by decree from above — had foreshadowed some of Lenin's views on party organization and the relationship between the revolutionary party and the proletariat. Tkachev, therefore, is often seen as the essential link between Chernyshevsky and Lenin, the legatee of Narodnichestvo and the precursor of Bolshevism.

A special place within the conspiratorial trend belongs to SERGEI NECHAEV (1847–82), a revolutionary fanatic who developed the idea of an utterly immoral, ruthless, and dedicated revolutionary conspiracy to its extreme logical conclusion. He formulated his principles in what is probably the most famous and certainly the most astonishing document in the history of the nineteenth-century Russian revolutionary movement, *The Catechism of a Revolutionary* (1868). It was meant to be a code of rules by which the revolutionary should be guided. It depicts the revolutionary as someone who has severed all ties with society and whose single purpose in life is revolution. Here are some of the rules from the *Catechism:*

- The revolutionary is a doomed man. He has no interests, no affairs, no feelings, no habits, no property, not even a name. Everything in him is wholly absorbed by a single, exclusive interest, a single thought, a single passion — the revolution.

- In the very depths of his being, not just in words but in deed, he has severed every tie with the civil order, with the educated world, and with all laws, conventions, ethics, and generally accepted rules of this world. He is an implacable enemy of this world, and if he continues to inhabit it, it is only to destroy it more effectively.

- He despises public opinion. He despises and hates the existing social customs and all of their motivations and manifestations. For him everything that promotes the revolution is moral; everything that hinders it is immoral.[8]

Nechaev's rejection of the all-human moral norms, his negation of all moral inhibitions, led him to embrace totally the principle of "the ends justify the means." He actually tried to enforce his extraordinary rules in his underground revolutionary group. Nechaev demanded from his associates unquestioning obedience, treating them as cogs in the machine of destruction. His extreme amoralism led him to murder the student I. I. Ivanov, a member of his circle, who had allowed himself to disagree with the group's dictator and criticize him. Having committed the crime, Nechaev fled abroad but was caught in Switzerland and extradited to Russia as a common criminal. He died in prison.

As an ideological tendency within the revolutionary movement, NECHAEVISM came to signify a combination of boundless devotion to the revolution with the utter ruthlessness in the choice of means of achieving it. Its pathological traits gave an early warning of the possibility of a criminal degeneration of lofty ideas. Despite his notoriety, Nechaev would be later acknowledged by Lenin and his Bolsheviks as a precursor of Bolshevism. Indeed, some of his ideas, such as the indispensability of a conspiratorial organization, strict subordination, elements of planning of an uprising, and his formulation of the "morals" of the revolution make it possible to consider him as a precursor of the Bolsheviks.

In the late 1860s and early 1870s a number of groups under the ideological influence of revolutionary Narodnichestvo sprang up among the youth and students. None of the groups were strict adherents of Lavrov's, Bakunin's, or Tkachev's methods of struggle. The revolutionary underground drew on their theoretical recommendations selectively, adopting mixed tactics, depending on the situation. In 1874 these young people initiated a massive "GOING-TO-THE-PEOPLE" movement under the banner of Bakunin's slogans of insurrection and Lavrov's calls for revolutionary propaganda. Thousands of young intellectuals, both men and women, left their homes, universities, and employment and joined in a crusade to spread the socialist gospel throughout the Russian countryside. They were motivated by genuine sympathy for the sufferings of the peasantry and fired up with youthful enthusiasm to serve a noble cause.

The whole affair proved a miserable fiasco. Many became disillusioned with the sullen and conservative nature of the peasants; others were arrested by the local police; and some were actually detained by the suspicious peasants and handed over to the authorities for "speaking against God and the tsar." Hundreds were imprisoned and later put on public trial in St. Petersburg and Moscow. The failure of the intelligentsia to establish contact with the people was a clear and tragic illustration of the continuing gulf that separated Russia's educated classes from the *narod*.

The Turn to Terror

The failure of the "movement to the people" campaign forced the revolutionaries to reappraise the situation and search for new ideas and different methods. It had revealed the utopianism of Bakunin's assertions about the peasantry's "readiness" for insurrection, as well as the organizational weakness of a movement decentralized in a network of uncoordinated groups. Certain theoretical positions had to be revised, including the belief in the peasants' innate socialist qualities. Agitation for socialism was replaced by more simple and popular slogans such as "land" and "liberty." To many radicals the propaganda approach had been completely discredited. The path of conspiracy and terror against the autocratic regime now seemed to be the only possible way forward.

The revolutionaries began to focus their efforts on the creation of strong secret organizations capable of taking direct political action and terrorizing the mighty imperial government. The better known of these underground groups was "LAND AND LIBERTY," founded in 1876. This centralized, fighting formation, which was built on the principles of conspiracy, strict discipline, and rigorous selection of new members, adhered to the populist goals of transferring all land to the peasants and empowering the communes to administer public affairs. These objectives were to be achieved by the mixed tactics of a more sustained seditious agitation among the peasantry and efforts to disorganize the government by acts of terrorism including "the elimination of the most harmful or eminent members of the government."

Given the peasants' general apathy, government repression, and the absence of democratic institutions, the revolutionaries increasingly focused their direct political action on the tactics of individual terror against the tsar and his most prominent ministers. In 1879 the "Land and Liberty" group split over the issue of terrorism into two separate organizations: "BLACK REPARTITION" and "PEOPLE'S WILL." The "Black Repartition" wanted to continue to prepare the country for revolution by the old means of propaganda and agitation. By contrast, the "People's Will" had set itself the task of staging a political coup, of using terrorism to achieve the country's political transformation.

In the view of the members of the "People's Will," the past failures of Narodniks were inevitable given the despotic character of the tsarist system. Without the freedoms of speech, press, and assembly, and in the atmosphere of arbitrary repression, it was impossible, they argued, to conduct sustained socialist propaganda. Their conclusion was that the revolutionaries' immediate task should be the overthrow of the autocratic regime. Only after that would it be possible to hold elections to a Constituent Assembly. The Assembly, they hoped, would endorse their specific demands, including popular representation, regional self-government, administrative and economic independence of the communes, the transfer of the ownership of land to the peasants and of factories to the workers, civil liberties, and universal suffrage.

The members of the "People's Will" further rationalized their recourse to political terror by arguing that they were entitled to use it as a means of self-defense against the repressive government. In their view, acts of terrorism were the only effective way to defend society against the unrestrained arbitrariness of the state, protect their populist ideals, and safeguard Russia's collectivist future. They hoped to bring down the hated regime by assassinating its key political leaders. In the late 1870s the "People's Will" staged a number of terrorist acts directed against high government officials, but gradually they decided to focus all their energy on the main task: the assassination of the tsar himself.

There had been attempts on the life of Alexander II even before the "People's Will" unleashed its deadly terrorist campaign (the tsar suffered six assassination attempts in total). However, the motivation behind the earlier attempts on the sovereign's life had been somewhat different. The earlier attempts were connected with certain real events — there was some concrete pretext for the acts of the terrorists. In 1866 Dmitri Karakozov shot at the tsar as revenge for the "deception" of the peasants by the 1861 reform; the following year Berezovsky made his attempt in order to avenge the crushing of the Polish revolt of 1863; Alexander Soloviev's attempt in 1879 was in revenge for the repression against the peaceful propagandists of the going-to-the-people movement.

By the late 1870s and early 1880s the assassination attempts against the tsar were no longer connected with concrete events. The motivation behind them became more complex and not immediately obvious. The revolutionaries were increasingly worried about the growing signs that their cherished ideals of equality and justice, based on the free communal organization of the future life of the people, were under threat from some new phenomena and processes generated by the reforms of Alexander II. Despite the half-and-half nature of the reforms and the fact that the commune had been retained, new capitalist relations — the growing stratification of the peasantry into better-off and poor — were undermining the commune and eroding the traditional conditions of village life. But without the village commune the populist ideal did not exist; it simply fell to the ground. For these reasons, by the late 1870s, the revolutionaries had come to regard the outcome of the reforms not only as the deception of the popular masses, but as a much more serious crime — as an attempt to deprive the people of the very possibility of a radiant socialist future.

In these circumstances all means of struggle were justified and permissible following the precept of "the ends justify the means." Terror became for the Narodniks a matter of principle, a method of achieving political and social transformation. The direct, uncompromising confrontation between the revolutionaries and the Winter Palace resembled a duel (at that time duels were an accepted way of settling quarrels among the gentry). In the end it led to a tragic situation in which Alexander turned into the executioner of revolutionaries, while the revolutionaries ended up as the executioners of the Tsar Liberator.

The terrorists were firmly convinced that they were acting in the name and best interests of the Russian people, and, indeed, they enjoyed a certain amount of sympathy among Russia's educated and well-to-do classes. However, the toiling masses, with the exception of a very small number of worker-revolutionaries, never showed any signs of sympathy for the men and women who were staking their lives, as they believed, on the people's behalf. Popular reactions to terrorism ranged from violent condemnation to irritation or, at best, indifference. The emperor remained sacrosanct as the "Tsar Liberator," while the educated revolutionaries represented, in the eyes of the peasants, the very people who were hoping to enslave them again. The peasants believed that the assassination attempts were the wicked deeds of the landowners, seeking revenge for the loss of their slaves.

After several unsuccessful attempts the Tsar Liberator was finally blown to pieces on 1 March 1881 by a terrorist bomb. Five leaders of the conspiracy — members of the "People's Will" — were arrested, tried, and publicly hanged. The rest of the radical intelligentsia was decimated by imprisonment, exile, and emigration. The "People's Will" had rocked the country's political system to its foundation. However, it failed to achieve the overthrow of tsarism.

The struggle of the "People's Will" played an important role in the Russian revolutionary movement. Its greatest contributions were the principle of taking direct action against the tsarist regime and its emphasis on the political struggle. The important lesson of the revolutionary crisis of the late 1870s and 1880s was that the peculiar conditions in Russia did make it possible for a tiny group of revolutionary intellectuals-conspirators to create a deep-seated political crisis, to throw the whole machinery of government into disarray and nearly bring the government to its knees in the absence of a mass movement or even of mass support. The lesson was not lost on a later generation of revolutionaries.

Following the assassination of Alexander II, revolutionary Narodnichestvo entered a period of decline. Its followers deeply felt the acute ideological crisis of the movement and the gulf that still separated them from the "people." Yet the decades of theoretical inquiries and practical work of agitation and political action had not been in vain. The generation of the *raznochintsy* had formulated the goals of overthrowing autocracy and stirring up the masses to revolution; it had begun to lay down the principles for the creation of a political party; it had set up a whole network of secret organizations; and, finally, it had produced the type of intrepid Russian revolutionary whose revolutionary energy and fanatical devotion to the cause were combined with highly developed conspiratorial skills.

Chapter Seven

Appearance of Marxism

Main Tenets of Classical Marxism

Russia's development in the postreform era made clearer with each passing year the utopianism of the Narodniks' hopes of a peasant revolution. Some of them began to question the belief in a special destiny of the Russian people and its predetermined movement toward a communal organization of life. The experience of Western Europe seemed to suggest that capitalism was, after all, a necessary stage on the road of human progress. The era of the bloody revolutions of the 1840s, which had so unsettled Alexander Herzen and made him spurn Western European socialist theories, was now in the past. European workers had won the right to participate in the political process. The popularity of Social-Democratic parties that expressed the interests of wage labor was on the rise. And so was the influence and reputation of Marxism as the ideology of the working class.

Marxism represented a particular type of socialism. Its founders were two German philosophers, KARL MARX (1818–83) and his lifelong friend and collaborator FRIEDRICH ENGELS (1820–95). Working for several decades, starting in the turbulent 1840s, they had constructed a huge and comprehensive, albeit not entirely consistent, philosophical system. Their ideas were first presented in a systematic form in 1848 in the celebrated *Manifesto of the Communist Party*. They were then developed more thoroughly in the three volumes of Marx's *Capital*. The intellectual roots of Marxism included the eighteenth-century Enlightenment, classical economics, utopian socialism, and German idealistic philosophy — in other words, some of the main traditions of Western thought. Most importantly, Marx and Engels tried to find a rational formula, a comprehensive social hypothesis, that would sum up the evolution of humankind and indicate the course of its future development.

One of the key elements of their theory was the idea of the NATURAL-HISTORICAL CHARACTER of social development. The essence of the theory was that society developed in accordance with its own intrinsic laws, which were no less objective than the laws of nature. For this reason each social formation appears only then and there, when and where appropriate conditions have matured for it. It subsequently gives way to a next formation when that new formation has been prepared by a different set of objective and subjective conditions. In this sense, Marx presented social development as a natural social-historical process. To use a metaphor, just as a foetus in a mother's womb has to pass through necessary preliminary stages before it becomes a self-sustaining living organism, so, too, social systems are conceived, develop, and pass from one qualitative stage to the next in accordance with certain objective laws.

The second fundamental Marxist principle in the explanation of historical process is MATERIALISM. Unlike idealism, which believes that consciousness determines existence, materialism looks for objective foundations of consciousness itself. It finds them in the material life of people, in their concrete social conditions. Materialism as a methodological principle was used by Marx to uncover an economic base of society in the form of the mode of production. He argued that the mode of production of the material means of existence conditioned the whole process of social, political, and intellectual life. It was not consciousness that determines existence, but, on the contrary, social existence determines consciousness. Thus, in a complex description of historical events and social structures a certain objective foundation was discovered that seemed to hold the key to the understanding of the evolution of human society.

The significance of Marx's discovery of the role of the mode of production was likened by Engels to that of Darwin's theory of evolution:

Just as Darwin discovered the law of evolution in organic nature, so Marx discovered the law of evolution in human history; he discovered the simple fact, hitherto concealed by an overgrowth of ideology, that mankind must first of all eat and drink, have shelter and clothing, before it can pursue politics, science, religion, art, etc.; and that therefore the production of the immediate material means of subsistence and consequently the degree of economic development attained by a given people or during a given epoch, form the foundation upon which the state institutions, the legal conceptions, the art and even the religious ideas of the people concerned have been evolved, and in the light of which these things must therefore be explained, instead of vice versa as had hitherto been the case.[1]

According to this theory, the mode of production or relations of production of the same type generate similar sociopolitical structures and even ideological forms. By using this approach, Marx singled out five socioeconomic formations: the primitive type of society; slavery; feudalism; capitalism; and communism. The capitalist stage and the capitalist mode of production and exchange were described and analyzed by him most exhaustively. The central idea in his analysis of capitalism, as expressed in his *Manifesto of the Communist Party,* was a remarkable "acceleration" that this phase of history, dominated by the bourgeoisie, had brought to global development:

> The bourgeoisie, during its rule of scarce one hundred years, has created more massive and more colossal productive forces than have all preceding generations together. Subjection of Nature's forces to man, machinery, application of chemistry to industry and agriculture, steam-navigation, railways, electric telegraphs, clearing of whole continents for cultivation, canalization of rivers, whole populations conjured out of the ground — what earlier century had even a presentiment that such productive forces slumbered in the lap of social labor?[2]

Marx's main conclusion from his analysis of contemporary capitalism was that the bourgeoisie would be unable to control this rapid expansion of the productive forces it had itself unleashed and would completely antagonize the proletariat by driving it to utter destitution and poverty. Capitalism was, inevitably, heading for self-destruction:

> Modern bourgeois society with its relations of production, of exchange and of property, a society that has conjured up such gigantic means of production and of exchange, is like the sorcerer, who is no longer able to control the powers of the nether world whom he has called up by his spells.[3]

On the basis of his analysis, Marx drew up the prediction that anti-capitalist revolutions would occur in the most developed capitalist countries. The current phase of history would be terminated by a proletarian revolution that would abolish the minority rule of the bourgeoisie and also do away with individual property as the economic foundation of its political power and usher in the era of communism with a workers' government running society "in the interest of the immense majority."

First Russian Followers of Marx

In the mid-nineteenth century Marx's ideas seemed to have little relevance for a backward and agrarian country like Russia. Moreover, many
Russian intellectuals did not believe their country would ever be capitalist. They shared the vision of a unique destiny for Russia conjured up
by Slavophiles and, later, by Narodniks. However, the crisis of Narodnichestvo of the early 1880s made many dissidents disillusioned with
peasant socialism. By that time, as a result of the "Great Reforms,"
Russia's industrial proletariat and, with it, the working-class movement
began to emerge. This attracted the attention of some revolutionary-
minded intellectuals who became increasingly interested in the Marxist
idea of a socialist revolution led by the urban proletariat.

In 1883, in exile in Switzerland, the first Russian Marxist group was
set up under the leadership of GEORGE PLEKHANOV (1856–1918). The
members of this small organization — "EMANCIPATION OF LABOR" —
had been active Narodniks in the past, former activists of the "Black
Repartition" group, which had emerged as a propagandist wing of
"Land and Liberty" after its split in 1879. Plekhanov and his associates
were deeply concerned by the ideological crisis in which Narodnichestvo
had found itself by the early 1880s, and they sought to find a solution
by subjecting their views to a complete overhaul. They did not abandon
their basic socialist ideals, but they now came to see capitalism as a necessary evil, an unavoidable stage in evolution — one that more advanced
countries and nations had already pursued and that Russia would not
be able to escape.

Their theoretical inquiries led them to the following conclusions:
postreform Russia was taking the *capitalist* path, and this would inevitably lead to the complete disintegration of the peasant commune.
Therefore the Narodniks' belief in the triumph of "communal socialism" was groundless. The pauperization of the peasantry would lead to
the growth and consolidation of the proletariat. It would be the proletariat who could and should lead Russia to socialism by establishing
its dictatorship and carrying through necessary changes in all spheres
of life. In order to prepare the proletarian revolution, it was necessary
to give the emerging labor movement a right direction, provide it with
a scientifically based ideology, and arm it with a program of action.
These tasks could only be carried out by the revolutionary intelligentsia,
steeped in the spirit of Marxist teaching.

The members of the "Emancipation of Labor" group sought to forge
this new intelligentsia by converting to Marxism as many former sup-

porters of Narodnichestvo as possible. They translated key writings of
Marx and Engels and their followers into Russian, and they produced
their own works in which they analyzed the situation in Russia from
Marxist positions. A particularly important role in the dissemination of
Marxism in Russia was played by Plekhanov's books *Socialism and Political Struggle* (1883) and *Our Disagreements* (1885). By subjecting the
main propositions of Narodnichestvo to severe criticism and by persis-
tently affirming the theoretical supremacy of Marxism, Plekhanov and
his adherents hoped to bring at least part of the revolutionary-minded
public under the banner of the new ideology.

At the beginning, Plekhanov's group seemed to make little headway
in Russia, as most Russian socialists continued to believe that Russia would bypass capitalism. However, the industrial upsurge of the
1890s made the Marxist approach seem more relevant to Russia, and
the "Emancipation of Labor" group began to attract disciples among
a younger generation of revolutionary intellectuals. Marxist literature
widely circulated among the intelligentsia, provoking heated arguments
and debates, in the course of which the new movement of social thought
acquired both vehement opponents and avid supporters. Marxist circles
began to spring up inside Russia. These were made up of university students who wanted to study Marxist theory and establish contacts with
factory workers.

In the 1890s Marxism made important inroads among Russian intellectuals, gaining adherents in academic circles and in the radical and
revolutionary movement. Among them were the young intellectuals
VLADIMIR ULIANOV (1870–1924), who was to adopt the underground
name of Lenin, and JULIUS MARTOV (1873–1923). Both decided to
dedicate their lives to revolutionary struggle, and they soon emerged
as leaders of the Russian Marxists. In the 1890s Marxism appealed
to many young intellectuals, including many future liberals, like Peter
Struve (1870–1944), Nicholas Berdyaev (1874–1948), and Sergei Bulgakov (1871–1944), who would later renounce their early Marxist
leanings.

In the 1890s the Marxists appeared to be winning their argument
with the Narodniks, when they emphasized the continuing growth of
capitalism and the proletariat in Russia. The government-sponsored industrialization accelerated the growth of an industrial working class.
With all due qualifications, the proletariat now constituted a significant
component of the Russian population and had an essential role to play
in Russian economy. Its significance as a factor in Russian politics was
also constantly rising. Thus, the actual development of Russia toward

the end of the nineteenth century seemed to follow the Marxists' rather than the Narodniks' blueprint.

In 1895 the Marxist movement reached an important new stage when diverse Marxist groups in St. Petersburg united into a citywide "LEAGUE OF STRUGGLE FOR THE EMANCIPATION OF THE WORKING CLASS." The leader of the new organization was the twenty-five year old Vladimir Lenin. "The League of Struggle" conducted revolutionary agitation among the St. Petersburg proletariat. The climax of its activity was the coordination of a big strike of textile workers in 1896, which involved nineteen factories. Unlike the early disparate Marxist groups, the "League of Struggle" had a larger membership, was more disciplined, and had a well-defined organizational structure. It was the first Marxist organization capable of providing effective leadership of the workers' movement.

St. Petersburg's "League of Struggle" served as a model for the creation of Marxist organizations in big industrial centers like Moscow, Kiev, and others across Russia. In Minsk in 1898 the first attempt was made to join the forces of Russian Marxism: a congress of Marxist organizations was held, at which the establishment of a unified RUSSIAN SOCIAL-DEMOCRATIC LABOR PARTY was announced. However, no program nor rules of the new party were adopted at the congress, and no firm links were established between local party organizations and the leadership center. Besides, nearly all the participants were arrested soon after the congress, and a number of local organizations were crushed. The task of creating a Marxist party still lay ahead.

The Fate of Narodnichestvo

The theoretical struggle between Narodnichestvo and Marxism was intense. Throughout the 1880s Narodniks fiercely defended their ideological system, trying to maintain its dominant position within Russian social thought. However, the postreform capitalist development, the disintegration of the village commune, and the conservatism and apathy of the peasantry compelled a growing number of intellectuals to give up old dogmas and turn to the study of Marxism instead. Life increasingly seemed to give more substance to the theoretical inquiries made by Russian Marxists such as Plekhanov and Lenin who argued that the future Russian revolution would be a proletarian one. The proletariat, in alliance with and as leaders of the peasantry, would carry through the

socialist transformation. Marxism seemed to show the way forward for
Russia in the new circumstances.

The growing popularity of Marxism cannot be attributed simply to
the crisis of the rival socialist ideology of Narodnichestvo. The spread of
Marxism in Russia must be seen in the wider context of the modernizing
processes that were beginning to affect postreform Russia. The development of capitalism, the appearance of elements of civil society, and the
government-sponsored industrialization of the 1890s seemed to indicate
that Russia, after all, took the road followed by the leading group of
industrialized nations. The Western model of development appeared to
display major advantages manifested in an accelerated cultural, economic,
and technological progress, the establishment of a parliamentary system,
and the expansion of democratic freedoms. All this gave credibility to
the arguments of the Russian advocates of "Westernism."

However, the new generation of the socialist-minded opposition
saw the process of "Westernization" and "Europeanization" of Russia
through the prism of Marxist theory — as the struggle for the ultimate
victory of the ideal of social justice. The conversion of Russian radicals to Marxism was, to a great extent, influenced by the successes of
the West European Social-Democratic movement, which in those days
adhered to the theoretical tenets of Marxism. The appearance of labor
legislation and trade unions and a recognition of the social and political
rights of workers represented real achievements in the struggle for social
equality in the West. Russian radicals were convinced that the European Social-Democratic movement was an influential force that helped
to bring about these progressive developments, making a significant contribution to the democratization of Western European society. These
achievements were proof enough for them of the scientific correctness
of Marxism.

But the growing preoccupation of more and more radical intellectuals with the revolutionary theories of Karl Marx did not mean that
the tradition of Narodnichestvo died out. In the 1890s the popularity of Narodnichestvo reached its lowest point, but at the start of the
twentieth century the movement overcame its crisis and revived. Representing two different currents within the general tradition of socialist
thought, Marxism and Narodnichestvo continued to develop side by
side, influencing each other and stimulating the common quest for a socialist alternative to capitalist development. Russian peasant socialism
and proletarian socialism were, as one writer has put it, "two skeins en-
tangled." And it was not just the socialist goal that they had in common.
Both Russian Marxists and Narodniks also agreed about the special role

of the intelligentsia in the liberation movement, and both sought to identify and mobilize a social class (the proletariat or the peasantry) that could become the main agent of revolutionary change.

It is important to note that Marx himself in the later years of his life devoted much attention to the Russian question, in particular to the peasant commune. In the preface to the Russian edition of the *Manifesto of the Communist Party* of 1882 he and Engels noted the big strides that Russia had made in its advance to capitalism, observing at the same time that the continued prevalence of the communal ownership of the land held the prospect of a direct transition to the communist form of ownership:

> *The Communist Manifesto* had as its object the proclamation of the inevitably impending dissolution of modern bourgeois property. But in Russia we find, face to face with the rapidly developing capitalist swindle and bourgeois landed property, just beginning to develop, more than half the land owned in common by the peasants. Now the question is: can the Russian *obshchina*, though greatly undermined, yet a form of the primeval common ownership of land, pass directly to the higher form of communist common ownership? Or on the contrary, must it first pass through the same process of dissolution as constitutes the historical evolution of the West?
>
> The only answer to that possible today is this: If the Russian Revolution becomes the signal for a proletarian revolution in the West, so that both complement each other, the present Russian common ownership of land may serve as the starting point for a communist development.[4]

Marx studied the views of Russian Narodniks with intense interest, making up hundreds of pages of notes. Their ideas about the road to socialism through the *obshchina* allowed him and Engels to take a fresh look at developments outside Western Europe, in countries of "nonclassical" capitalism, and led them to pose the question of the possibility of a noncapitalist road to communism.

Marx's scholarly reputation was highly regarded by the leading Narodniks. The program of the "People's Will," for example, contained references to the revolutionary activism of the proletariat and the possibility of enlisting workers' help in the matter of agitation and propaganda among the peasantry. Nevertheless, many intellectuals still felt that, since Marx's revolutionary philosophy was based on a study of the industrial history and political economy of the advanced capitalist societies of Western Europe, his class-based ideas of "bourgeois-democratic" and "proletarian-socialist" revolution were inapplicable to backward, agrarian, autocratic Russia. At the turn of the century Narodnichestvo was reinvigorated and received a new purpose and direction that reflected the general mood of the Russian peasantry. The demands for the transfer of all land to those who farmed it and the idea of cooperative socialism formed the core of the programs of *neo*-Narodnichestvo: both of its revolutionary wing, represented by the Party of Socialist-Revolutionaries, and its moderate-reformist wing, represented by the Party of People's Socialists.

Peasant socialism, with its belief in the need for a noncapitalist road of development, was thus to remain a powerful force in the Russian political scene until and beyond 1917. In addition, it exerted a major influence on the evolution of the emerging Marxist movement. Yet despite all this, the Russian socialist revolution was to be accomplished not in the name of Herzen, but in the name of Marx.

Chapter Eight

The Last Romanovs

Government Reaction

The reign of ALEXANDER III (1881–94) and the reign of NICHOLAS II (1894–1917) until the Revolution of 1905 formed a period of continuous reaction. Narrow-minded and convinced traditionalists, the son and grandson of the Tsar Liberator not only rejected political change, but tried hard to reverse or limit the effect of the many reforms that had already been implemented.

The chief characteristic of Alexander III's reign was political stagnation coupled with growing aggressiveness toward any attempts, however feeble, to limit the monolithic power of the autocratic government. In the 1880s the arsenal of the autocratic "police state" was augmented by the introduction of new instruments of control and repression, "departments on protection of order and public security," which came to be known simply as *okhrana*. They took over many of the duties of the Third Section of the Imperial Chancellery abolished by Loris-Melikov as a concession to liberal opinion in the last year of Alexander II's reign. The *okhrana* had the functions of secret political police, including the setting up of a network of undercover agents and informers in all social sectors.

New legislative measures were enacted to give the coercive apparatus of the state unlimited prerogatives. Laws on local administration were revised in order to reduce the influence of the liberal element in the *zemstvos* and to strengthen the conservative gentry membership in them. As a result, the *zemstvos* were put under the tight supervision of the central government. The popular press was subjected to rigorous censorship with many progressive periodicals forced to close down. Even book collections in public libraries came under the scrutiny of censors, who purged them of any publications deemed "subversive." These retrograde measures served to undermine the fragile foundations of formal legality laid down in Alexander II's reign.

The excessive aggressiveness with which the tsarist regime protected its power monopoly served merely to antagonize further the left-wing opposition and provided it with moral arguments to justify the use of revolutionary terror. The radicals' hatred of the authorities only grew more bitter, while their doctrines became ever more extreme. Alexander III's government's reaction was not, however, limited to repression against the radical left. It rejected outright any compromise even with the liberal opposition. For many years the Russian press was forbidden even to mention the idea of a national representative assembly in whatever form. The idea would resurface again only in conditions of revolutionary crisis on the eve of the Revolution of 1905.

The government's policy of suppressing every current of opposition thought and its refusal to engage in any meaningful political interaction with society were combined with an attempt to resurrect the outdated official doctrine of Orthodoxy-Autocracy-Nationality devised in the conservative era of Nicholas I. This was now "repackaged" as the theory of "PEOPLE'S AUTOCRACY," which presented Russia's autocratic form of government as a most ideal and advanced political system. The ideologues of the new official theory, such as Konstantin Pobedonostsev (1827–1907), Procurator of the Holy Synod and one of the key advisers to Alexander III, promulgated the notion of a close unity of the tsar and the people. However, this notion was in principle different from the ideas of the liberal-minded Slavophiles, who saw the clearest expression of such unity in a popular assembly. By contrast, the official theory upheld the privileged position of the nobility as "the live link between the tsar and the people."

Based on the chauvinistic idea of the superiority of all things Slavic in general and Russian in particular, the official doctrine was translated into the enforced policy of Russification, a policy that could hardly cement together a multiethnic empire like Russia, where ethnic Russians, at the end of the nineteenth century, made up only 45 percent of the whole population. Jews, Polish Catholics, Baltic Protestants, Central-Asian Muslims — all fell victim in a greater or lesser degree to this ill-conceived policy. A whole battery of discriminatory legislation was devised aimed at suppressing various manifestations of non-Russian national identity and un-Orthodox religious practices. Even the use of native languages — for example Polish in Polish schools — was selectively banned and the learning of Russian made compulsory in some of the non-Russian borderlands.[1] Even the East Slavs, Ukrainians, and Belorussians, who were ethnically and culturally most close to Great Russians, were denied their cultural identity and were officially regarded as "Russians," while their language and culture were not recognized as being separate from Russian.

The only national region that was allowed to retain its special legislation, a representative assembly, and its own monetary system was Finland, although its autonomy was constantly under threat. In the period between 1898 and 1905 Finland was subjected to particularly harsh Russification, which provoked a violent nationalist backlash culminating in the assassination of the governor-general of Finland, Bobrikov, in 1904.

The Jewish community was singled out for particularly vindictive treatment and racialist attacks. It was an open secret that Alexander III was a convinced anti-Semite. Under him special legislation was introduced that restricted the rights of Jews and forbade them from living outside the so-called Pale of Settlement, which was limited to twenty-five provinces in the territory of Russia and Poland. The discrimination against the Jews eventually led to the emergence of a "Zionist" movement in search of a separate Jewish homeland.

Despite the authorities' preoccupation with maintaining a privileged status for the Russians, their policies had no beneficial effect on the economic well-being of the ethnic Russian population. The standard of living in the Russian heartlands was often lower than on the ethnic periphery. In Ukraine, the Caucasus, Poland, the Baltic, and Finland, the government's policy of systematic Russification not only failed to halt the emergence of nationalist movements, but stimulated ever stronger demands for greater cultural and political autonomy.

Nicholas II

The last two Romanovs to rule Russia upheld similar principles and policies, but they differed markedly in character. Alexander III was a strong man, Nicholas II, a weak one. Under Nicholas (1868–1918, reigned 1894–1917) confusion and indecision further complicated the fundamentally wrong-headed efforts of the government.

Nicholas became tsar in 1894 at the age of twenty-six. He was, undoubtedly, a well-educated young man, spoke several European languages, but his tutoring was somewhat one-sided. He showed more interest in applied military subjects than in political and social studies. The issues that agitated the educated society of the day left him cold. He was completely ignorant of the Narodnik and Marxist theories that caught the imagination of a considerable part of his progressively minded subjects.

As a human being, Nicholas possessed certain attractive qualities. He was a simple and modest man, devoted to his family. Yet these positive personal traits mattered little in a situation that demanded strength, determination, adaptability, and vision. Nicholas's estimate of Russian conditions and needs became increasingly unreal. It may well be argued that another Peter the Great could have saved the Romanovs and Imperial Russia. It is obvious, however, that the last tsar could not. A good man, but a miserable ruler lost in the moment of crisis, Nicholas did not possess the qualities necessary to rescue the archaic, rotten Russian system from imminent collapse.

The home background of Nicholas's childhood years may hold a key to understanding much of his political behavior as Russia's sovereign. He was thirteen years old when his grandfather was mutilated by the "People's Will" bomb. There can be no doubt that this incident must have been one of the strongest and most decisive impressions of his childhood. Alexander II's tragic death was followed by repeated attempts to revive the spirit of the "People's Will" in new terrorist organizations that appeared one after another, plotting new assassinations, including attempts on the life of Nicholas's father, Alexander III. Strict security measures at the palace of Gatchina in the suburbs of St. Petersburg, where his family had spent virtually all the years of his father's reign, rare trips into the capital, and a narrow circle of acquaintances formed the background to the daily life of the future Russian emperor. Few people around him could provide the prince with a truthful picture of the country's life, and least of all his mother, a Danish princess, who often had a less than adequate understanding of what was happening. She sincerely blamed the "nihilists" for all the troubles in the country.

The enforced isolation from the realities of everyday life in Russia and the general atmosphere of insecurity and fear that had permeated his childhood years were largely to blame for a strong aversion that Nicholas developed not just to the opponents of autocracy themselves, but practically to any idea or demand that arose from the liberal-minded section of society. Brought up to believe fully in the divine origin of autocratic power, he was probably even psychologically unable to understand the fact that, as one Russian journalist observed, the very realities of life in Russia placed bombs in the hands of those who would far rather have held a pen.[2]

A home background of this kind helps to explain a significant episode that took place in January 1895, practically three months after his accession, when the new tsar met the representatives of the nobility, the *zemstvos,* and the towns at the Winter Palace. There is an inescapable parallel between this meeting and Alexander II's public appearance before Moscow's nobility forty years earlier. Both tsars used the occasion to make public announcements of their political intentions. However, whereas Alexander II in his speech broke the news of the impending reform of serfdom, his grandson chose to dash any hopes of political reform by expressing himself in words that seemed to some a "spiteful trick":

> I am pleased to see representatives of all estates who have journeyed here to profess their loyal sentiments together. I believe in the earnestness of these sentiments, that have been inherent in every Russian since time immemorial. But I know that recently in some rural assemblies the voices have been heard of people carried away by senseless daydreams of the representatives of the zemstvos participating in the business of domestic administration. Let all be appraised that I, dedicating all My efforts to the well-being of the people, shall preserve the principle of autocracy as firmly and steadfastly, as it was preserved by My unforgettable late Parent.[3]

The offensive phrase "senseless daydreams" referred to the idea of a modest consultative role in the national government requested by the representatives of the *zemstvos.* Their liberal proposals were thus dismissed by Nicholas offhand, completely, and without reservation. His unwillingness to consider even moderate plans for reform dashed the liberals' hopes for peaceful change and pushed them to the left of the political spectrum. They began to turn a sympathetic ear to the radicals' call for a violent opposition to tsarism.

A dark shadow over Nicholas's reign was also cast by the tragic event that marred his coronation celebrations in the spring of 1896. The festivities, which were to be accompanied by the distribution of commemorative gift packages and a program of popular entertainment, brought huge masses of people to KHODYNKA FIELD in Moscow. The field had not been properly leveled for the occasion, and the kiosks with gifts were put too close to one another. According to one witness:

> A mass of people half-a-million strong, pressed together as tightly as possible, staggered with all its unimaginable weight in the di-

rection of the kiosks. People by the thousand fell into a ditch and ended standing literally on their hands at the bottom. Others fell straight after them, and more, and more, until the ditch was filled to the brim with bodies. And people walked on them. They could not help walking on them, they were unable to stop.[4]

According to the official statistics, 2,690 people suffered in the crush, 1,389 of whom died. The incident produced an unpleasant impression on the tsar, but the festivities continued as planned. On the night of that very day Nicholas and his wife, Alexandra, attended a ball in the Kremlin and danced. Next day they went to dinner at the German ambassador's.

Nicholas and his government would never be able to erase a negative impression that the Moscow festivities made on public opinion. One of the émigré pamphlets published in Geneva the same year accused the tsar of being incapable of observing even the outward forms of decency. From this time on, in wide sections of the populace Nicholas II came to be known as "the Bloody."

The Khodynka incident had clearly revealed, at the very outset of Nicholas's reign, his inability to react adequately and sensitively to changes in the situation and to make suitable adjustments in response to popular feelings and public opinion. As one writer notes: "In all probability he simply had not been endowed with the proper capacity to respond to the living, changing course of public life. But, if this is of little significance in the fate of a private individual, for the head of such an authoritarian state as the Russian Empire, it was a shortcoming fraught with the most serious consequences."[5] Some analysts attribute a truly symbolical significance to the tragic episode during the coronation festivities, seeing it as a projection in concentrated form of Nicholas II's entire reign.

Tsarist Industrialization

One of the remarkable characteristics of Alexander III's and, particularly, of Nicholas II's reign was a contrast between internal oppressive politics and more liberally oriented economic and financial policies of the government. While they both tried to halt political change, the last Romanovs were persuaded to permit the government to sponsor a massive modernization program designed to boost the country's industrial capacity and introduce modern capitalist forms of production and exchange.

The industrial revolution had arrived in Russia half a century later than in many of the leading countries. However, in the years following the Peasant Reform of 1861 capitalist development had been gaining pace, and by the end of the century the industrial output had grown seven times, promoting Russia to fifth place in the world industrial league table. In the postreform era industrial growth had been achieved mainly through the expansion of textile industries of all sorts and the production of consumer-oriented goods for the domestic and international markets. After grain, textile exports occupied the second most important place in Russian exports, competing successfully in Eastern markets with their European rivals.

In the final decade of the nineteenth century, largely on the initiative of the government, Russian industrialization was given a new direction toward the development of the heavy industrial sector. The guiding figure in the program of speedy industrialization was SERGEI WITTE (1849–1915). He was an economic planner and manager of the type common in the governments of Western Europe and the United States, but exceedingly rare in the high officialdom of Imperial Russia. His background was unusual for a tsarist minister, because he was not a noble but had made his career in business and railway administration. It was therefore natural for him to encourage closer contacts between the government and business when he became the minister of finance under Alexander III and continued in that post under Nicholas II until 1903.

This was the key ministerial position, for a minister of finance held the reins of command over the empire's entire economy. Witte's remarkable energy and ability were devoted, in particular, to the stabilization of finance, the promotion of heavy industry, and the building of railways. In 1897, after accumulating a sufficient gold reserve, he established a gold standard in Russia, thus fixing the value of the rouble against other currencies and against gold. This measure did much to add stability and prestige to Russian economic development, and to attract foreign capital. Witte encouraged heavy industry by virtually every means at his command, including government orders, liberal credits, unceasing efforts to obtain investment from abroad, an improved transportation system, and heavy indirect taxation on items of everyday consumption to squeeze the necessary funds out of the peasants. He put into effect a massive state-sponsored program of railway building, including the construction of the Trans-Siberian Railway, which was completed in 1905 and extends 7,416 kilometers (5,500 miles) to the shores of the Pacific Ocean. The rapid growth of railways depended on government orders for iron, coal, locomotives, and equipment, which helped boost the development of Russian heavy industry and engineering. Thus, in Russian conditions, the state played a leading role in bringing large-scale capitalist enterprise into existence.

Toward the end of the century Russia possessed eight basic industrial regions. Alongside the old industrial centers of Moscow, St. Petersburg, the Urals, and the Polish region, which contained textile industries, metal-processing, machine-building, and chemical, coal, and iron industries, new industrialized areas had emerged. The recently developed southern region centered round the Russian city of Novorossiysk and the Ukrainian Donbass area, which was at the cutting-edge of technological innovation and supplied coal, iron ore, and basic chemical products. The southwestern region specialized in beet-sugar. The Transcaucasian manganese-coal region supplied substantial amounts of its two products. Finally, the Baku sector by the Caspian Sea was a rapidly growing area of oil extraction.

In the final decade of the nineteenth century the Russian government's strategy of economic development yielded spectacular rates of industrial growth, which have rarely been equalled in the industrial history of any country: about 8 percent a year. However, Russia's big strides in developing its industrial capacity led to structural imbalances in the economy that adversely affected the agricultural sector. Of all the population groups, the peasants paid a particularly heavy price for the government's industrial policy. To finance economic modernization, Witte relied on Russia's traditional fiscal structures, such as the village commune, which played a crucial role in the collection of government taxes and redemption dues. On top of the heavy fiscal burden of direct taxes, peasants also paid for the industrialization as consumers, through high tariffs on imported goods and rising indirect taxes on consumer goods such as vodka. There was no welfare program to help cushion the ruinous effects of home-grown capitalism on the peasant economy. Lack of social provisions, combined with a bad harvest and an epidemic of cholera, resulted in the mass hunger of 1891–92. The neglect of the social consequences of rapid capitalist development was clearly a weak side of the government-sponsored industrialization. The tsarist economic strategy meant preserving the autocracy, for only an autocratic government could exert this degree of fiscal pressure on the population. Protests about the results of government economic policies began to mount from the late 1890s and contributed to the social discontent, which eventually culminated in the Revolution of 1905.

Characteristics of Russian Capitalism

By the end of the nineteenth century the system of Russian capitalism was in place and displayed certain distinctive as well as common features as compared with the leading capitalist nations of the West. What were its more salient characteristics?

High Degree of Concentration of Production and Labor

Because Russia industrialized late and rapidly, advanced Western technology was borrowed wholesale, with the result that Russian factories were often more modern than their Western counterparts. Almost overnight Russia acquired huge plants and large-scale industries in a few industrialized regions. The result was a high concentration of workers in very large-scale industrial enterprises. In 1900 almost half the industrial labor force was located in factories that employed more than a thousand workers — a very high number by contemporary European standards. Not impressive in quantity in proportion to total population (about 3 million out of a population of about 170 million in 1914), the Russian proletariat was therefore more densely massed than in other countries, forming large and closely knit groups in industrial centers, including St. Petersburg and Moscow. This heavy concentration of labor in the few nerve centers of the empire would pose a great danger to the imperial government after the workers discovered in 1905 the powerful weapon of a general strike to pressure employers and the authorities.

Formation of Monopolies

The high concentration of production inevitably led to the formation of monopolies. The owners of large-scale enterprises belonging to the same branch of industry began to cooperate with one another in regulating output and setting prices for their goods. This allowed the monopolists to establish control over the market, dictate their terms to the consumer, and thus extract maximum profits. The monopolies first appeared in the form of syndicates in which individual companies maintained their autonomy in matters of production while cooperating in setting prices for their products. By the early twentieth century syndicates began to turn into trusts in which enterprises were incorporated into a single production system managed from one center of command. Monopolies existed in all major branches of industry, including oil extraction, sugar-production, railway rolling-stock production, coal-mining, and the metallurgic industry.

High Concentration of Financial Capital

The process of the formation of trusts led to radical changes in the organization of production and required huge financial resources. Industry was beginning more and more to depend financially on banks. The concentration of industrial production went hand in hand with the concentration of financial capital. In the early twentieth century the five biggest banks controlled most of the finances. They eagerly invested in industry and to a considerable degree subordinated it to their control. As a result, the confluence of financial with industrial capital took place. Major financial tycoons sat on governing boards of industrial enterprises, while leading industrialists and entrepreneurs became closely linked with banking. The financial oligarchy that emerged had concentrated in its hands huge financial and industrial resources. In the early twentieth century this new force would begin to vie with the government for the right to direct the country's economic development.

State-Led Economic Growth

The new force — the financial oligarchy — was closely connected with the state. The state in Russia had always kept most important branches of industry under its control; and it continued to exercise control in the new conditions. In the early twentieth century special bodies were set up that reflected the close relationship between the government and leading capitalists, such as, for instance, a "Shipbuilding Council" or a "Congress of Transport Affairs." These organizations oversaw the allocation of government orders, gave subsidies and tax benefits, and so on. Comprised of industrialists and government officials, they allowed the government to regulate production in close contact with the representatives of major monopolies. For these reasons the emerging Russian bourgeoisie had an ambivalent attitude toward the autocratic-bureaucratic regime. On the one hand, as its wealth increased, it began to crave political power and thus found itself in opposition to autocracy. On the other hand, the continual financial support from the ruling bureaucracy and the dependence on government orders, subsidies, and other benefits rendered the bourgeoisie's opposition fairly weak, inconsistent, and predisposed toward political compromises. Because of its political servility and social egotism, the bourgeoisie commanded little respect in Russian society.

Preponderance of Foreign Capital

Russia's new industries were to a large extent dependent on foreign capital. The establishment of the gold standard created conditions that attracted investment by banks and stockholding companies from France, Britain, Germany, and Belgium. With its inexhaustible resources of raw materials and cheap labor, Russia quickly became a magnet for Western European investors. The biggest share of foreign capital went into metallurgical companies, oil extraction, machine-building, and oil-processing industries. Investment in Russian heavy industry yielded huge rates of profit — much higher than could be gained from investment in French, British, or Belgian production. In addition, foreign investment was strongly encouraged and protected by the Russian government. As a result, at the start of the twentieth century in key branches of industry such as mining, metal-processing, and machine-building the share of foreign investment was higher than the domestic one.

This did not make Russia completely dependent on Western European capital. Yet this peculiarity had one important consequence. Profits earned from Russian investment returned to Western Europe. They increased the wealth of Western European bourgeoisie, which could direct part of its income to ease domestic problems and diffuse social tensions. In the early twentieth century in Western Europe the workday was shortened considerably, wages were rising, and the system of an old-age pension provision was introduced. Gradually a significant stratum of qualified, well-paid workers had emerged, and the Western labor movement increasingly acquired a peaceful, reformist character. The Russian bourgeoisie, on the other hand, could not afford social concessions to the workers — it simply did not have enough wealth. It also tried to export capital to less-developed countries, but it could not compete in this sphere with its more powerful foreign rivals. Russian capital could establish footholds only in a few regions such as in central Asia, northern Iran, and northern China. Profits from investments from these regions were comparatively modest. All this limited the Russian bourgeoisie's means of resolving social conflicts in a peaceful and amicable way.

Hard Conditions of the Working Class

At the beginning of the twentieth century the Russian working class remained the most oppressed and impoverished in Europe, representing an excellent example of a destitute and exploited labor force, char-

acteristic of the early stages of capitalist development described so
powerfully by Marx in *Capital*. Workers' wages were a quarter to a
third of those in Western Europe; the proportion of well-paid workers was very small. The majority of Russian workers worked and lived
in squalid conditions; hours of work were long, accident rates were
high, and discipline was harsh. Not surprisingly, the Russian workers began to organize to better their lot. They developed monolithic
social solidarity and were open to revolutionary agitation. This restricted even further the bourgeoisie's freedom of maneuver and made
it even more cautious as a would-be agent of political change. It saw
the autocracy as less of a threat to itself than the revolutionary-minded
working class.

Survivals of Serfdom

Finally, the social and economic backwardness of the countryside was
a feature of Russian capitalism that arguably was to have most fatal consequences. The pace of the development of capitalist relations
in agriculture lagged far behind the rapid growth of industrial production. The vestiges of serfdom, untouched by the reform of 1861,
considerably slowed down agricultural development. Village communes
tended to perpetuate backward and archaic agricultural production
methods. They persisted in their traditional, ignorant ways, including
the partitioning of land into small strips, which discouraged the use
of modern agricultural techniques. Above all, they lacked capital, education, and any initiative for modernization. Russia still remained an
overwhelmingly agrarian country.

At the turn of the century capitalist development was beginning to
transform the country, but its effect on different branches of the national economy was uneven, resulting in marked disproportions within
its overall structure. The accelerated construction of the railway network across the whole country was drawing vast remote regions into a
single domestic market, but this process was far from complete. Despite
Russia's impressive economic growth, its per capita industrial production and per capita national income were still far behind the leading
group of industrialized nations. Huge newly built modern industrial
plants coexisted with thousands of small archaic mills. The agrarian sector remained dominant, and capitalist relations in agriculture developed
at a slower pace due to the numerous vestiges of the old serfdom system.
According to the general census of the population of 1897, about five-
sixths of the total population were still engaged in agriculture, and only

about one-sixth in large and small industry, trade, on the railways, in building work, and the like. Even a decade and a half later, in 1913, only 18 percent of the population lived in towns, and industry still produced only 20 percent of national income.[6] This shows that although capitalism was making rapid progress, Russia was still a mainly agricultural, underdeveloped country.

Chapter Nine

The Birth of Bolshevism

Lenin's Brand of Marxism

The part played by Vladimir Ulianov (Lenin) in determining Russia's destiny in the twentieth century is a remarkable demonstration of the role of personality in historical events. He was born in 1870 into an intellectual family — his father was a school inspector in a town on the Volga named Simbirsk, now Ulianovsk. A striking parallel exists between Lenin's and Nicholas II's early periods of life: both experienced a tragic bereavement in the family. Whereas for Nicholas the assassination of his grandfather must have been one of the most lasting memories of childhood, Lenin was greatly influenced by the death of his eldest brother in 1887, who was executed for participating in a plot to assassinate Alexander III. At the time of his execution Vladimir was only seventeen. He greatly admired his brother, and his death has sometimes been considered a turning point for Lenin, who became a radical early on.

He soon found an ideological base for his radicalism in Marxism, quickly rising to the role of the leader in the "League of Struggle for the Emancipation of the Working Class," an underground Marxist organization established in St. Petersburg in 1895. In 1896 he suffered imprisonment for his illegal activities and was exiled to Siberia for three years. While in exile, he produced a massive work called *The Development of Capitalism in Russia* whose main contention was that Russia was, indeed, becoming a capitalist nation. In 1900 he left Siberia and traveled abroad, where he participated, together with the "father of Russian Marxism," George Plekhanov, in the publication of a Social-Democratic newspaper, *The Spark,* and in other revolutionary activities, often under the pseudonym of Lenin. Lenin quickly rose to positions of leadership in a newly created Social-Democratic Party; he became head of the party's extremist Bolshevik wing in 1903. Before long he became one of the most important Marxist theoreticians in Russia.

Lenin's theoretical contribution to Marxism could in no sense rival the contributions of the two German originators of the doctrine. He strove to adapt Marxism to the changing conditions in the world and to Russian circumstances, and he produced certain important additions to and modifications of the basic teaching. The need for some of these arose from the fact that Marx had analyzed the contemporary capitalist society and predicted that, as a result of a proletarian revolution, it would be replaced by a communist society, but he had little to say of a concrete nature about how the postrevolutionary society would be run, or indeed, about how the revolution itself should be organized and guided. Lenin, on the other hand, in his long career as an exiled revolutionary, wrote at length on the conduct of the revolution and on society in the immediate postrevolution phase.

Dictatorship of the Proletariat

Lenin's chief contribution to the Marxist canon was the development of Marx's concept of the dictatorship of the proletariat, which would be exercised during and after the revolution by the Communist Party acting as the vanguard of the proletariat.

The Marxist concept of the dictatorship of the proletariat should not be confused with the concept of dictatorship as a specific form of government, which is the opposite of democracy. In Marxist teaching, the concept of dictatorship denotes the system of political domination of a certain social class. For example, under the capitalist system a given country may have a democratic form of government. But the trappings of democracy only conceal the political and economic domination, or dictatorship, of the bourgeoisie as the ruling, dominant class of the capitalist socioeconomic formation. The class struggle in capitalist society necessarily leads to the overthrow of the minority dictatorship of the bourgeoisie and to the establishing of the majority dictatorship of the proletariat. This dictatorship itself only constitutes a transition to the abolition of all classes and to a classless communist society.

In the writings of Marx and Engels the concept of the dictatorship of the proletariat was most clearly elaborated with regard to the experience of the Paris Commune of 1871, which the founders of Marxism viewed as the first proletarian revolution in human history, insofar as it brought to power a government of the working class — the bloc of proletarian and petty-bourgeois revolutionaries. This was government of a new type — the first example of a dictatorship of the proletariat in history. The main conclusion that the two founders of Marxism reached in their analysis of the lessons of the Paris Commune was that the chief reason for its downfall was an insufficient toughness on the part of the proletarian government, evident in its hesitancy to suppress the counterrevolutionary forces and in its tactics of "passive defense."

In developing the Marxist concept of the dictatorship of the proletariat, Lenin also attached great importance to the study of the lessons of the defeated Paris Commune and insisted on the form of an iron dictatorship that would be utterly ruthless and merciless toward the enemies of a workers' republic of the future. Lenin left no doubts about what he meant by dictatorship:

> Dictatorship is rule based directly upon force and unrestricted by any laws.
>
> The revolutionary dictatorship of the proletariat is rule won and maintained by the use of violence by the proletariat against the bourgeoisie, rule that is unrestricted by any laws.[1]

Lenin used the phrase "the dictatorship of the proletariat" to describe a government representing the majority of the population, but prepared to use force to control the minority that opposed it. According to him, immediately after the revolutionary overthrow of capitalism there would be an intermediate period during which dictatorship of the proletariat would perform the function of suppression of the exploiting classes with the consequent destruction of the very foundations on which the activity of exploiters was based (such as private property) and even the physical annihilation of the exploiters themselves. However, the new government would be more democratic than any that had existed previously, as it would represent for the first time in history the interests of most Russians, rather than those of a privileged minority.

In Lenin's view, the new proletarian government would need to build and maintain a coercive machinery of power and use it not just against its internal enemies, but also to withstand "direct attempts on the part of the bourgeoisie of other countries to destroy the victorious proletarian socialist state." Only with the triumph of the proletarian-socialist revolution on a worldwide scale and with the achievement of the ultimate, communist, stage would class struggle finally be over, would society become classless, and would the coercive apparatus of the state no longer be needed. The state would die out (or, to use Friedrich Engels's famous phrase, simply "wither away"). The dictatorship of the proletariat would come to an end.

If the Paris Commune of 1871 was the first attempt in history to establish a dictatorship of the proletariat, then Russia in 1917 became the first country in the world where, under the determined leadership of Lenin and his Bolshevik Party, the dictatorship of the proletariat triumphed and consolidated.

Role of the Peasantry

Lenin's next major adaptation of the classical Marxist doctrine stemmed from his determination to stage an anti-capitalist proletarian revolution in a predominantly peasant country where capitalism barely existed. A land of peasants, Russia could not afford to rely for its future on the proletariat alone, and at least the poor peasants, if not the wealthier ones, had to be assigned the role of agents of revolutionary change in order to bring theory into some correspondence with reality. This was contrary to the views of Marx, Engels, and Marxists in general, who had neglected the peasants in their teachings and relegated them, as petty proprietors, to the bourgeois camp. Lenin, however, came to the conclusion that, if properly led by the proletariat and the party, poor peasants could be a revolutionary force. As early as 1905, during Russia's first revolution, he put forward the slogan: "A Revolutionary Democratic Dictatorship of the Proletariat and Peasantry."

Lenin hoped to create a government that would represent an alliance of peasants and proletarians and would thus be based on the social support of most Russians. His recognition of the role of the peasantry in a "proletarian" revolution shows that he made use of many propositions previously asserted by the Narodniks. Nicholas Berdyaev has pointed to this fact as evidence that Leninism had absorbed the revolutionary elements of Narodnichestvo in a changed form:

> Lenin was a Marxist and believed in the exclusive mission of the proletariat. He believed that the world was approaching a period of proletarian revolutions, but he was a Russian and he made his revolution in Russia, a country of an entirely peculiar character. ...He had to bring about in a peasant country the first proletarian revolution in the world. He felt himself free from any of the stereotyped [Marxist] doctrines. ...He proclaimed a workman and peasant revolution, a workman and peasant republic; he decided to make use of the peasantry for the proletarian revolution, and he succeeded in this, to the embarrassment of the Marxist doctrinaires.[2]

Lenin's reconsideration of the role of the peasantry in bringing about the establishment of the new order was a vital corrective that made

Marxism more relevant to Russian conditions and helped bolster the revolutionary optimism of Lenin and his followers.

Two Revolutions in One

Since Russia was behind the rest of Europe, Russian Marxist revolutionaries had to plan for *two* revolutions. In the first, the BOURGEOIS-DEMOCRATIC REVOLUTION, the workers would aid the bourgeoisie to overthrow tsarism and establish a democratic republic. This would set the stage for a long period of capitalist development during which Russia would become an industrialized country. The factory workers would grow in numbers and would organize, but the political power would be in the hands of the bourgeoisie. Eventually, the PROLETARIAN-SOCIALIST REVOLUTION would take place. The workers would revolt, seize political power from the capitalist owners of industry, establish the dictatorship of the proletariat, and create a proletarian state.

The orthodox Marxists, such as Plekhanov and Martov, saw a clear distinction between the bourgeois and socialist revolutions. In their view, the bourgeois revolution would usher in a long transition period in which the power would be in the hands of the bourgeoisie, while capitalism would flourish, building up both the material and social preconditions for a socialist revolution. They believed that the second — socialist — revolution was far in the future.

Lenin, however, came to believe that in Russia the two revolutions would run into each other. In his opinion, the Russian bourgeoisie was too conservative and reliant on a strong autocratic government to push for a radical bourgeois revolution. In Russian conditions it fell to the working classes to push the bourgeoisie into making radical political demands that would speed up the development of capitalism in Russia. In 1905 the revolutionary activity of peasants and workers so impressed Lenin that he began seriously to consider the possibility of using their energies to radicalize the revolution and to establish a working-class government even during the bourgeois revolution.

He saw his chance of putting into practice the idea of "telescoping" two revolutions into one soon after the overthrow of the tsarist regime in February 1917, when a "bourgeois" Provisional Government was set up. In contrast to moderate Marxists who did not question its legitimacy, Lenin called for the overthrow of the Provisional Government and the establishing of a working-class government. This call transformed the proletarian revolution from a distant dream into an immediate reality. The decision to stage an anti-capitalist revolution gave

Lenin's Bolsheviks a huge advantage in the search for working-class support. The commitment to revolution also infused his party with a sense of purpose that the moderate socialists lacked. Its members could now concentrate on the task of seizing power.

The Party of a New Type

Because Lenin believed that proletarian revolution was at hand, he took it seriously and prepared for it carefully. Lenin understood that in tsarism Russian Marxists had a formidable opponent, the struggle against which required a high level of unity and discipline. He therefore attached great importance to organizational problems and to the preparation of organizational structures of a future Marxist party. Lenin also saw more clearly than most that a working-class party would need the leadership skills of radical intellectuals like himself. This was partly because in Imperial Russia, in contrast to, for example, Germany, Marxism never acquired a legal standing or a mass following, remaining essentially a conspiracy of intellectuals. If Lenin wanted results, he had to depend on intellectuals steeped in Marxist teaching and united in a small dedicated party of professional revolutionaries. This places the Bolshevik leader firmly in the tradition of Russian radicalism, the tradition of Chernyshevsky and Tkachev, and even, broadly speaking, of such Narodniks as Lavrov, who emphasized the role of the "critically thinking individuals" as the makers of history. Though he rejected the ideology of Narodnichestvo and their tactics of terror, Lenin admired the organizational cohesion of the "People's Will," the populist group that had assassinated Alexander II.

In 1902 Lenin produced *What Is to Be Done?* The title of this seminal work on the party's organization directly echoed the name of Chernyshevsky's novel. In the book Lenin laid down a detailed plan for the building of the party of the working class. He severely criticized those within Russian Social-Democracy who argued that the party should concentrate the workers' attention on the *economic* struggle against capitalism as the means of raising proletarian political consciousness. Lenin believed that this trend of "economism" within Marxism would encourage the workers to develop merely a "trade-union consciousness" and distract them from the vital political task of overthrowing tsarism.

In other words, Lenin believed that the workers, left to their own instincts, would choose reforms in wages and working conditions over political revolution. To Lenin, trade unionism meant the ideological enslavement of the workers by the bourgeoisie. In his view, only a strong

organization of revolutionaries could provide leadership to the spontaneous movement of the proletariat, free it from its subordination to
bourgeois ideology, and transform its struggle into a genuine "class
struggle." It was the party's task "to divert the working-class movement from this spontaneous, trade-unionist striving to come under the
wing of the bourgeoisie, and to bring it under the wing of revolutionary Social-Democracy."[3] This meant that the party's chief mission was
to mobilize and direct the workers toward the goal of overturning the
existing political and economic order.

What the proletariat needed then was "a party of a new type" that
would not simply drag at the tail of the labor movement, passively reg-
istering what the masses of the working class feel and think. On the
contrary, the party would stand at the head of the movement, forming
the "VANGUARD OF THE PROLETARIAT," capable of elevating the workers
above their momentary economic interests to the level of strategic class
interests. In practice, this meant that in the particular circumstances of
Russia, where the working class was only beginning to form, the Marxist Party would not wait for the Russian proletariat to evolve into a
fully fledged political class, but would assume an active and decisive
role in shaping the working class itself and spearheading the proletarian revolution. It would be the party of a new type in the vital sense
that it would not be deterred by the quantitative and qualitative inadequacy of the Russian proletariat but would substitute itself for the
working class. The Russian revolution would be made not by a class,
but by a party proclaiming itself to be the representative and vanguard
of a class.

As to the structure and composition of the party, Lenin believed that
in an autocratic state, where political parties were not allowed to operate legally and where tsarist police agents had much experience in
fighting and infiltrating such organizations, the success could only be
achieved by a party that was comprised of people professionally engaged
in revolutionary activity and led by a hierarchy of authoritative leaders.
Lenin wrote:

> I assert, that no revolutionary movement can endure without a
> stable organization of leaders that maintains continuity...; that
> such an organization must consist chiefly of people profession-
> ally engaged in revolutionary activity; that in an autocratic state
> the more we *confine* the membership of such an organization to
> people who are professionally engaged in revolutionary activity
> and who have been professionally trained in the art of combating

the political police, the more difficult will it be to wipe out such an organization.[4]

This was the concept of a monolithic and militant underground party with a clearly defined organization, in which members must submit to strict party discipline. It would operate as a revolutionary headquarters with a military-style commitment to subordination, unity, and secrecy.

Lenin's views on the organization of the party are extremely important for understanding the Russian Revolution and much of Soviet development. According to Nicholas Berdyaev:

> The very organization of the party, which was centralized in the extreme, was a dictatorship on a small scale. Every member of the party was subjected to this dictatorship of the center. The Bolshevik party which Lenin built up in the course of many years was to provide the pattern of the future organization of the whole of Russia, and in actual fact Russia was organized on the pattern of the Bolshevik party organization. The whole of Russia, the whole Russian people, was subjected not only to the dictatorship of the communist party but also to the dictatorship of the communist dictator.... Lenin denied freedom within the party and this denial of freedom was transferred to the whole of Russia.[5]

With his single-mindedness and determination Lenin set out to achieve his vision of a revolutionary organization that would be capable of becoming an active, history-making force. Its firm leadership of a proletarian revolution, its scientific knowledge of the laws of history, and its exceptional commitment to unity and discipline would more than compensate for all those inadequacies of Russian capitalism that made more orthodox Marxists view the prospects of an early proletarian revolution in Russia with skepticism. "Give us an organization of revolutionaries, and we shall overturn the whole of Russia!" was the challenge with which Lenin concluded *What Is to Be Done?* By 1917 Lenin had this organization in the Bolshevik Party, and his prophesy, made fifteen years earlier, was finally fulfilled.

The important thing about Lenin's additions to and development of the original Marxist doctrine in questions of both ideology and organization is that they appeared to work in Russia to the embarrassment of more orthodox Russian Marxists. They led to the creation of a revolutionary government of the working classes. Whether they succeeded in creating a genuinely socialist society is, however, an altogether different matter.

Bolshevism and Menshevism

Lenin's uncompromising stand on party organization, discipline, and leadership initially outlined in *What Is to Be Done?* was the chief cause of the split in the newly created Russian Social-Democratic Labor Party (RSDLP) at its founding congress in 1903. (Technically, this was the party's second congress, as the first had met in 1898, only to be dispersed by the police.) The congress was held abroad in secret, first in Brussels and then in London. One of the most important items on its agenda turned out to be the question of the criteria for party membership. Lenin's hitherto close comrade, Julius Martov, proposed that a party member must, first, accept the party program; second, support the party financially; and, third, be prepared to work under the direction of one of the party organizations. Lenin agreed with the first two principles but objected to the third. In his formulation, a party member must work "*in* one of the party organizations."

The seemingly insignificant variation in wording exposed two widely differing views as to what type of party there should be. Martov's formulation envisaged a broad party of sympathetic supporters prepared to render "personal cooperation" with party organizations. Lenin, true to the organizational principles of the party elaborated by him only a few months before in *What Is to Be Done?*, wanted the party to be a narrow, secret band of fully dedicated activists. In contrast to Martov's wording, his formulation required of party members a higher degree of discipline, professionalism, and commitment to the cause.

At the congress Lenin lost the vote on the question of party membership to Martov. On a later item, however, which also concerned the question of party leadership and organization, he won a slender majority. Armed with this tenuous numerical advantage, Lenin promptly dubbed his supporters the "majority-ites." The Russian word for "majority" is *bolshinstvo* — hence Lenin's followers became known as BOLSHEVIKS. His opponents, led by Martov, were called the "minority-ites" or MENSHEVIKS.

The 1903 congress also adopted the party program, consisting of two parts: minimum and maximum. The two parts of the program corresponded to the two revolutions that Russian Marxists were to prepare for. The minimum program set the task of achieving a bourgeois-democratic revolution, in which the workers would aid the bourgeoisie to overthrow tsarism and establish a democratic republic. The maximum program planned for a proletarian-socialist revolution in which the workers would seize power from the capitalists and establish the dictatorship of the proletariat.

For moderate Marxists, such as Plekhanov and Martov, this maximum goal looked very distant indeed. Nevertheless, the very fact that the Russian Social-Democratic Party had set itself the ultimate objective of establishing a dictatorship of the proletariat put it into an altogether different light, making it a radical, extremist organization. The goal of a proletarian dictatorship made any compromise and cooperation with other reform-minded social and political forces extremely difficult, not to say impossible. The adoption by the congress of the maximum program signified the victory of the radical wing of the RSDLP — i.e., of the Bolsheviks with Lenin as their leader. Their opponents, the Mensheviks, insisted that the party should adhere in its work only to the minimum program. The inclusion of the clause on the dictatorship of the proletariat also marked the parting of ways between Bolshevism and European Social-Democracy: programs of West European Social-Democratic parties did not contain such a goal.

Although for the moment they were technically two factions of a single party, and despite several later attempts at reunification, the split between the Mensheviks and Bolsheviks proved irreparable. Only for a short period during the heady days of the Revolution of 1905 were the two wings of Russian Social-Democracy able to overcome their differences. However, after 1905, disagreements among Russian Marxists surfaced again, and the split between them began to widen. The Mensheviks continued to believe in a mass organization, open to all revolutionaries who were free to engage in democratic discussions within the party. They were in favor of an alliance with all other revolutionary and liberal parties and gave support to trade unions pursuing better wages and conditions for workers. They were circumspect in their assessment of the viability of a proletarian revolution in Russia and insisted that the bourgeois stage had to occur first, so as to enable all the necessary preconditions for a socialist revolution to mature.

By contrast, Lenin's faction proceeded to organize itself on the principles of a tight-knit underground party of professional revolutionaries subordinated to the will and authority of its supreme leadership in the form of the Central Committee. It rejected cooperation with other parties and dismissed the struggle for improved conditions of workers as playing into the hands of the bourgeoisie and distracting them from their vital political task of revolution. The Bolsheviks also gradually fell in line with Lenin's unorthodox idea of merging the bourgeois and the proletarian revolutions into one.

1898–1917   Russian Social-Democratic Labor Party
1917–1918   Russian Social-Democratic Labor Party (Bolsheviks)
1918–1925   Russian Communist Party (Bolsheviks)
1925–1952   All-Union Communist Party (Bolsheviks)
1952–1991   Communist Party of the Soviet Union
1993–   Communist Party of the Russian Federation

By 1912 the split between the Mensheviks and the Bolsheviks had become permanent, with the two factions evolving effectively into two separate parties. In the years and months leading to the October Socialist Revolution of 1917, as the workers' mood became more militant, the Mensheviks lost their working-class support to the Bolsheviks. As they believed that capitalism would exist for some time, the Mensheviks were reluctant to undermine the property rights of capitalists and landlords and to force the pace of events toward revolution. As a consequence of this view, they were perceived by the working classes to be a less radical party with closer links to the bourgeoisie. The Bolsheviks, on the other hand, saw no need to compromise with a bourgeoisie they intended to overthrow. They could therefore support workers' control in industry, and peasant control of the land. For Russia's peasants and workers such a program had much greater appeal. They increasingly sided with the Bolsheviks, whom they saw as more "working-class" and more revolutionary.

Marxism *and* Leninism or Marxism-Leninism?

The deplorable results of the communist experiment in the Soviet Union have seriously discredited the idea of "socialism" as an alternative to "capitalism." Those who still cling to the socialist ideal as a model of social development try to dissociate Marx from Lenin, insisting that the Bolshevik leader made a radical revision of classical Marxism and completely transformed it into the militant ideology of a totalitarian state. They find instances of complete reversals of Marx's conclusions, for example, in Lenin's assertion about Russia's readiness for a proletarian revolution. Marx repeatedly emphasized that the new communist society would be the result of a highly developed capitalism. Socialism would triumph simultaneously in several economically most-advanced countries. In this regard Russia was viewed by Marx as a very unlikely place in which to have a proletarian revolution, because the industrial revolution there had hardly started.

Some analysts, however, are convinced that Leninism rests firmly on the doctrinal foundations of classical Marxism. They argue that both Marxism and Leninism recognize the central role of class struggle in human history. They both share the belief in the necessity of establishing a proletarian dictatorship and the conviction that a communist party must play a preeminent role in the political process. Fundamental to both Leninism and Marxism is a negative attitude toward private property. Finally, Lenin stood firmly on the platform of Marx's "revolutionary dialectics," which saw revolution as a necessary and legitimate way of social transformation and which justified the use of all available means of political coercion and force.

It is possible to list a range of Marxist principles by which Lenin was guided in his activities first as the leader of the Russian proletarian revolution and later as the head of the victorious workers' government. These ideas formed part and parcel of Leninism and were thoroughly assimilated by it. They became the immutable dogmas that underpinned the construction of socialism in the former USSR. Only the most central of them will be summarized here:

- humankind in its development passes through five formations, with communism being the highest and final of them;

- humankind advances to communism, the essence of which will be "from each according to his abilities, to each according to his needs";

- private ownership of the means of production is connected with exploitation; with the abolition of private property, exploitation will disappear;

- class struggle is the essence of world development: "the history of all hitherto existing society is the history of class struggle" (Marx);

- class struggle is waged by two main classes: the exploited working class and the exploiting class of the bourgeoisie;

- due to its social position the working class is naturally attracted to socialism;

- the state is an instrument created to protect the exploiters from the exploited;

- democracy under capitalism is merely one of the forms of the exploiting bourgeois state;

- the road to socialism lies through a violent revolution, the aim of which is the destruction of the bourgeois state and private ownership and the creation of a workers' state — the state of the dictatorship of the proletariat;

- the state of the dictatorship of the proletariat is a necessary stage in the transition to a classless society, a society without the state;

- the essence of socialism and of the transition to communism is a gradual abolition of money-commodity relations (in other words, of the market);

- the essence of a socialist economy is a high degree of centralization and of planning in all aspects of economy;

- dictatorship of the proletariat is unthinkable without the Communist Party's dominant position within the state.

Marxist tenets with Lenin's amendments would become gospel in the Soviet Union, where the entire ideology was frequently referred to as "Marxism-Leninism," a phrase coined by Stalin to describe the conflation of basic Marxist theory with the ideas of Lenin. From 1917 until the collapse of the Soviet Union in 1991 Marxism-Leninism provided the foundations of Soviet ideology and organization.

Chapter Ten

The Revolution of 1905–7

Anti-autocratic Opposition on the Eve of Revolution

By the start of the twentieth century, as a result of the government-sponsored modernization, which had created a demand for experts of many kinds, the intelligentsia, represented by doctors, lawyers, teachers, and other professionals, had increased enormously. Many nobles had been forced to take up intellectual work of various kinds. However, the predominant place in the composition of the intelligentsia was now firmly occupied by the "men of mixed ranks," the *raznochintsy*. Poorly paid, excluded from participation in the affairs of state, they had few reasons to preserve an unquestioning loyalty to the regime. Some felt so alienated that they became revolutionaries, imparting to the Russian anti-autocratic movement its characteristic democratic spirit and radicalism. In contrast to their working-class followers, members of the intelligentsia were better educated and therefore had a clearer understanding of how the tsarist system worked. They provided most of the leaders of the revolutionary movement and of the left-wing of Russian Liberalism.

Despite their shared opposition to the autocracy, different groups within Russia's educated classes fought for different visions of their country's future and had conflicting ideas about how to achieve them. "Down with autocracy!" was the only slogan they were unanimous about. As for the rest, divisions between different factions of the intelligentsia seemed to be insurmountable. To begin with, the intelligentsia was divided into a liberal and a socialist camp. The liberals were split further into supporters of constitutional monarchy, parliamentary monarchy, or a republic. Some of them advocated gradual reforms; others were in favor of more radical, rapid changes. Socialists were equally disunited, separated into neo-Narodniks and Marxists. The latter were further split into Bolsheviks and Mensheviks. The significance of the division within Russian Marxists was not yet obvious at the time of the Revolution of 1905–7. Its dire consequences would be revealed only several years

ANTI-AUTOCRATIC OPPOSITION ON THE EVE OF THE 1905 REVOLUTION

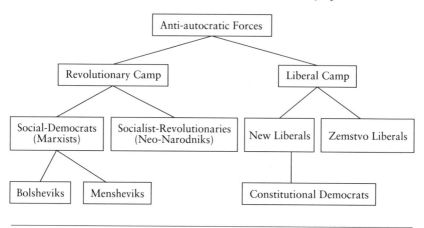

later, in 1917, when it would become one of the chief reasons why the autocracy, after a short period of constitutional monarchy and an even shorter interlude of democracy, was swept away by a communist tyranny.

Social-Democrats, represented by the Bolshevik and Menshevik wings of the RSDLP, were not the only political party in the early twentieth century in Russia that advocated a revolutionary transformation of the country's political and economic system. By no means had all of the revolutionary-minded members of the intelligentsia converted to the Marxist version of socialism. Many continued to adhere to the populist tradition of peasant socialism that had first appeared in the 1860s. At the end of 1901 and the beginning of 1902 these "neo-Narodniks" established a new illegal organization, the SOCIALIST-REVOLUTIONARY PARTY. Its most important thinker and leader was VICTOR CHERNOV (1873–1952). The new party, which imitated the organizational and tactical methods of the "People's Will," set up a terrorist wing that assassinated many prominent officials, including one of the tsar's uncles, Grand Duke Sergei Aleksandrovich, in February 1905. The SRs, as they were known, also conducted revolutionary agitation among the peasantry.

Socialist-Revolutionaries and Social-Democrats represented the revolutionary camp in the political forces for change. They shared a similar outlook and strove for the common goal of socialism. However, leaders of the two parties had different visions of the ways to achieve socialism. Their disagreements created insuperable ideological and organizational divisions within the revolutionary camp. Any attempts to unite Socialist-

Revolutionaries and Social-Democrats were mutually rejected. Only unofficial contacts were allowed between the two parties.

The revolutionary camp was not the only force that strove to undermine the foundations of autocracy. Dissension had spread to many liberal-minded intellectuals, too, who also saw an urgent need for reforms. The liberal intelligentsia tried at all cost to prevent revolution and social upheavals. However, they realized that the regime's procrastination over the issue of reform only served to aggravate social tensions. For this reason, the liberals sought to do everything possible to compel the tsar and the ruling circle to take the road of reform.

The ideological and social complexion of Liberalism itself was undergoing change. In the mid-nineteenth century Liberalism had been an ideology of disgruntled nobles concerned to reduce the powers of autocracy and its bureaucracy. Since 1864, the *zemstvos* had provided the institutional base for this "GENTRY" (or ZEMSTVO) LIBERALISM. Its chief aim had been to create institutions through which forces outside the bureaucracy could shape government policy. Liberal nobles had proposed to the tsar the creation of a national *zemstvo*, or Duma, as far back as 1862, and again in 1895. Though they saw this purely as an advisory body, the government regarded the idea as a threat to autocracy. In 1895 Nicholas II dismissed the idea as no more than a "senseless daydream."

The late 1890s saw the development of a new, radical trend within Liberalism which became known as "NEW LIBERALISM." Many of the "new liberals" were ex-Marxists (particularly those who used to belong to the so-called legal Marxists[1] and the right-wing of the "economists") or former Narodniks who disagreed with the terrorist tactics of Socialist-Revolutionaries. In contrast to the older "gentry" Liberalism, the new trend relied more on the *raznochintsy* element within the intelligentsia. New Liberalism sought to combine the basic principles of old Liberalism with social programs of democratic socialism but rejected the Marxist conception of socialism. The intellectuals representing this trend emphasized the need for democratic and social changes. They also tried to free Russian Liberalism from some of its outdated Slavophile ideas and give it a more westernizing orientation.

The most prominent ideologists of the new liberal trend were, among others, Sergei Bulgakov, Paul Miliukov, Vladimir Nabokov, Fedor Kokoshkin, and Peter Struve. In 1902 in Germany members of the liberal-minded intelligentsia, with the financial support of *zemstvo* liberals, published the first issue of an illegal paper, *Liberation*. Its editor-in-chief, Struve, had been a prominent legal Marxist in the mid-1890s. The first issue contained an appeal to the autocratic government

to launch a far-reaching political reform. It was written by the historian
PAUL MILIUKOV (1859–1943), who sought to convince the tsar about the
necessity of adopting a constitution. Miliukov believed that it was possible to combine the Marxist and the liberal visions of Russia's future
and thus form a united front of the entire opposition to exert maximum
pressure on the authorities.

In the pages of *Liberation* Miliukov came up with the idea of establishing an illegal liberal organization. This proposal received broad
support among the intelligentsia. Numerous circles began to spring up
that shared the liberal platform of the newspaper. However, it proved
impossible to unite the two main strands of Russian Liberalism. In July
1903 the "new liberals" established an illegal liberal organization called
the "Union of Liberation," whose program borrowed some of its more
radical ideas from Marxism. Their demands included an elected Legislative National Assembly with real legislative powers. Their chief aim
was the abolition of autocracy, though many of them favored a constitutional monarchy of some sort. A few months later, in November 1903,
the "Union of Zemstvo Constitutionalists" was set up by constitution-
ally inclined members of the liberal bourgeoisie. The members of the
more radical "Union of Liberation" were against a merger with the *zemstvo* constitutionalists, whom they perceived as being too right-wing.
The *zemstvo* liberals, in their turn, were reluctant to make concessions
to the radicalism of the intelligentsia.

As the revolutionary mood in the country deepened, however, the liberal intelligentsia realized the urgency of forming a united front with the
liberal bourgeoisie in order to galvanize its representatives in the *zemstvos* into making more resolute demands for constitutional reforms. In
addition to exerting pressure on the *zemstvo* liberals, the "Union of Liberation" sought to spread its influence among broader sections of the
population. Its tactics included agitation for the setting up of professional associations and trade unions that would have elected boards (or
bureaus). The intention was to join these boards into a unified network
of trade unions — a "Union of Unions." The liberals hoped that the
"Union of Unions" would bring together not just members of liberal and
democratic intelligentsia, but also workers and peasants. They would
form a united front to voice moderate political demands as well as to advance their professional and economic interests. The idea of the "Union
of Unions" was supported by Socialist-Revolutionaries and Mensheviks
but rejected by Bolsheviks.

Most of the trade unions that eventually joined the "Union of
Unions" represented intellectual professions, such as university lecturers,

writers, lawyers, teachers, doctors, pharmacists, and statisticians. This was a convenient forum for expressing economic demands and political positions. In the course of the 1905 Revolution the "Union of Unions" underwent a political evolution. Following the general strike in October 1905, it radicalized its demands to reflect the mood of the popular masses. The members who disagreed with this shift to the left quit the organization.

The radicalization of the "Union of Unions" did not last, however. After the defeat of the revolution a large part of the intelligentsia swung to the right, reacting to the change of political situation by a return to the liberal camp. Many abandoned political activity altogether. Others joined the ranks of a new, liberal political party that grew out of the "Union of Liberation." Established in October 1905, this was called the PARTY OF CONSTITUTIONAL DEMOCRATS (or KADETS). Miliukov became one of its most important leaders and the head of its Central Committee.

Under normal circumstances, the educated classes would be called upon to act as an intermediary between the government and the popular masses. In early twentieth-century Russia, however, the attitudes and inclinations of the radical intelligentsia precluded it from playing that vital role. Inspired by a near-religious belief in revolution, it sought to direct the growing social discontent of the working classes toward the goal of the overthrow of the hated autocratic government.

The Revolutionary Masses

Until the Revolution of 1905 the dissent in the milieu of the gentry and *raznochintsy* intellectuals had existed alongside the popular risings of the discontented masses, but they had never really come together in one powerful anti-autocratic movement. Earlier intellectuals-revolutionaries, like the Decembrists, for example, were concerned about the unpredictability and violence of a spontaneous popular revolt. The inability of the educated members of society to find a common language with the "people," as well as the peasants' natural distrust of "squires," had ensured that for decades the revolutionary intelligentsia and the masses had been unable to overcome mutual suspicion and misunderstanding.

However, at the turn of the nineteenth century socialist and liberal-democratic doctrines began to filter into the popular movement. The influence of various social-political organizations and parties of the intelligentsia among the worker and peasant masses started to grow. This combination of radical ideas with the revolutionary energies of the masses produced an explosive mix that totally transformed the situation in the country. At the start of the twentieth century popular discontent began to assume all-Russian proportions. The numbers of strikers, rebels, and dissenters multiplied dramatically. Calls for a violent overthrow of autocracy were becoming ever louder, imparting an increasingly revolutionary character to popular protests.

The result was an unprecedented rise of popular discontent that erupted into three revolutions in a space of twelve years. The Revolution of 1905–7 and the February and October Revolutions of 1917 were the three great peaks and the culmination of popular movements in Russia. They had a momentous effect not just on Russia's future but on the course of worldwide developments in the twentieth century. The Russian revolutions were in many ways different from the earlier revolutions in the West and from the revolutions in the East at the start of the twentieth century. Their singularity was in the way in which the struggle against the remnants of the antiquated feudal system was combined with the protest against capitalist exploitation, in the way in which various currents of rural and urban unrest blended in one democratic movement, in the way in which the working class and the radically minded intelligentsia spearheaded revolutionary action, and in the way in which socialist ideas caught the imagination of the masses.

There was also much in these three great revolutions that was reminiscent of the age-old Russian revolt against authorities and traditions that went back deep into Russian history. It was precisely this powerful element of spontaneous, unrestrained, destructive insurrection inherent in popular movements that had made the aristocratic revolutionaries of the nineteenth century wary of the prospect of a popular rising. Born out of the enduring ignorance of ordinary people and their hatred toward the authorities, this unbridled anarchic spirit reflected Russia's almost complete lack of firm democratic traditions, an authoritarian mentality of the masses, and a poorly developed political culture in all sectors of society.

The rebellious mood of the people was also heightened by their destitution and poverty. In Russia, the institution of small- and medium-scale private ownership, particularly the ownership of land, was dangerously underdeveloped. There was a near absence of a middle class that might have grown on the basis of such ownership and that might not have been so vulnerable to radical, extremist slogans. It was hardly surprising that in Russian circumstances popular movements became breeding grounds for ultra-radical elements that manipulated public consciousness and the social behavior of the masses and claimed to speak and act on their behalf. By the start of the twentieth century Russia was ready for its first revolution. The soil for it had been prepared by a series of crises that affected the country's economy, its social and ethnic relations, and its political system. The situation had been aggravated by the fact that the industrial modernization had drawn Russia more closely into the circle of other industrialized capitalist nations and thus also made it vulnerable to world cycles of economic booms and slumps. The world economic crisis of 1900–1903 hit Russia particularly hard as it was combined with a poor domestic harvest.

To make matters worse, Russia's population also felt the strains of the RUSSO-JAPANESE WAR (1904–5), which had broken out as a result of a conflict of interests between the two countries in Manchuria (a region in northern China) and in parts of Korea. The Japanese repeatedly sought a Russian withdrawal from Manchuria, but the Russian government refused to give in to Japanese demands, believing that Japan was only a weak military adversary. However, during a year and a half of hostilities Russia suffered an unbroken series of military defeats both on land and on sea. The conflict ended with a relatively mild peace settlement for Russia, mainly due to the diplomatic and political skills of Sergei Witte, the former minister of finance, who negotiated the truce. The war, however, had badly damaged the government's prestige.

The general discontent quickly spread to the whole of society and, in particular, to its lower strata. "Down with autocracy!" was the revolutionary slogan and the battle cry that was supported and even enthusiastically embraced by an ever-growing part of the population. The workers, in particular, became restless. They were no longer prepared to put up with the outdated economic and legal conditions of their existence. They had developed new cultural and material needs, a feeling of human dignity and formidable class solidarity. The workers' movement now fought to resolve a broad range of vital social and political issues. Its growing strength was revealed in the dramatic increase in the volume of strikes — with more than 530,000 striking workers over the period of 1901–4.[2] Despite this unprecedented growth of working-class unrest, the workers, for the most part, voiced their grievances and demands by means of strikes and protests that would be regarded as legitimate and permissible by the standards of civilized states. To the tsarist government, however, such expressions of popular discontent appeared unlawful. The Russian authorities interpreted the workers' economic demands as an attempt to alter the foundations of the existing order, and they severely suppressed them.

Much of the workers' dissatisfaction arose from Russia's lack of proper labor legislation that would regulate relations between capitalists and workers. There was no legal provision for the operation of trade unions, for national insurance for illness and work-related accidents, or for a system of old-age pensions. If the government had had the wisdom to give thought to comprehensive labor legislation of this kind, it is possible that this policy might have diffused an explosive social situation. However, such a policy would have conflicted with the interests of the employers. Foreign investors in particular demanded firm protection of their business interests in Russia, and the government was reluctant to quarrel with them. It found it easier to pursue its traditional policy of the suppression of discontent instead.

As a result, the government unwittingly forced the workers to adopt a more radical, revolutionary course of struggle for their legitimate demands. They began to establish closer links with the radical intelligentsia and, above all, with the Marxists. This new alliance would rock the Romanovs' empire to its foundations and would ultimately destroy it. By dismissing the very possibility of Western-type reformism in Russia, the government pushèd the masses into making ever more radical demands and taking revolutionary action.

In the early twentieth century the popular anti-autocratic movement had entered a new and crucial stage. It became nationwide in scale and was increasingly guided by the revolutionary parties as well as organizations of a liberal-democratic orientation. The situation was pregnant with cataclysmic consequences. The social, political, and ethnic unrest that had been gathering in the preceding years erupted in the First Russian Revolution of 1905.

The Course of the Revolution

The spark that ignited the revolutionary conflagration was provided by a terrible tragedy in St. Petersburg on Sunday, 9 January 1905, when a peaceful march by more than a hundred thousand workers and members of their families was ruthlessly fired upon by government troops, causing thousands of casualties, including women and children. The workers wanted to present their grievances to the tsar at the Winter Palace and ask for his protection against the arbitrariness of factory owners and corrupt officials. The unheard-of brutality of the police action to disperse the protesters and the cynicism of the authorities, who tried to portray the shooting as a legitimate response to an anti-government rising of a disorderly rabble, were too much even for a country accustomed to despotism. The "Bloody Sunday" massacre provoked a tidal wave of indignation in society that swept away any remaining respect for the authorities. Along with its numerous human victims, it killed Russia's age-old popular trust in the tsar as the people's protector.

The irony was that a detonator of popular revulsion against the regime had been provided by an organization that had been set up under the patronage of the police and the church. The ill-fated workers' march had been the initiative of the "ASSEMBLY OF RUSSIAN FACTORY WORKERS OF ST. PETERSBURG," which was led by a priest, FATHER GRIGORI GAPON. The "Assembly," which was a strictly legal organization of patriotic and educational orientation for workers, stood apart from political parties. Despite the fact that only about 3 percent of St. Petersburg's workers had joined by the start of 1905, the organization's standing with the proletariat in the capital was high and it was more influential by far than any of the revolutionary parties at that time.

Writing a petition to the tsar was the idea of the members of the "Assembly." The text of the petition was composed by Father Gapon himself, who was aided in this by intellectuals from the liberal-democratic camp. (Social-Democrats and Socialist-Revolutionaries from the revolutionary camp tried to dissuade the workers from taking part in the protest march to the Winter Palace, arguing that the idea of presenting the petition was both useless and dangerous.) Couched in emotional religious language, the petition contained practically all the general democratic demands of the day. It reflected the workers' feeling of deep despair at the tyranny of employers and the arbitrariness of bureaucracy:

> Sovereign, there are thousands of us here; outwardly we resemble human beings, but in reality neither we nor the Russian people as a whole enjoy any human right, have any right to speak, to think, to assemble, to discuss our needs, or to take measures to improve our conditions.... All the workers and the peasants are at the mercy of bureaucratic administrators consisting of embezzlers of public funds and thieves who not only disregard the interests of the people but also scorn these interests. The bureaucratic administration has brought the country to complete ruin, has brought upon it a disgraceful war, and continues to lead it further and further into destruction....
>
> Sovereign, these are the problems that we face and these are the reasons that we have gathered before the walls of your palace.

Here we seek our last salvation. Do not refuse to come to the aid of your people; lead them out of the grave of disfranchisement, poverty, and ignorance; grant them an opportunity to determine their own destiny, and remove from them the unbearable yoke of bureaucrats. Tear down the wall that separates you from your people and let them rule the country with you.[3]

The biblical idiom of the petition made its message clearer to the workers, many of whom came from the countryside and were proletarians in the first generation. Some had never been involved in any political activity before. They believed in the tsar and hoped he would intervene to protect them. They saw the petition as a last chance to settle intractable social conflicts peacefully. Thus, the movement led by Father Gapon reflected some of the elemental hopes and longings of the Russian people.

The shooting of the peaceful demonstrators caused horror and dismay all over the country. But already by the evening of that fateful Sunday barricades had been erected in St. Petersburg, and skirmishes of workers with the government troops and the police soon took place. At midnight Father Gapon wrote a new proclamation, this time addressed to the workers, in which he denounced the tsar as a traitor to the people, released the soldiers from their oath of allegiance to Nicholas II, and called the people to the barricades, permitting them, by the authority of the church, the use of dynamite and bombs. Gapon then went into hiding abroad, where he liaised with the leaders of the Russian socialist emigration, including Plekhanov and Lenin. He wrote several more inflammatory proclamations that reached Russia through various channels and were widely circulated there.

Despite this, Gapon failed to establish himself as a popular leader. Many workers became disappointed in him after the tragic denouement of the protest march and the mysterious disappearance of its chief organizer. Rumors spread that Gapon was an agent in the pay of the police. The branches of his "Assembly" in the capital were shut down, and the leadership of the unrest now passed firmly into the hands of the revolutionaries, Social-Democrats in particular, who had warned of the danger and futility of Gapon's plan to present the petition. The idea of negotiating with the regime was now totally discarded in favor of the slogan of an armed insurrection.

The popular outrage over the shooting of 9 January and the anger at the government's continued procrastination over long-overdue reform sent waves of unrest across the whole empire. Hundreds of thousands of workers, students, and members of the democratically minded intelligentsia took to the streets to participate in mass rallies and demonstrations. In the first three months of 1905 alone over eight hundred thousand workers took part in strikes, with over 40 percent of them putting down their tools in political protest. They were joined by about forty thousand Russian university students who decided to boycott their classes for the rest of the academic year.[4] The discontent spread to liberal circles, the urban middle class, and the peasantry. Even Russian factory owners began to articulate guarded political demands.

The major industrial cities and regions provided the focal points of the unrest. Strikes and demonstrations continued throughout the spring and summer of 1905. Some of the biggest protest actions were these: the seventy-two-day strike of textile workers in the town of Ivanovo-Voznesensk, east of Moscow; the general strike of Polish workers in Lodz; the general strike at the Black Sea port of Odessa, accompanied by the mutiny of sailors on the battleship *Potemkin.* Because workers' trade unions were still weak and inexperienced, the leadership of the strike movement was provided by the so-called left bloc of the two main revolutionary parties of Social-Democrats and Socialist-Revolutionaries, as well as nonparty worker activists. Sympathy with the striking workers was widespread and was felt by many sections of the population and, in particular, by democratically and liberally minded members of the intelligentsia and university students. Universities opened their doors to the protesters, making their buildings available for public meetings and anti-government rallies. Some factory owners continued to pay wages to the striking workers, realizing that they were fighting in the interests of the entire nation.

Such broad-based solidarity created a unique atmosphere in which the ruling circles felt more and more isolated and under enormous pressure from public opinion. In August, in the face of the united opposition of most levels and sections of the population, the government faltered and promised to convene an elected national assembly with a consultative role. Such a concession might have worked in January, but in August it was no longer enough. On 19 September Russian print workers went on strike; they were soon joined by other workers in both capital cities. On 7 October railway workers declared a strike crippling the government's ability to dispatch troops to centers of unrest. Transport and communications of all kinds came to a standstill, paralyzing the machinery of state. In a matter of days Russia was in the grip of the first general strike in its history.

The OCTOBER STRIKE was a nationwide political strike that embraced all of Russia's vitally important regions. Nearly two million people took part in it, including eight hundred thousand factory workers, seven hundred thousand railway workers, and nearly five hundred thousand students, white-collar workers, and intellectuals.[5] The strikers were no longer prepared to accept petty concessions from the government and their employers. They demanded the convocation of a Constituent Assembly, political freedom, political amnesty, and an eight-hour workday. But their paramount slogan, which was intoned and amplified by countless rallies and strikes, demanded nothing short of a revolution. "Down with autocracy!" became the October Strike's rallying cry and the measure of the nation's disaffection with the authorities.

During the October Strike, St. Petersburg's workers, drawing on the experience of the strike in Ivanovo-Voznesensk several weeks earlier, set up a SOVIET OF WORKERS' DEPUTIES to coordinate the strike action in the city. This quickly became the model of a new working-class organization that was reproduced across the empire. The Russian word "Soviet," which means advice or counsel, was also applied to meetings, such as the peasant commune. Indeed, it was probably traditions of the commune that inspired the first Soviet. Just as communes consisted of all heads of households in the village, a Soviet was elected from all workers in the town. Soviets were set up in towns and cities across the country, including in Moscow, Baku, Ekaterinburg, Irkutsk, Odessa, and Saratov. In some places they gained much wider powers than simple strike committees, spreading their control from working-class districts to entire towns and effectively acting as city councils or the local administration.

The St. Petersburg Soviet was by far the most important of them, rapidly rising to the dominant position among Soviets throughout the country. Among its 562 members were workers, teachers, doctors, trade-union officials, and representatives of the revolutionary parties. The most influential of the political parties represented in the Soviet was the Russian Social-Democratic Labor Party and, in particular, its Menshevik wing. The leader of the St. Petersburg Soviet was a young Marxist, LEV TROTSKY (1879–1940). He was independent of both Menshevik and Bolshevik factions and became one of the revolution's most inspiring public speakers.

The OCTOBER STRIKE quickly gained the support of most strands of the opposition movement. The rare display of unity by the opposition finally forced the government to its knees. Frightened by the scale of the workers' protest, terrified by the growing unrest in the army and peasant disturbances in the countryside, and unable to move troops by rail to quell the dissent, the authorities found themselves in a critical situation.

On 17 October 1905 Nicholas II, on the advice of Sergei Witte, signed a manifesto that granted his subjects basic civil and political rights and promised the convocation of a State Duma, an elected *legislative* national assembly (instead of the purely consultative assembly proposed by the government in August). A few days later, on 21 October, the government also announced partial political amnesty.

The OCTOBER MANIFESTO undermined the united revolutionary coalition forged in the days of the general strike. The right-wing of Russian Liberalism immediately accepted the Manifesto as a satisfactory conclusion to the revolution. On 4 December it established a new liberal party, the UNION OF 17 OCTOBER (the "Octobrist" Party), whose leader was a major industrialist, ALEXANDER GUCHKOV (1862–1936). In contrast, the left-wing liberals, who had already set up their own Constitutional-Democratic Party (or Kadets) at a founding congress held in October, denounced the Manifesto for its failure to meet their main demand to grant an elected legislative assembly that would be empowered to draft a new constitution. However, they were willing to accept the new system as a starting point for reform and were prepared to end revolutionary activities.

Though it was not radical enough to satisfy fully the revolutionary parties and even many of the liberals, the Manifesto signified a major victory of the prodemocratic forces. The promises contained in the Manifesto were wrung out of the tsarist government mainly by peaceful means, with only a few instances of serious street fighting between workers and troops and the police. For a brief moment following the publication of the Manifesto there was a fragile equilibrium between the government and the opposition.

This was soon broken, however, by the conservative elements of Russian society who mounted a counteroffensive to avenge the humiliation suffered by the tsar at the hands of the revolutionaries. Right-wing elements stirred up a horrendous wave of anti-Semitic pogroms, carried out by hooligan gangs with official support at the highest level. The pogroms claimed several thousand lives across Russia. The massacres of Jews were organized with the aim of intimidating the revolutionaries, worker activists, and members of the radical intelligentsia. By fanning the flames of chauvinist and monarchist hysteria, the right-wing elements also hoped to impel the tsar to take tougher actions against the revolution.

Revolutionaries themselves were not ready to stop the fighting. They continued to incite the workers with inflammatory calls for an armed insurrection in order to bring the struggle against the autocracy to its logical end. Their aim was to secure, this time by force, what could not be achieved by peaceful means in October: the convocation of a Constituent Assembly and the establishment of a republic. The revolutionary opposition felt intoxicated by the atmosphere of freedom that followed the announcement of civil liberties in the October Manifesto. Censorship was hardly enforced. Social-Democrats could now operate almost openly without fear of repression. In some places they persuaded workers to begin stocking up weapons and to form armed detachments.

The government, however, had somewhat recovered from its October capitulation and now thirsted for revenge. By provoking the opposition to an armed insurrection before it was properly ready, and then ruthlessly smashing it, the authorities hoped to teach it another lesson along the lines of the "Bloody Sunday" crackdown. Neither side was willing to give in or agree to a compromise.

The confrontation flared up with new intensity in December 1905. Its focus had now shifted from St. Petersburg to Moscow, where the workers were not as worn out by fighting as their comrades were in St. Petersburg, and where the government did not have as many troops and police. On 7 December, acting on the decision of the local Soviet of Workers' Deputies, supported by all revolutionary parties, Moscow workers went on a political strike. Within two days the strike escalated into street battles with troops and police. These raged for the next ten days. The insurrectionist camp was comprised of diverse social elements, including workers, students, high school pupils, women, white-collar workers, and intellectuals. The city's population openly sympathized with the fighting workers. Many joined them on the barricades.

However, the military leadership of the rebellion was no match for the actions of the regular army and the police. The insurrection was suppressed with great bloodshed. In one of the city's districts the government even resorted to the use of artillery against the rebels. The casualty figures are incomplete, but at least fifty-five people were killed and over a thousand wounded, many of the victims innocent bystanders.[6] The responsibility for the tragic events of December 1905 did not entirely rest on the tsarist government. The revolutionaries were also to blame. Their fanatical fervor and doctrinaire extremism served to inflame the rebellious mood of the workers. At the same time, the revolutionaries themselves were under enormous pressure from the spontaneous radicalism of the masses.

After the defeat of the Moscow insurrection in December 1905, the revolutionary tide started to ebb. Strikes continued throughout 1906 and the first half of 1907. They were now better organized, and the strikers' demands were well thought-through and wide-ranging. Yet, fewer and fewer strikes ended in victory for the workers. In the conditions of an economic slump and relative stabilization of the tsarist regime, the workers found it increasingly difficult to compel the employers to meet their demands.

Results of the Revolution

The two and a half years of discontent from 1905 to 1907 had produced a wave of strikes, mutinies, and disorders unprecedented in Russian and world history. Although the revolution failed to achieve its ultimate objective — the overthrow of autocracy — different sections of the Russian population made gains as a result of their struggle. The industrial working class in particular had wrested certain improvements in its condition from the government and from employers, thanks to its discovery of the general strike as a powerful new means of exerting political pressure. In some regions the workers succeeded in securing significant wage increases compared to the prerevolutionary level, although in real terms the average wage across the country remained approximately the same because of the rise in the prices of some staple commodities. In addition, the workers compelled the bosses to reduce the number of minor offenses in the workplace punishable by fines and also to cut the working hours. Most factories now operated a nine- or ten-hour day, and some had an eight-hour day. There was even a small number of companies in which workers secured collective agreements with employers that guaranteed benefits such as annual paid leave and sick benefits. However, there was still no national labor legislation to guarantee welfare provisions of this kind for the majority of workers.

Certain achievements had been made in widening the political rights of the workers. Those of them who worked in companies employing fifty workers or more had now the right to participate in elections to the State Duma. Economic strikes were legalized, and so too were trade unions, which could now openly engage in their activities. The revolution had tremendously raised the workers' class consciousness, their awareness of their political potency, the cohesion of their ranks, and their class solidarity. Because the workers bore the brunt of the battle against the autocracy, the ups and downs of their struggle affected all sections of the Russian society, from government circles and business classes to the millions of peasants. Their fighting spirit, courage, and determination were an example and a source of inspiration for other underprivileged social strata in the struggle for the betterment of their conditions. The labor movement was the backbone of the First Russian Revolution and the backdrop against which all major events of the years of turmoil unfolded.

The peculiar circumstances of Russia's backwardness — with its predominantly peasant population downtrodden and illiterate, middle classes weak and amorphous, and bourgeoisie still in its infancy — had propelled the relatively small proletariat to the forefront of political struggle and into the role of chief agent of the anti-autocratic, "bourgeois" revolution. This allowed Russian Marxists such as Plekhanov and Lenin to advance the theoretical proposition about the proletariat's leading role, or HEGEMONY, during the anti-autocratic stage of the revolution. Lenin and his Bolsheviks came to interpret the idea of proletarian hegemony as meaning that the politically active workers and Marxist revolutionaries held ideological and organizational leadership over the nonproletarian toiling masses and, above all, over the peasantry.

Other classes of the Russian population took an active part in the revolution alongside the workers. In this sense the democratic Revolution of 1905–7 is interpreted by some analysts as a sum total of component elements, including workers, peasants, soldiers, students, national liberation, and other currents of revolution, with their individual issues, aims, and peculiarities.[7] In particular, the Revolution of 1905–7 is sometimes seen as a "PEASANT" REVOLUTION in recognition of the scale of the peasant movement directed against the landowners and the government. Historians have uncovered about twenty-six thousand instances of disturbances in the countryside during the years of the revolution, involving several million peasants. The peasant unrest peaked in November and December 1905, when many peasants interpreted the October Manifesto as permission to seize the gentry's land they had long believed was theirs by right.

The chief demand of all sections of the Russian peasantry — from poor and middle to well-to-do peasants — was the transfer of all land to those who cultivated it. The vast majority of peasants rejected the idea of paying redemption fees for the gentry's land and demanded its confiscation and equal distribution among peasant families in line with communal egalitarian traditions. The issue of whether to hold the land in private ownership or to make it subject to nationalization or "socialization" by the peasants was hardly ever seriously considered. The majority of peasants insisted that land could not be treated the same as other property — like farm tools, animals, buildings, for instance — and no one should have the right to buy, sell, or mortgage it. The land was

"God's" and "no one's," and as such was the asset of the entire nation. Equally, the preservation of the commune in those regions where it had traditionally existed was never put into doubt.

As a result of the powerful rise of the peasant movement in 1905–7, the peasants had won certain concessions from the government and the landed proprietors. These somewhat relieved the economic and fiscal pressures on the village. The outstanding redemption payments were cancelled, land rent fees were lowered, and the wages of hired agricultural laborers increased by some 10 percent. However, a radical settlement of the agrarian issue, sought by the peasant movement, had not been achieved.

With the defeat of the First Russian Revolution, the socialist parties entered a period of deep ideological reflection and organizational crisis. Both Social-Democrats and Socialist-Revolutionaries broke down into a number of splinter groups, currents, and factions, which reflected a variety of views on the postrevolutionary political situation and advocated different party tactics. As the revolutionary mood of the masses abated and their fascination with ultra-radical slogans was replaced by disappointment in the revolution's results, the membership of the socialist parties shrank dramatically, as rank-and-file members deserted in droves. In addition, the revolutionary parties were badly damaged by the repeated and large-scale arrests of their activists. Party organizations were continually smashed by the police, which were kept informed about the parties' activities by undercover agents who had infiltrated both central and regional party organizations. Many party leaders were arrested and languished in internal exile. Others, like the Marxists Lenin, Martov, and Trotsky, or the Socialist-Revolutionary Chernov, fled abroad to escape persecution. As a result, the central committees of the revolutionary parties could now operate only outside Russia. They had to rely on an inadequate network of "travelling agents" and written correspondence to keep in touch with surviving local committees in Russia.

The sharp decline in the membership of the socialist parties was also an indication that despite their considerable influence and active agitation, they failed to captivate the masses completely by socialist slogans. The socialists' influence was particularly weak among the peasantry, which made up the overwhelming majority of the country's population. Even the Socialist-Revolutionaries, who claimed to be chief champions of peasants' interests, relied for their main support on urban social structures. Although partially indoctrinated by socialist ideologies, the worker and peasant movements retained much of their spontaneity and autonomy.

The crisis of 1905 revealed the extreme vulnerability of the autocratic government, which had survived because of the cultural and economic gulf between Russia's educated elites and the mass of rural and urban working people. However, as long as Russia's upper classes remained discontented with the existing political system, there was the possibility that, in a moment of crisis, they might reluctantly support a working-class insurrection.

The defeat of the Revolution of 1905–7 led to some stabilization of the autocratic regime. The turbulent upheavals of the revolutionary years were now giving place to apathy, pessimism, and withdrawal into private life. The workers were exhausted after years of strikes. A large part of the intelligentsia was subdued by a penitent mood, repenting the part it played in inciting the workers to ill-prepared and violent protests. All political parties were in crisis. The revolutionary mood was further dissipated by factors such as the drawn-out economic slump of 1904–9, the launching of the government's agrarian reform, and sterner police measures against violations of public order.

Despite all its casualties and excesses, the First Russian Revolution signaled a new phase in the process of modernization and democratization of the country's social and political structures. As a result of the revolution, Russian society had become more open, dynamic, and independent from the authorities. It was characterized by a more mature civic consciousness and greater ideological pluralism. Yielding to the pressure of the powerful mass movements of 1905–7, the government had to concede new reforms associated with the names of its ministers Witte and Stolypin. Yet they were not bold or far-reaching enough to effect the kind of socioeconomic and political change needed to forestall a repetition of the unrest of 1905 and all the unpredictable consequences this could bring to society.

Chapter Eleven

Russia between Revolutions

Constitutional Experiment

The social upheavals of 1905 had finally forced out of the government the promise to introduce a constitutional system with an elected
parliament. However, Nicholas's reluctance to allow any weakening
of his autocratic powers ensured that the government's attempt to devise a workable constitutional framework would be halfhearted and
incomplete. When drawing up the Fundamental Laws early in 1906,
Nicholas did all he could to limit the powers of the Duma. The electoral
system discriminated heavily against peasants and workers; elections
were to be indirect; and votes were to be cast and counted by separate constituencies (called *curias*), set up for each class or property
group.

Moreover, the powers vested in the new legislative forum were
severely limited. Ministers remained responsible solely to the tsar and
continued to be appointed and dismissed solely by him. The Duma had
the power to reject only parts of the state budget. The new constitution transformed the traditional supreme body within the bureaucracy,
the State Council, into an upper house, many of whose members were
to be appointed by the tsar or nominated by the government. The tsar
retained the power to veto all legislation, while Article 87 of the Fundamental Laws enabled him to rule by decree when the Duma was not
in session. In addition, Nicholas insisted on referring to his own authority as "autocratic," though he agreed to drop the word "unlimited"
from the traditional formula describing the sovereign's power. This now
read: "Supreme autocratic power belongs to the emperor of all Russia"
(Article 4).

The FIRST DUMA, which sat from 27 April to 8 July 1906, was dominated by Kadets, led by Paul Miliukov, and by peasant deputies who
formed their own Duma faction called the Trudovik (Labor) Group. Socialist parties, except for the Mensheviks, boycotted the elections. The
Kadet majority in the Duma took the lead in issuing a series of demands

for far-reaching reforms, including changes to the constitution to allow the appointment of a government responsible to the Duma and a radical land reform. The government refused to discuss these demands out of hand, though it did consider appointing some prominent Kadets and Octobrists as ministers. When negotiations broke down, the government dissolved the assembly. The Kadets and some other radical deputies issued a manifesto calling for a protest in the form of passive resistance. However, they failed to muster public support strong enough to unsettle the government.

The SECOND DUMA met in February 1907. Although it saw a small increase in the number of right-wing deputies and the decline in the number of the Kadet deputies, it was, nevertheless, even more radical than the First, because the Social-Democrats and Socialist-Revolutionaries, who had boycotted the First Duma, sent delegates to the Second. The radical left-wing deputies bitterly denounced the government for the harsh measures it was taking to quell political unrest. Unable to find any common ground between its proposals and the demands of the Left, the government dismissed the Second Duma on 3 June 1907.

On the same day the government used Article 87 to issue a new electoral law, which drastically altered the franchise on which subsequent Dumas were to be elected. The new law favored Russia's traditional classes — the landed nobility and the peasantry — while the representation of the urban population, and the working class in particular, was cut to a fraction. The indirect curial electoral system meant that, first, the electoral constituencies, defined by estate, sent "electors" to provincial electoral assemblies; the electors in the provincial assemblies could then elect delegates to the Duma. Under the new law, the *curia* of landowners chose one elector from just 230 of its voters, while it took 1,000 wealthy business people to choose a single elector; 15,000 lower-middle-class voters; 60,000 peasants; and 125,000 urban workers. In the provincial electoral assemblies the new norms of representation also favored the landowners: 50.2 percent of electors in these bodies came from the landowning constituency.[1] Here was a clear indication of the conservatism of a government that still found it easiest to work with its traditional supporters, the landed nobility.

The new electoral legislation had been enacted by the government in breach of the Fundamental Laws, which forbade any changes to the electoral system without the consent of the Duma and the State Council. There were few protests, however, and the new law succeeded in its immediate aim. The makeup of the THIRD DUMA (1907–12), which was considerably more conservative than the first two Dumas, was dominated by landed nobles and the Octobrist Party, led by Alexander Guchkov. The Left was markedly reduced, and the Kadet opposition had toned down some of its more radical proposals. For the first time the government found itself dealing with an assembly broadly sympathetic to some of its legislation.

The Third Duma was the only one to complete its full five-year term. However, though it managed to avoid controversies such as those that had brought the first two Dumas to an early end, the Third Duma found it increasingly difficult to cooperate constructively with the reactionary government. Toward the end of its term, the Duma's relations with ministers had deteriorated markedly, and it became clear that it would not be able to hold together a political alliance between the government and the landowners, officials, and capitalists who supported the Octobrist Party. The Octobrists themselves split into separate factions. The core of the party, which had suffered major political defections to the Right, moved close to the Kadets and became more outspoken in their criticism of the government.

The FOURTH DUMA (1912–17) marked the end of the constitutional experiment in Russia. By the time the Duma recovered, it had become abundantly clear that the tsar had never accepted the dilution of authority wrung out of him by the Revolution of 1905. In 1913 and 1914 he and his ministers seriously considered returning Russia to the political system that had existed before 1905. Another possibility considered was to end the Duma's authority in making laws, leaving it with only advisory powers. Thus, as Russia approached the Great War, Nicholas continued to see the Duma as an unnecessary and even dangerous institution. Even with the outbreak of war in 1914, when the Duma deputies called a halt to all criticism of the government and rallied behind it, Nicholas was unwilling and unable to enlist the support that Russia's new political elite offered for the war effort.

By refusing to take the Duma seriously, the government alienated not merely the new upper classes of intellectuals and entrepreneurs, but also its more traditional supporters among the landed nobility. It had also deprived itself of their advice and expertise, which were so crucial for mounting an effective war effort. From then on the regime had as little support among Russia's upper classes as it had in 1905. Enthusiastic supporters of autocracy could be found only on the far Right of Russian politics, and among anti-Semitic, proto-Fascist organizations such as the "UNION OF THE RUSSIAN PEOPLE," first formed in 1905. The "Union" blamed all of Russia's problems on socialists, the democratically minded intelligentsia, and the Jews, calling on the population to combat the

RUSSIA'S MAIN POLITICAL PARTIES
DURING THE CONSTITUTIONAL PERIOD

Party's name	Main aims	Support base
Russian Social-Democratic Labor Party (1898)	minimum: overthrow of autocracy maximum: proletarian revolution	radically minded intelligentsia
Socialist Revolutionary Party (1901)	Socialization of all privately owned land	small owners: peasants, town-dwellers, artisans, small traders
Constitutional Democratic Party: Kadets (1905)	a new order on the Western constitutional model	liberal intelligentsia, part of liberal-minded landowners, medium and big bourgeoisie, the professions
Union of 17 October: Octobrists (1905)	constitutional monarchy	big industrial and financial bourgeoisie, the new business class
Union of the Russian People (1905)	preservation of the autocratic system	big landowners, merchants, shopkeepers, the police, the clergy, lower middle class in towns, wealthy peasants

"enemies of the Tsar and Fatherland." It waged open chauvinist propaganda in the press and from the church pulpit, while its activists, united in the so-called BLACK HUNDREDS, helped the government disperse workers' strikes and students' rallies and staged mass pogroms of Jewish communities.

The constitutional reform had failed to bridge the gap between the government and Russia's rapidly changing educated elites. The new upper classes were politically disaffected, antagonized by Nicholas's attempts to stifle the potentially democratic institution of the Duma and his refusal to introduce a Western-style government. Even the backing the regime could expect from its traditional supporters, such as the landed nobility, was hesitant and uncertain. Its power rested now on the bureaucracy and the army alone. The most dangerous aspect of the government's position was the political blindness of the tsar, who still believed in the loyalty of the masses of the peasants, the army, and the nobility. Nicholas simply was unable to see how isolated his government was and how narrow was the base of support for a government about to lead its country into a devastating international war.

Prewar Economic Development; Stolypin's Land Reform

In the period from the 1860s–70s to 1913 Russia was gradually overcoming its economic backwardness it had inherited from serfdom. On the whole, in the period from 1860 to 1900 industrial production in Russia increased sevenfold. In the last twenty or so years of its existence — particularly from 1909 — tsarist Russia was a world leader in industrial growth and well positioned to do justice to the country's enormous natural resources. Growth in industrial output in this period may have been as rapid as 6 percent a year. This is below the remarkable 8 percent growth rate of the industrial boom of the 1890s, but it is impressive nonetheless. Having surpassed France in the volume of industrial production, Russia began gradually to catch up with Britain, Germany, and the United States, growing with remarkable speed in the years preceding the Great War.

It is important therefore to discount the widespread misconception that Russia before the 1917 Revolution was something like a Third World underdeveloped country. The official Soviet propaganda during the time of Stalin's dictatorship did much to promulgate the proposition about Russia's economic backwardness on the eve of the First World War in order to emphasize and extol the achievements of Stalin's own industrialization drive and to give him the credit for transforming Russia into an industrialized country. The thesis about Russia's prerevolutionary backwardness was designed to perpetuate the myth epitomized in Winston Churchill's well-known words that Stalin "took Russia with a wooden plough and left it with a nuclear bomb."

This was not quite so. During the last years of the tsarist regime Russia was well advanced and heading for industrial "take-off." Particularly impressive was the accelerated growth of railway construction and machine building. It was largely to the government-sponsored railway construction that Russia owed its initial industrial boom in the 1890s, and it continued at an intensive pace in the early twentieth century. In 1905 a most spectacular project, the 7,416-kilometers-long Great Trans-Siberian railway, was completed, linking the rail networks of European Russia with the Pacific coast. By 1913 the overall length of railways in

RAILWAY CONSTRUCTION IN RUSSIA
(LENGTH OF TRACK IN KILOMETERS)[2]

1851	1860	1900	1913
0	3,000	40,000	71,700

THE GROWTH OF INDUSTRIAL OUTPUT IN RUSSIA (IN POODS)[3]

	1895	1914	grew by how many times
Coal	466 million	1983 million	4.3
Cast iron	73 million	254 million	3.5
Iron and steel	70 million	229 million	3.3

Russia reached 71,700 kilometers. The railways created a big demand for metal (for rails, locomotives, and rolling-stock), and also for increasing quantities of fuel — coal and oil. This led to the development of the metal and fuel industries.

Many commentators now agree that even based on a modest extrapolation of its prerevolutionary industrial growth-rate, Russia would have become a great industrial and military power without revolution and communist planning and, more particularly, without the unheard-off human suffering and sacrifices imposed by Stalin's regime with its concentration camps, mass deportations, and show trials. In other words, Russia would have become a great industrial power much more smoothly and quickly if the Soviet system had never been.[4]

After 1905, capitalist development in industry was accompanied by extensive reforms in peasant agriculture. The powerful peasant movement in the years of the First Russian Revolution had demonstrated that the peasants had never fully accepted the new land arrangements institutionalized by the reform of 1861 as a just solution. They continued to dream, after emancipation, of a new partition of land to be ordered by the kind tsar, once he was able to overcome the resistance of the nobles and his ministers. They looked with increasingly covetous eyes on the broad acres of the nobles' estates, which adjoined their narrow strips, hoping that one day they would be able to lay their hands on this land.

Nevertheless, until 1905, the peasants had by and large acquiesced to the conditions of the emancipation settlement and used legal methods to alleviate their land hunger. They bought some land from landlords, but, more commonly, they leased additional land, often on difficult terms.

Decades of hardships and privation had accumulated abundant explosive material for a revolutionary upheaval at the village level. The spark was provided in 1905 by the unrest in the cities, which soon spread throughout the countryside. In 1906 and 1907 the peasant deputies in Russia's new parliament, the Duma, clamored for the distribution of estate lands. And, as fifty years before in the days of the emancipation reform, the peasants' demands were generally supported by all progressive elements of Russian society.

The most radical solution of the land issue was proposed by Socialist-Revolutionaries, heirs to the nineteenth century's Narodniks. They advocated the Narodniks' idea of "SOCIALIZATION" of all privately owned land, by which they understood "its transfer from private property of individual owners to public domain and administration by democratically organized communes . . . on the basis of equalized utilization."[5] The liberals, such as the Kadets, also agreed that the landowners would have to give up a considerable part of their estate lands in order to increase holdings of the poorer peasants, but argued that the landlords should get a fair compensation. In 1905 even some big landowners were prepared to accept that the compulsory redistribution of some gentry land was the only way to solve the problem of rural discontent.

However, as an alternative to the radical and liberal proposals, in November 1906 the tsarist government enacted its own kind of agrarian reform. This reform was connected principally with the name of PETER STOLYPIN (1862–1911), the last leader of notable talent to serve Nicholas II. In 1906 he was first appointed minister of the interior and then chairman of the Council of Ministers (i.e., prime minister). As minister of the interior, Stolypin waged a merciless struggle against the revolutionary movement, suppressing any remaining discontent by force. Under him the government tried oppositionists in courts-martial and made free use of the hangman's noose, known as "Stolypin's necktie." Nevertheless, he realized that there were genuine reasons that fueled revolutionary attitudes in society and that reform was the only way to stamp out revolution completely. A hereditary landowner and convinced monarchist himself, Stolypin, nevertheless, clearly saw the impossibility of going back to the old order — the autocratic system — with the landed gentry as its main pillar.

As a result, Stolypin's policies as prime minister were of a contradictory nature. He sought to give maximum prerogatives to the ruling bureaucracy, yet he also found it necessary to preserve the elected Duma. While protecting the property rights of the landed gentry, he at the same time tried to widen the social base of the regime by enlisting the support of the big bourgeoisie and of more well-to-do groups of the peasantry.

Land reform was Stolypin's most important policy, as it promised to have a far-reaching effect on the internal life of the country. The policy had a clear and concrete objective, namely, creating in the Russian village a powerful layer of well-to-do peasants who would become reliable supporters of the government. They would form a new class of independent, economically viable proprietors in the countryside who would be attached to the principle of private property, and therefore better co-exist with the manor system and act as a bulwark against any future revolution in the village. The essence of Stolypin's approach was epitomized in his famous slogan: a "wager on the sturdy and the strong." From the landlords' point of view, the main attraction of Stolypin's plan was that it did not require the surrender of their land. The creation of a new propertied class of small landowners was to be achieved at the expense of other sections of the peasant population. A way had to be devised to speed up the disintegration of the egalitarian village commune in order to allow this new class of small capitalist farmers to emerge. Thus the destruction of the peasant commune became the cornerstone of Stolypin's agrarian reform.

Stolypin's land decrees came into effect in late 1906, although they acquired full legal force only when they were passed by the Duma in 1910–11. The new laws abolished compulsory communal land tenure, and turned the land into the private property of the male heads of households, rather than it being the collective property of the commune. The new individual owners could now demand the consolidation of their scattered allotment of land into a single block to form a separate farm. Thus, individually owned farmsteads were "cut out" of the collective, communal land. These measures were designed to encourage the appearance of small-scale capitalist farming. The government also set up special "land settlement commissions," which helped negotiate and implement the complex rearrangements of communal landholdings into private farmsteads.

It is difficult to gauge the success of Stolypin's reform since it was interrupted by the Great War and the revolution. What is clear, however, is that the process of the disintegration of the commune remained slow, and a new class of wealthy and independent peasants did not arise overnight. By 1915, about 30 percent of all peasant households had requested individual ownership of the land, and 22 percent had received it.[6] Most of the new farms appeared in the empire's western and southern provinces where peasants were already familiar with individual landholding. The reforms had least effect in the overpopulated central regions, where the problem of land shortage was particularly severe. In these areas, the village commune provided considerable protection to destitute peasants, and most households clung desperately to this support.

Stolypin's policies certainly benefited some of the richer peasants (*kulaks*) but did very little to alleviate the distress of the poorer villagers still suffering from shortages of land. The major deficiency was, however, Stolypin's failure to tackle the agrarian problem as a whole. His legislation dealt only with peasant land and did nothing to touch the property interests or the private estates of the landed gentry. This was an issue that the peasants themselves were to address by direct action in the turmoil of 1917. Stolypin has received much praise from some analysts who believe that the determined prime minister was in fact saving the empire and that, given time, his agrarian reform would have achieved its major objective of transforming and stabilizing the countryside. They contend that Stolypin also planned a broader program of reforms in which the agrarian reform played a pivotal role. Agrarian reform was to be complemented by the improvement of local *zemstvos*: these representative institutions were to be extended to regions of the empire that for various reasons still did not have them. Stolypin also planned to address the deficiencies of the judicial system, which had been put in place by Alexander II but which was later distorted by the retrograde measures of Alexander III. He had plans to boost popular education in order to close the cultural gap between the illiterate masses and the educated classes. Finally, Stolypin considered the introduction of measures of social protection, such as mandatory insurance of workers against illness and work-related accidents. If Russia could have had several decades of peace and stability, and had Stolypin's reform program been implemented in full, this group of analysts argues, then it is possible that the projected bulwark against an agrarian revolution in the shape of the politically conservative rural society might have been created, and future historians would have hailed the period when he was at the head of the Russian government as a second, after Alexander II's reign, era of the "Great Reforms."

But Stolypin's numerous critics have pointed, for example, to the limited scope of Stolypin's land reform, which represented, in a sense, one more effort to save gentry land by making the peasants redivide the land they already possessed. Some peasants were compelled to sell their land and move to towns, where they joined the ranks of the urban wage workers. This suggests that the Stolypin reforms, far from solving the

problems of discontented peasants, may have driven them to the towns
and turned them into radicalized dispossessed proletarians.

In Stolypin's own time his agrarian policy was attacked by critics from the far left to the far right of the political spectrum. Some
of his most implacable opponents came from the ranks of Socialist-
Revolutionaries who had every reason to think that the implementation
of the new measures would cut directly against their revolutionary aspirations, spelling the end of their dreams of peasant socialism in Russia.
Fearing the disintegration of the commune, the neo-Narodnik propagandists agitated against the right of peasants to leave the commune and
against the privatization of the communal land. At the other end of the
spectrum the new policy was not supported by many conservatives, who
feared a sharp break with the paternalistic tradition. And the prime minister's critics were by no means limited to the defenders of the commune
as such. Even the liberal opposition had its doubts. As Paul Miliukov,
the leader of the liberal Kadets, pointed out:

> The Stolypin reform tried to divert peasants from the division of
> the land of the nobles by the division of their own land for the
> benefit of the most prosperous part of the peasantry.[7]

Thus, argued critics, far from curing the basic ills of rural Russia, the
reform added new problems to the old ones, in particular by helping to
stratify the peasant mass and by creating hostility between the stronger
and richer peasants and their poorer and more egalitarian brethren. It
is worth noting that communal peasants disliked peasant-proprietors
even more than they did landlords; in 1917 the first lands they seized
belonged to neighbors who had left the commune.

Prospects of Democratic Capitalist Development

In 1911 Stolypin was assassinated under mysterious circumstances. But
even before the prime minister's death, it became clear that his policies,
which had had some stabilizing effect on the situation in the country, were unlikely to prevent a new revolutionary upheaval. In 1910
the workers' strike movement revived and continued to rise throughout
1911. The discontent was intensifying again among university students
and members of the democratically minded intelligentsia. Revolutionary
attitudes were heightened particularly in 1912, after the tragic events at
Lena goldfields in eastern Siberia, where workers on a peaceful march
to present their demands to the bosses were gunned down by the troops

and the police. One-hundred and seventy miners were massacred. Like the "Bloody Sunday" incident of 1905, the Lena shooting provoked a huge wave of sympathy strikes across Russia, involving over three hundred thousand people. In the same year the unrest spread to the army and the navy.

The revolutionary mood in the country continued to rise unabated up to the outbreak of the Great War. In 1913 and the first half of 1914 the number of striking workers in manufacturing industry grew to two million. In Russia's outlying regions movements for national independence gained momentum, especially in Transcaucasia, the Baltic region, and the Polish Kingdom. As in 1905, a general crisis was beginning to engulf the empire, and the specter of a new revolution was rearing its head. With its domestic affairs in such a perilous state, Russia, in August 1914, entered the First World War.

Historians often comment on the fact that wars have precipitated major changes of direction in Russian history. Many have been particularly fascinated with the question of Russia's involvement in the First World War and the relationship between this involvement and the 1917 Revolution. Put simply, the question boils down to this: did the war generate the domestic crisis that brought about the collapse of the tsarist regime; or was the crisis of Russia's sociopolitical system already of such a refractory nature as to make revolution in any case inevitable? Was Imperial Russia ruined by the war, or would it have disintegrated because of its own pressures and contradictions, war or no war?

The Optimistic View

In assessing Russia's prospects for peaceful political development prior to the war some analysts take an OPTIMISTIC view. They argue, for example, that the constitutional experiment and the establishment of the Duma not only provided representatives of the new political parties with experience of government and administration, but also helped to develop the political culture of various social classes, including the peasantry, by familiarizing them with the procedures of parliamentary elections. Besides, this group argues, the tsarist regime was not as isolated and vulnerable as it seems. There were many powerful groups, particularly among Russia's educated elites, who were willing and able to back a forward-looking government if it offered them some role in government. Bankers, entrepreneurs, landowners, and professionals had little to gain from revolution; they were much more interested in political stability.

In addition, the "optimists" continue, Russian society was becoming increasingly progressive and democratic every year. Modern education had spread rapidly at different levels and was remarkably humanitarian and liberal. Russian universities enjoyed virtually full freedom. Even the periodical press, in spite of various restrictions, gave some representation to every point of view, including the Bolsheviks'. To be sure, grave problems remained — economic backwardness and the poverty of the masses, in particular. Yet the economic revival that began in 1907 showed that the rapid economic growth of the late nineteenth century was no accident. Through continued vigorous industrialization and Stolypin's land reform, Russia's economic ailments were on the way to being solved. Despite enormous strains of modernization, there was every reason to think that a competent government would be able to cope with them and preside over a successful transition to some form of mature capitalist society. The conclusion that the "optimists" draw from all this is that had it not been for the intervention of the war, Russia would in all probability have followed a peaceful path of democratic capitalist development, and the revolution would have been avoided.

The Pessimistic View

Critics in the "PESSIMISTIC" school have drawn a different conclusion about Russia's chances of peaceful development. They argue that a violent overthrow of tsarism was inevitable. The restricted parliament that Nicholas II allowed in the aftermath of the Revolution of 1905 had made Russia nominally a constitutional monarchy. But it was sham constitutionalism because — both according to the Fundamental Laws and in fact — the executive branch of the government and the ministers in particular were not responsible to the Duma.[8] Nicholas and his ministers were hardly able to provide the skillful leadership that Russia needed. Besides, the tsar increasingly tried to emasculate this potentially democratic instrument. The Duma and mass participation in the political process was systematically stifled. The tsar went through four Dumas in the twelve years between the Manifesto and his abdication. The purpose of this high turnover of Dumas was to get a legislature that would be politically tame and obedient to the will of the autocrat. All this showed that he was still unwilling to learn the lessons of the crisis of 1905. His attempts to minimize the concessions he had granted and to preserve what he could of the traditional structures of autocracy made it more and more difficult to rebuild support for the government in a rapidly changing society.

Other aspects of the life of the country, ranging from political terrorism both of the Left and of the Right, to Russification and interminable "special regulations" to suppress unrest, emphasized further the distance that Russia had to travel before it could be considered progressive, liberal, and law-abiding. Russia's long tradition of arbitrary rule and the authoritarian political culture it had fostered meant that notions of a "legally based" state were very slow in penetrating both the official and the popular consciousness. The country remained essentially a police state with the punitive organs still enjoying extensive powers of arrest and punishment without trial of persons deemed to be socially or politically undesirable. In times of social unrest, martial law in the form of the government's "special regulations" was frequently imposed, overriding the civil courts and allowing the use of corporal and even capital punishment in the suppression of popular disorder.

Social and economic problems were still more threatening, according to the "pessimists." They point to the deep cultural and economic divisions that still existed in Russian society. Land hunger generated discontent among the semi-proletarianized peasantry, with millions of impoverished peasants coveting the large estates of the gentry. The urban workers had to endure appalling living and working conditions and very low wages. They were becoming more radical, exceptionally militant, and apparently willing to follow the Bolsheviks. Still more ominous was the fact that the upper classes themselves were disenchanted with the existing political system that denied them any effective role in government. Even the loyalty of the government's traditional supporters among the nobility was undermined by their declining wealth and influence. As long as the upper classes remained discontented, there was always a possibility that, in a moment of crisis, they might reluctantly support a working-class insurrection.

In this unstable situation, all the discontents that had led in 1905 to widespread support for the underground revolutionary parties were again fomenting unrest in the summer of 1914. Russia was headed for catastrophe, and the Russian government, accustomed to ruling only by autocratic methods, did not possess the political skills and flexibility to forestall it. Thus, unlike the "optimists" who believe that Imperial Russia was ruined by the First World War, the "pessimists" maintain that the war provided merely the last mighty push to bring the whole rotten structure tumbling down.[9]

Russia in the First World War

The warring powers had entered the hostilities in the conviction that they would relatively quickly achieve their principal military objectives. The governments of the Allies — Britain, France, and Russia — believed that they would be able to crush their main enemy, Germany, by attacking it on two fronts: from the west and the east. The Central Powers, on the other hand, represented by Germany, Austro-Hungary, and Turkey, hoped to prevent the Allies' joint operations, and isolate and rout them one by one, with powerful military strikes. It was soon clear, however, that such hopes were unfounded. The war escalated into a worldwide, drawn-out conflict that required from the belligerents the mobilization of their entire human and economic resources. In such a war victory, as never before, depended not just on military success at the front but also on the strength of the home front. It required a robust, modern industry, reorganized for the conduct of war, an efficient and reliable transportation system, and, above all, domestic peace and the cooperation of various sections of society for the war effort. Torn apart by intense internal conflicts, Russia had little chance of winning a war of this kind.

On the whole, the Russian people entered the war in a heightened mood of patriotic euphoria, which showed that, despite everything, traditions of loyalty to tsarism had survived among many sections of the population. Within a few weeks after the declaration of the war on 20 July 1914, the Russian government responded to the popular mood by renaming the country's capital PETROGRAD. The new name had a patriotic Slavic ring to it, in contrast to the old name of St. Petersburg, which now seemed too German.

The upper classes rallied around the government. In the Duma, all criticism of the government ceased. In July 1914 its deputies met for one day and voted war credits. A provisional committee of Duma members was set up under Michael Rodzianko, the Duma president, to organize aid for victims of the war. *Zemstvos* and town councils throughout Russia held conferences to consider how they could support the war effort. By August, the "All-Russian Union of Zemstvos for the Relief of the Sick and Wounded" had been formed. In May 1915 representatives of industry and trade set up another body — the Central War Industries Committee — to coordinate war production. Alexander Guchkov, the Octobrist leader, was elected its chairperson. In June 1915, *zemstvos* and municipal organizations merged in the "All-Russian Union of Zemstvos and Cities." These voluntary organizations did much to coordinate Russia's war effort.

Even on the Russian Left most socialists, with the exception of the Bolsheviks, followed the example of the veteran socialist Plekhanov and adopted a prowar stand. This attitude was motivated by the conviction that a victory by the Central Powers would mean the triumph of reaction and militarism and spell unshakeable domination of Europe by Germany.

However, by 1915, when Russia's first major military setbacks occurred, the patriotic euphoria started to wane, as it became increasingly clear that the country's economic, social, and political systems, as well as its armed forces, were failing the ultimate test of war. It became more and more obvious that the imperial government had again failed in its tasks, as in the Crimean War and the Russo-Japanese War, but this time on a much larger scale.

Russia had entered the war unprepared MILITARILY. A large-scale rearmament program, designed to modernize the Russian army and navy and upgrade their weaponry to the technological level of leading industrial nations, had started shortly before the Great War broke out. According to the government's estimates, the modernization of the armed forces was to be completed in 1917. When starting the war, the Germans knew about the Russian rearmament program and understood that in 1917 the Russians would have a much more formidable army than it had in 1914. The outbreak of hostilities prevented the Russian government from implementing its ambitious plans of rearming the armed forces. In the test of war Russian weapons turned out to be inferior to those of its enemies and Russian ammunition was in short supply.

The ECONOMIC EFFECTS of the war were devastating. The mass mobilization of 15 million conscript troops between 1914 and 1917 had serious repercussions on both agriculture and industry. Conscription of peasants from the large private estates, which produced mainly for the market, resulted in reduced output of agricultural production. Labor productivity in industry also declined as skilled workers were replaced with inexperienced laborers, women, children, and prisoners-of-war. With more and more enterprises converting to military production, output of consumer goods plummeted, adding more hardships for the civilian population. Moreover, these difficulties were compounded by problems of transportation. Most railway rolling-stock was commandeered to carry troops and munitions to the front, leaving little to deliver much-needed foodstuffs from the grain-growing regions to the towns. In big cities — in Petrograd and Moscow, particularly — there were shortages of bread, meat, sugar, and other basic commodities.

The war also caused an acute financial crisis. Poland and large areas of western Russia were occupied by enemy troops, with consequent loss not only of industrial resources, but also of a tax-paying population. Naval blockades of the Baltic Sea by Germany and the Black Sea by Turkey effectively cut off Russia's foreign trade and deprived the government of customs revenues. Even more disastrous was Nicholas's high-minded decision, in August 1914, to prohibit the production and sale of alcoholic drinks during the war. The ban on alcohol deprived the government's treasury of the 30 percent of its revenue that came from its monopoly over liquor sales.[10] Thus, at a time when the government was faced with the exceptional expenses of the war, its revenues took a precipitous fall. Starved of cash, it had to resort to printing money, inaugurating the twentieth century's first great inflation.

In the POLITICAL SPHERE, the war was marked by the failure of the monarchy, its ministers, and its generals to direct the military effort adequately. Some responsibility for Russia's military disasters rested with the imperial couple themselves. Against the advice of his ministers, Nicholas had personally assumed command of the army in 1915, leaving the everyday conduct of home affairs in the hands of his wife. The Empress Alexandra was herself under the influence of a scandalous group at court headed by GRIGORY RASPUTIN (1864–1916), a Siberian peasant and sectarian, the "man of God" who in an incredible manner had been propelled into the highest court circles. His apparent powers to cure the bleeding of Nicholas's hemophiliac son Alexei gave Rasputin a powerful hold over the imperial couple and, in particular, over the empress, who saw him not only as the healer of her only son but also as a genuine oracle whose word she believed absolutely.

Rasputin's St. Petersburg period, according to the reports of the agents who kept him under constant surveillance, was marked by ever-growing unrestrained debauchery, drinking bouts, and orgies, embroiling even highly placed figures. His drunkenness and sexual antics were widely publicized by the press. Yet for the imperial couple and their children his "holiness" and "piety" were not a matter for question. The great paradox in the relationship between Rasputin and the royal family was that Nicholas and Alexandra were so blinded by their faith in Rasputin's ability to prolong the life of the heir to the throne that they did not actually see the direct threat posed by this relationship to the throne itself and, indeed, to the very continuation of the dynasty.

It has to be said that Rasputin's actual influence in the making of the most important political decisions — for example, the role he played in influencing appointments to positions of state — was considerably exaggerated not only during his time, but particularly afterwards. What really mattered about Rasputin was not his actual political influence but the fatal impact he had on the monarchy's prestige. This relationship greatly undermined the honor and reputation of the royal family.

This situation gave rise to constant and ever-growing discontent in circles around the tsar and attempts to push the dissolute monk aside and get him away from court. Eventually, as all attempts to remove him from court by political means had failed, the idea of physically disposing of him was born in a small circle of conspirators. On 30 December 1916 Rasputin was murdered by a group that included Prince Felix Yusupov, husband of the emperor's niece, the Grand Duke Dimitri, who was Nicholas's first cousin, and Vladimir Purishkevich, a Duma deputy of the far Right.

The fact that Rasputin was murdered by figures from ultraconservative and high-society circles reflected the great fear in those quarters of the impending revolution. They regarded Rasputin as a great threat to the throne and to the idea of monarchy, believing that his relationship with the royal family might spark a revolution. Two months after the murder of Rasputin the autocracy collapsed, but the scandal that had surrounded Rasputin's name was merely a symptom, not a cause, of the acute malaise which afflicted an incompetent and unpopular regime. Rasputin was a logical end product of the political bankruptcy of tsarism, which had allowed a narrow-minded, superstitious woman and an ignorant, grotesque peasant to hold the destinies of an empire in their hands.

The war had far-reaching PSYCHOLOGICAL EFFECTS on society, inducing a corrosive demoralization of the army at the front and a deepening sense of alienation from the government among various sectors of the population in the rear. At the front, several factors explain the decline in the army's reliability. The first was the sheer scale of the war and the staggering Russian human losses that resulted from it. In the course of the war the Russian army mobilized 15,500,000 troops and suffered great casualties: 1,650,000 killed, 3,850,000 wounded, and 2,410,000 taken prisoner.[11] Yet these enormous human sacrifices seemed to have been made without avail. For three years the Imperial Army went from defeat to defeat; by 1917 it had lost a significant portion of the empire's western provinces.

Second, heavy losses at the front and enhanced conscription in the rear meant that the composition of the Russian army itself was changing. The increasingly unreliable troops were not so much trained and loyal fighters for tsar and country as hastily drafted and poorly equipped "peasants clad in uniform." The traditional officer corps, drawn from the ruling class, was also becoming diluted by what perhaps may be described as the "intelligentsia clad in uniform," in other words, young professionals who would never have contemplated a military career in the time of peace. Many of these newly recruited officers were not imbued with the automatic loyalty to the regime typical of the traditional officer corps.

Finally, even the general staff at the top of the military command were becoming alienated from their sovereign, whom they blamed for his inexperienced military meddling in his role as commander-in-chief.

The defeats and demoralization at the front inevitably began to effect the rear. As the initial upsurge of patriotic enthusiasm for the tsar and the motherland began to wane, the war came under careful scrutiny, primarily by the Duma politicians and various political factions.

Chapter Twelve

February and October Revolutions

Collapse of Tsarism

To the liberal opposition, Russia's heavy defeats of 1915 had clearly demonstrated that the autocratic regime was incapable of bringing the war to a victorious end. The realization that a lost war would inevitably lead to a revolutionary explosion galvanized the Kadets, Octobrists, and other liberal and moderate-conservative groupings in the State Duma to form a broad parliamentary alliance in opposition to the government. Members of the alliance, which was called the "PROGRESSIVE BLOC," harshly criticized the tsarist ministers for the incompetence with which the government led the war effort, called on the tsar to sack his obviously inept administration, and even openly accused the government, the tsar, and the empress of treason. Above all, the "Progressive Bloc" demanded a competent set of ministers, a cabinet that would enjoy "the confidence of the nation." As the military situation continued to deteriorate, the "Progressive Bloc" hardened its demands, calling for a Western-style government with a limited monarchy and a ministry responsible to a majority in the Duma.

The tsar, however, flatly refused to satisfy the demands of the Duma opposition. Nicholas had never really accepted the dilution of autocracy brought about by the introduction of the Duma. When the war started, he seized on the military emergency to rule almost without convening the Duma, and thus also without trying to enlist the support that the liberal opposition offered for the war effort. This policy, together with the ascendancy of Rasputin and his influence over Empress Alexandra, who in effect governed while Nicholas was away at the front, looked to the opposition in the Duma like a coup d'état against the constitutional order. In the face of the tsar's unwillingness to make any concessions to the opposition, the liberals began to plot the overthrow of Nicholas II.

The diverse leftist groups embraced a variety of attitudes toward the war. Most Socialist-Revolutionaries and other peasant-orientated socialist groupings, such as the Trudoviks, advocated "defensism." The essence of this approach was expressed by the Trudovik spokesman Alexander Kerensky, who urged the working people first to "defend our country and then set it free." Many Mensheviks were in favor of pacifism, while the Bolshevik leader, from his exile in Switzerland, preached outright defeatism, insisting on "turning the imperialist war into a civil war."

The scale of the war confirmed Lenin's radicalism. To him it was an irrefutable proof that the final crisis of capitalism had arrived. In the work *Imperialism, the Highest Stage of Capitalism,* published in 1916, Lenin argued that by the end of the nineteenth century capitalism in advanced capitalist countries had reached its highest and last stage — IMPERIALISM. The war arose from the irreconcilable internal contradictions of "bourgeois" societies and the growing conflicts between imperialist capitalist powers over colonial profits. The class struggle became ever more intense. Mounting economic crises escalated into a general crisis of the capitalist system, which spilled over in the catastrophe of worldwide war. The war marked the death agony of capitalism and opened the way to revolution. The task of the proletariat and of Social-Democratic parties in the countries at war was to transform the imperialist war into a series of revolutionary civil wars against their capitalist governments, which would ultimately lead to the triumph of a world revolution.

At Lenin's insistence the slogan of "REVOLUTIONARY DEFEATISM" was adopted by the Central Committee of the RSDLP as early as the autumn of 1914. The Bolsheviks denounced the war as unjust and predatory on all sides of the conflict and called on the workers of the warring nations to seek the defeat of their own "bourgeois" governments. Lenin and his adherents hoped that the implementation of this slogan in practice would lead to the collapse of the imperialist states and the transformation of the First World War into a world revolution.

The decision of the German Social-Democratic Party to support the German government in 1914 confirmed Lenin's fear that, at the moment of truth, moderate socialist parties would support the bourgeoisie. From this time on he saw the moderate socialists as enemies, fighting for, rather than against, the bourgeoisie. Lenin's suspicion of them was further vindicated at two international conferences of the socialist Left in Switzerland, the first in Zimmerwald in 1915 and the second at Kienthal in 1916. Lenin presented his "defeatist" program at the conferences, but his defeatist views were rejected as extreme even by these radical leftist gatherings. Only a small minority supported his stand that it was impossible to attain socialist revolution without wishing for the defeat of one's government and actively working for such a defeat.

Undisturbed by the objections to his strategy in the ranks of the leftist socialists, Lenin continued to work, with his characteristic stubbornness and ruthlessness, for the realization of his ideas. By 1916 the defeatist slogans began to gain popular support, leading to the rise of the pacifist movement in the army and navy. Instances multiplied of insubordination to officers, refusals to advance, mass surrenders, and desertions. At some parts of the eastern front Russian soldiers even fraternized with the enemy troops. The continual growth of the Bolsheviks' influence — both at the front and in the rear — spelled grave dangers to the authorities.

Increasingly the population began to voice its discontent, not only with the military reverses, but also with the domestic hardships that were directly attributed to the government's incompetence. The short-lived mood of national solidarity at the outbreak of war had now evaporated. Industry was battered by a renewed wave of strikes. Most members of Russia's upper classes, who at the start of the war had rallied behind the government, were now united in opposition to it. In the Duma and in voluntary organizations such as the All-Russian Union of Zemstvos and Cities and the War Industries Committee, and through other networks and connections, they already had the embryo of a new, alternative government without the tsar. A constitutional crisis was threatening to paralyze Russia's war effort. But the ruling classes hesitated to take that last step alone.

The final push came from the streets of Petrograd. On 22 February 1917 a lockout at the giant Putilov metalworks brought many metal workers into the streets. Next day large numbers of women textile workers, concerned with mounting food shortages, went on strike. In the following days demonstrations rapidly spread across the city. By the end of February 1917 over 80 percent of Petrograd's workers were on strike. They were joined by white-collar employees, teachers, and students. The city's central avenue was flooded with mass rallies and demonstrations, held under the red banners and slogans "Down with the tsar!" All attempts by General Khabalov, the commander of the Petrograd garrison, to maintain order proved futile. On 27 February soldiers of some regiments mutinied and went over to the demonstrators. On 28 February General Khabalov lost control over the situation in the capital completely and felt compelled to order the remaining loyal defenders of the old regime to lay down their arms.

Thus, a massive outburst of social discontent erupted in the midst of a war that was being lost, while the economy was beginning to break down, and with the government and the ruling elites locked in a constitutional crisis. Only the combination of these circumstances could lead to a revolutionary explosion. This became the February Revolution of 1917. Resolute action, such as promptly bringing in loyal forces from outside the capital, might have saved the imperial government. Instead, with Nicholas II away at the front, authority simply collapsed, the main institutions of government crumbled, and many officials went into hiding. The question now was which political forces would be daring enough to fill the power vacuum produced by the crisis.

In these extraordinary circumstances, on 27 February, a group of leaders of all parties represented in the Duma met to discuss the formation of a new government that would be able to take the situation under control. A week later, the first PROVISIONAL GOVERNMENT emerged, composed of a score of prominent Duma leaders and public figures. Prince George Lvov, formerly chairperson of the All-Russian Union of Zemstvos and Cities, assumed the positions of chairperson of the Council of Ministers (i.e., prime minister) and of minister of the interior. His more important colleagues included the Kadet leader Miliukov as minister of foreign affairs, the Octobrist leader Guchkov as minister of war and of the navy, and Alexander Kerensky, the only socialist in the cabinet — associated with the peasant-orientated Duma faction — as minister of justice.

The new government closely reflected the composition and views of the "Progressive Bloc" in the Duma, with the Kadets obtaining the greatest single representation. Thus, the newly created government, although catapulted into power by the action of the revolutionary workers and soldiers of Petrograd, represented the political interests of the middle and upper classes.

Nicholas heard the news of the unrest in Petrograd at his military headquarters in the town of Mogilev. On its way back to Petrograd, the imperial train was stranded by railway strikes at Pskov, the headquarters of the northern front. There he found he no longer had the support of his army commanders, who recommended to Nicholas that he abdicate. The tsar bowed to the inevitable and on 2 March abdicated for himself and his only son, Alexei, in favor of his brother, Michael. But Michael refused to take the throne, and the monarchy disappeared. Thus ended the rule of the Romanovs in Russia. In five days the autocracy, without putting up the slightest resistance, collapsed like a house of cards.

The collapse of the three-century-old Romanov dynasty in Russia was an important turning point not only in Russian but in world history. It is comparable to the downfall of the French monarchy at the end of the eighteenth century. The war and revolution caught the tsarist empire in the middle of a process of transformation (industrial, agrarian, educational, and military), at a point when most of the reforms undertaken during the constitutional period were beginning to produce their first results. However, the tsarist empire's political evolution could not keep pace with its rapid socioeconomic progress. The failure to adapt Russia's antiquated government structure to the fast-changing social and economic conditions was among the principal reasons for the downfall of tsarism.

The brutal and devastating war brought into stark relief the inefficiency, inadequacy, and rottenness of the autocratic regime, which became completely "detached" from its people. The alienation of Russian society from the tsarist government was at the root of the crisis that crippled Imperial Russia. The educated public, denied the possibility of participation in the affairs of state, was politically disaffected, with some groups even wishing for the military defeat of their own government. The rural masses (which still comprised some 80 percent of the population) were estranged by the regime's age-long neglect of the peasant problem. The masses of soldiery, half-buried in muddy trenches stretching for over two thousand miles from the Baltic to the Black Seas, were demoralized by the endless, hopeless battles in which they did not see any real meaning. The incapacity of the tsar and the tsarist regime in the face of the military and political crisis eroded even the loyalty of the tsar's traditional supporters: it was not the demonstrators in Petrograd but the army high command and the aristocratic members of the Duma who advised him to abdicate.

"Dual Power"

The February Revolution had brought about some radical shifts in the correlation of Russia's main political forces, affecting the standing of different parties. Monarchist groupings, in particular, had been quickly swept away by its tide, while the significance of parties that used to be close to monarchists, such as the Octobrists, was greatly diminished. By contrast, the liberal Kadets were swiftly transformed from a party of the opposition into a ruling party, while the Socialist-Revolutionaries and the Mensheviks were content to take on the role of constructive opposition.

The singularity of the February Revolution, however, was in the way in which it had resolved the most cardinal question of any revolution—

the question of power: who would pick up the reins of government after the old authority had collapsed? In Russia two governments simultaneously had emerged contending for the right to provide political leadership after the fall of tsarism: the liberal Provisional Government, which officially held the reins of power, and the unofficial government in the form of the PETROGRAD SOVIET OF WORKERS' AND SOLDIERS' DEPUTIES supported by the armed workers and soldiers of the capital.

The Soviet had been established on the initiative of socialist intellectuals who had been very imperfectly represented in the Fourth Duma. They saw the formation of the Provisional Government by the Duma as a challenge to themselves and decided to set up a separate governing body. They already had a model of a quasi-governmental working-class organization in the earlier St. Petersburg Soviet, established in October of 1905 and suppressed by the government in December of that year, and this they decided to revive. Hasty elections were arranged by the socialists at various factories and military barracks of Petrograd, and on 27 February the Petrograd Soviet was set up as a rival governing authority. Most members of the Soviet were Mensheviks and Socialist-Revolutionaries, with the Bolsheviks numbering some 10 percent of the delegates. The Executive Committee of the Soviet was composed predominantly of Menshevik intellectuals.

This simultaneous formation of the Provisional Government, on the one hand, and the second alternative government in the form of the Soviet, on the other, brought about the situation of "DUAL POWER," under which the "bourgeois" Provisional Government had to coordinate its decisions and share power with the "proletarian" Petrograd Soviet. The unstable situation of "dual power" characterized almost the whole of the period of several months leading to October 1917, during which Russia, with no head of state, had two governing bodies: one enjoyed formal authority without power, while the other had power without formal authority. The Provisional Government had the support mostly of Russia's traditional elites, as well as the remnants of the tsarist bureaucracy and the high command in the army. The Petrograd Soviet commanded the loyalty of urban workers and peasants, and spread its authority over other Soviets that sprang up in the towns and villages and at the front. From the outset, the Provisional Government was dependent on the goodwill of the Soviet, which expressed the distrust of the worker and soldier "masses" toward the "bourgeois" and "capitalist" ministry.

In addition, amid the February events, the Soviet issued its famous "ORDER NUMBER ONE" aimed at democratizing the army by electing soldiers' committees. The new law also demanded that troops submit themselves to the authority of the Soviet "in all political matters." In practice it meant that the Soviet had now control over the garrison troops of the capital. Soon the application of the decree was spread to rank-and-file soldiers even at the front. Soldiers began electing soldiers' committees or "Soviets," which reserved the right to reject officers' orders. This reduced the authority of officers and thus weakened the Provisional Government's control over its armed forces. Military discipline was further undermined by the ending of censorship, which led to the increase in antiwar propaganda within the army, and by the Provisional Government's decision to abolish the death penalty at the front.

The structures of the new, largely working-class, machinery of power developed at an astonishing speed. Within weeks Soviets sprang up throughout the country. In June at least 350 local Soviets sent their representatives to the first All-Russian Congress of Soviets in Petrograd. The Petrograd Soviet now presided over a network of local bodies, reaching across the entire country. In the spring, this new administrative machinery was still ill-organized and unreliable, but it ensured that the Soviet had more real power than the Provisional Government.

At this stage the Soviet could have seized power on its own if it had wanted to. Most socialist leaders, however, believed that Russia was not ready for a socialist revolution. They remembered that even Marx had warned against trying to build socialism before all the necessary preconditions had matured. They argued that the Soviet democracy was too young and inexperienced to claim government authority in the desperate conditions of war and disintegration. The Soviet had therefore to entrust the power to its class enemy, the propertied elements, which had the skills and experience necessary to keep the economy running. The bourgeois government would continue to rule the country and direct the development of capitalism for a long period. In the meantime the Soviets of Workers' and Peasants' Deputies would master the technique of administration from the bourgeoisie.

In addition to these ideological arguments for restraint, psychological factors may have been equally important.[1] Most socialist leaders came not from Russia's working classes but from the intelligentsia. Only seven out of the forty-two members of the Soviet's first Executive Committee were workers. The rest were intellectuals. Despite their radical political beliefs, they shared the culture and outlook of Russia's upper classes and feared that a working-class revolt in backward Russia could lead only to anarchy. Most socialist leaders also remembered the lessons of the 1905 Revolution, when the unrestrained agitation of radical intellectuals was partly responsible for the ill-prepared December insurrection in Moscow, which ended in bloodshed.

"Dual power" was an uneasy coalition of "bourgeois" and working-class institutions, claiming to represent both Russia's traditional elites and its popular masses. It recreated the fragile alliance of the upper and lower classes that had nearly brought the tsarist government down in October 1905. In principle, the coalition of the Provisional Government and the Petrograd Soviet had enough popular support to create genuinely democratic institutions for the first time in modern Russian history. However, the political and social antagonisms between upper classes and working classes proved insurmountable. Their alliance grew shakier with each day and was finally blown up in October when the Bolsheviks seized power.

Bolshevik Takeover

Much of the blame for the course of events that weakened the prospects of Russia's first attempt at democratic government must be borne by the Provisional Government. The Provisional Government, as its name implied, saw itself as a temporary administration whose main task was to prepare the elections to a CONSTITUENT ASSEMBLY. It was expected that the Constituent Assembly, when elected on the basis of a democratic electoral law, would consider and approve the key principles of Russia's future constitutional system and create permanently functioning governmental institutions. The majority of ministers in the Provisional Government were supporters of the rule of law; they did not want to prejudge or resolve issues that they thought were outside their mandate. These should wait until the convocation of the Constituent Assembly. The core of the Provisional Government was formed of liberal Kadets such as Paul Miliukov and Alexander Manuilov, who understood the importance of the idea of a proper, "legally based" democracy. They knew that without this, "democracy" would be a cloak for arbitrary decision-making based upon the principle "might is right," or on expediency. The awful paradox is that in this view the legalistically minded ministers were absolutely correct, but the situation they faced made such a view impossible to carry out.

The Provisional Government did not want to prejudge not only the decision on the form of the future Russian state, but also such vital questions as the ownership of land and the conclusion of peace with

Germany. For peasants (and the overwhelming majority of the Russian population, including most soldiers, were peasants) the real issue of the revolution was land. Yet the Provisional Government refused to act, arguing that only the Constituent Assembly could undertake so fundamental a redistribution of Russia's resources. In the meantime peasants started to take gentry land anyway, knowing that the government could no longer stop them.

Above all, it was the government's decision to pursue war-to-victory that proved to be its biggest mistake. The Provisional Government felt obliged to continue the war because it accepted its treaty obligations to Great Britain and France, which forbade the conclusion of a separate peace by any of the Allies. It was "legalistic" about this and also believed that since Russia was now on its way to "democracy," the "democratic allies" — Great Britain and France — were its natural partners against Imperial Germany and Austria. The ministers in the Provisional Government hoped that victory in the common struggle would entrench in Russia a form of government similar to the constitutional regimes of its allies. Also the Western allies themselves were all the time putting pressure on the new government in Russia to stay in the war. In addition, there was a huge logistical problem. In the spring of 1917 Russia had seven million men under arms. How could Russia cope with such numbers if the war ended and so many troops would have to be transported home? Later most of them "transported themselves" anyway, but the Provisional Government could not have officially "ordered" them to quit the trenches and go home.

Whatever the motivation behind the government's resolve to continue with the war effort, its decision was extremely dangerous, for it grossly underestimated the depth of the antiwar mood of the masses. Most of Russia's peasants, workers, and soldiers no longer had any desire to fight. Peasants in the army could not wait for the land repartition that they knew was about to take place. They deserted in increasing numbers to go back to their villages to ensure they did not miss out on their share of the gentry's land.

Thus, the reservations of the "legalists" in the Provisional Government prevented it from taking bold steps that would have gone at least some way toward meeting the expectations of the masses and significantly transforming the country's sociopolitical system. As a result, it restricted room for its own political maneuvering and lost the initiative to the ultra-radical political forces. A speedy convocation of the Constituent Assembly might have solved some of these problems. Yet the government claimed that wartime conditions made it impossible to hold elections. Eventually it set up an electoral commission in May and promised elections in November. However, its procrastination over the issue had planted the suspicion that a "bourgeois" government was deliberately avoiding elections that might result in its overthrow. Both the actions and the inaction of the Provisional Government increasingly alienated the working classes and the leftist forces. In their eyes the Provisional Government lacked legitimacy. The Soviet, by contrast, was "their" government, the symbolic representative of Russia's exploited classes.

Other reasons as well prevented the Provisional Government from taking stock of the situation and making right political decisions. The Russian bourgeoisie, which it mainly represented, had not yet accumulated enough political experience or mastered the skills of public administration. It was not adept, like its more experienced Western European counterpart, in reaching social compromises and making political deals. In addition, it was not always capable of differentiating clearly between its long-term strategic interests, such as holding on to power and maintaining its dominant position, and short-term, tactical ones. These latter, which often overshadowed the former, included the undisguised desire of the industrial and financial bourgeoisie to preserve large-scale private land ownership (many estates of the nobles by 1917 had passed into its hands). The bourgeoisie was also interested in the continuation of the war because war brought it huge profits and promised territorial gains and new trade and economic advantages in the event of victory.

The political force that was most successful in exploiting the situation of "dual power" and the weaknesses of the bourgeois Provisional Government to its own utmost advantage was Lenin's party of Bolsheviks. In March 1917 the idea that they would be ruling the country several months later appeared preposterous even to most Bolsheviks themselves. At that time they were the smallest of the major socialist parties. They had about twenty-five thousand members, and only forty representatives among the fifteen hundred or so members of the Petrograd Soviet. When the tsar abdicated, the main Bolshevik leaders were not in the capital. Joseph Stalin (1879–1953) and Lev Kamenev (1883–1936) were in Siberian exile, while Grigori Zinoviev (1883–1936) and Nicholas Bukharin (1888–1938) were in forced exile abroad. In March they were only starting to arrive in Petrograd.

Lenin himself had been living in exile abroad almost continuously since 1900, apart from a brief return in 1905. During the war he lived in Switzerland. After the fall of the autocracy he negotiated frantically to return through enemy country. The Germans decided that Lenin's return could only harm the Russian war effort and gave him and a group of his close Bolshevik associates safe passage to neutral Sweden. From there, in a special sealed train made available by the German government, the Russian revolutionaries entered Russia and arrived at Petrograd's Finland station on 3 April. There the Bolshevik leader addressed the welcoming crowds with a call for international socialist revolution.

This surprised even some senior Bolsheviks, who by and large were content with the accomplishment of the February, "bourgeois" revolution and had decided to support the "bourgeois" Provisional Government. (Stalin and Kamenev had made this decision after they returned from Siberian exile in mid-March and assumed control of party affairs.) Lenin's call contradicted classical Marxist theory, which clearly showed that the development of the productive forces of Russia had not attained the level that made socialism possible. In addition, socialism, according to Marx, should triumph in most of the economically advanced capitalist countries simultaneously.

Lenin's party comrades should, however, have had no reason for surprise. By 1917 Lenin believed firmly that a period of worldwide socialist revolutions was imminent. More than that, he believed that the Russian revolution would play a key role in the worldwide socialist revolution, for Russia would be the first country in which world capitalism would crack. In articles written during the war he suggested what Stalin would later call "brilliant deductions" that allowed him to stand Marxism on its head. Lenin discarded the notion that socialist revolution had to triumph in all countries simultaneously. He claimed that he had uncovered "an absolute law of capitalism" that made the socialist revolution possible first in several or even in one capitalist country, taken singly. This was the "LAW OF UNEVEN ECONOMIC AND POLITICAL DEVELOPMENT OF CAPITALISM":

> The development of capitalism proceeds extremely unevenly in different countries.... From this it follows irrefutably that socialism cannot achieve victory simultaneously in all countries. It will achieve victory first in one or several countries, while the others will for some time remain bourgeois or pre-bourgeois in character.[2]

However, the rest of the world would not remain capitalist for long. The victory of socialism in one country would trigger anti-capitalist revolutions all over the world, as the international proletariat would hasten to rally behind their victorious comrades and topple their own bourgeois governments:

> Uneven economic and political development is an absolute law of capitalism. Hence, the victory of Socialism is possible first in several or even in one capitalist country alone. After expropriating the capitalists and organizing their own socialist production, the victorious proletariat of that country will arise against the rest of the world — the capitalist world — attracting to its cause the oppressed classes of other countries, stirring uprisings in those countries against the capitalists.[3]

Lenin's most daring "deduction," however, was the assertion that Russia would be the country to initiate the world proletarian revolution. He argued that revolution was likely to break out initially not where capitalism was most strongly developed but "at the weakest link in the imperialist chain," which was Russia. Here capitalism had developed alongside a semifeudal agrarian structure, and the bourgeoisie had proved too feeble to overthrow the absolute monarchy. The first revolution on the agenda, therefore, was the bourgeois-democratic overthrow of tsarism and the abolition of feudal remnants. By taking the lead in the bourgeois-democratic revolution, the Russian proletariat, in alliance with the poor peasantry, could push straight forward to the socialist revolution.

Lenin realized that in the economic sense Russia was not ready for the introduction of socialism. He argued, however, that, though Russia remained too backward to build a viable socialist society on its own, it would be able to do so after a wider world revolution that would create a socialist Europe. Lenin was firmly convinced that Russia would not be left on its own, that its bold step toward socialism would be supported by the highly developed countries of Europe, which stood on the threshold of a world socialist revolution. Therefore it was the duty of the Russian working classes to overthrow their own bourgeoisie and detonate a European revolution. Thus, Lenin augmented Marxist theory in order to put Russia, its working classes, and its Marxist revolutionaries in the vanguard of the struggle for socialism, ahead of all advanced capitalist countries.

There was one more important reason why Lenin urged his comrades to get ready for a socialist revolution. He saw that the current unstable situation in Russia presented the Bolsheviks with a unique opportunity to take the reins of power in their hands. Once they were in control of Russia, they would be able to implement policies necessary to overcome

Russia's economic and cultural backwardness and make the leap into socialism. He was prepared to gamble as he saw that his chances were high. Lenin liked to quote Napoleon: "On s'engage et puis on voit," first engage in a serious battle and then see what happens. Being a "practitioner" of revolution, rather than a pure theoretician, he had always had a streak of recklessness and adventurism in him.

Lenin's analysis of the political situation in Russia and of the behavior of the liberal and moderate socialist parties during the first several weeks after the collapse of autocracy would be completely vindicated by the subsequent course of events. Lenin saw more clearly than most of his party comrades that the vacillation of the ruling political bloc, represented by the Kadet, Socialist-Revolutionary, and Menshevik politicians in the Provisional Government and the Petrograd Soviet, would inevitably destabilize the situation in the country. It became increasingly obvious that they were unable to meet the social expectations and demands of the popular masses and, most of all, to end the war, give land to the peasants, and improve food supplies in the towns. It was precisely the underestimation by the ruling circles of the degree of urgency and explosiveness of those issues, the procrastination over reform, and the continuation of the war that played into the hands of the extremist forces of the Left. They now had a good chance of gaining the support of the masses and seizing political control. What was needed, thought Lenin, was the right choice of strategy in the struggle for power.

On his arrival in Petrograd he immediately got down to formulating what exactly his party had to do to speed up the socialist revolution. In a condensed form his ideas first appeared in his celebrated April Theses, published in the Bolshevik newspaper *Pravda* under the title "The Tasks of the Proletariat in the Present Revolution," and then elaborated in other articles written in the spring of 1917. In the April Theses, Lenin advocated the overthrow of the Provisional Government by the Soviets. To achieve this, he offered a program designed to gain the support of the masses, secure the Bolshevik majority in the Petrograd Soviet, undermine the authority of the Provisional Government, and, ultimately, transfer all power from it to the Soviet. This was an outline of the strategy that, within seven months, was to bring the Bolsheviks to power.[4]

On the issue of war, Lenin rejected the Provisional Government's slogan of "revolutionary defensism," arguing that under the new government the war on Russia's part remained "a predatory imperialist war owing to the capitalist nature of this government." He called upon his party members to organize widespread propaganda among the army to the effect that it was impossible to end the war by a truly democratic peace without the overthrow of the capitalist ministry.

In the Theses Lenin underscored his idea of merging the two stages of the revolution into one by insisting that in February Russia had entered "a transition from the first stage of the revolution — which, owing to the insufficient class consciousness and organization of the proletariat, led to the assumption of power by the bourgeoisie — to the second stage, which must place power in the hands of the proletariat and the poor strata of the peasantry." This transition was made easier by the Provisional Government's reluctance to use violence in relation to the masses. The new liberal government consciously sought to create the conditions of a maximum freedom for its citizens (on Lenin's own admission, "Russia is now the freest of all the belligerent countries in the world"). This gave the revolutionaries a unique opportunity to accomplish the transition from the bourgeois revolution to the socialist revolution by peaceful means.

In order to achieve the establishment of a working-class government, the Bolsheviks should first renounce any support of the Provisional Government and then step up the propaganda campaign, portraying the majority bloc of moderate socialists in the Soviets as being under the "influence of the bourgeoisie and the conveyors of its influence to the proletariat." By criticizing the mild and conciliatory stance of the Soviets, the Bolsheviks would increase their own influence in them, and, as soon as they had secured a majority, they would declare the transfer of the entire government power to the Soviets of Workers' Deputies.

Lenin emphasized that the Soviets were the "only possible form of revolutionary government." In his April Theses he vehemently castigated the idea of a parliamentary system, insisting that what Russia needed was "not a parliamentary republic — to return to a parliamentary republic from the Soviets of Workers' Deputies would be a retrograde step — but a republic of Soviets of Workers' and Peasants' Deputies throughout the country, from top to bottom." Lenin understood that the Bolsheviks stood little chance of becoming a ruling party as a result of the planned elections to the Constituent Assembly. They had, however, a very good chance of coming to power by seizing control of the Soviets.

Despite the unquestionable respect that he commanded in his party, Lenin had to use all his powers of persuasion to get the Bolshevik leaders to accept this radical program. However, many rank-and-file party members from the working class shared Lenin's outlook and gave support to his arguments in party committees, with a result that a party conference early in May adopted the April Theses as official party policy. This decision distinguished the Bolsheviks from all the other socialist parties, for they were now the only political force committed to the creation of a working-class government. The decision to overthrow the Provisional Government also meant that the Bolsheviks had no need to compromise with the "bourgeoisie" and court Russia's upper classes. They could now concentrate on building up support from the working class and soldiers by offering the masses a simple but attractive program: an end to the war, land to the peasants, bread to the hungry, freedom to the empire's oppressed nationalities. Whether they could satisfy these demands was an altogether different matter. The party's commitment to revolution also meant that Bolsheviks now had a sense of purpose that the moderate socialists lacked.

In the meantime events in Russia appeared to vindicate Lenin's strategy. In April the minister of foreign affairs of the Provisional Government, Paul Miliukov, sent a diplomatic note to Russia's war allies in which he reaffirmed his government's determination to pursue the war against Germany until it could reach a "just peace." The document was published in the popular press and provoked huge shows of public indignation in Petrograd and other cities. Miliukov was forced to resign from his post, together with Guchkov, the minister of war and the leader of the Octobrist Party. In early May some ministerial posts in the Provisional Government were given to the leaders of moderate socialists — such as Chernov, the founder of the Socialist-Revolutionary Party; the Menshevik Tseretely; and others — in order to restore the declining prestige of the bourgeois government. The Provisional Government now became a coalition cabinet. However, this had little effect on the nature and direction of its policies.

In this situation Bolshevism was gaining in strength and popularity. Bolshevik Party membership began to rise. In February the Bolsheviks had only about twenty-five thousand members — far fewer than either the Mensheviks or the Socialist-Revolutionaries. By May they had the support of most factory committees in the capital. By June the rise in Bolshevik strength was clear to everyone. At the first All-Russian Congress of Soviets of Workers' and Soldiers' Deputies, held in that month, the Bolsheviks had 105 delegates; the Mensheviks, 248; and the Socialist Revolutionaries, 285. At the congress Lenin bluntly declared that his party was "ready to take all power." This declaration was backed up by mass rallies, organized by the Bolsheviks in Petrograd and other major cities. These were held under the Bolshevik slogans of "All power to the Soviets!" "Down with the war!" "Down with minister-capitalists!" and caused a new, June crisis of the Provisional Government. They showed that the Bolsheviks were now a serious political force in the capital.

In June the government tried to rouse patriotic feelings with a huge military offensive on the southwestern front. The beginning of July, however, brought the news of the collapse of the Russian army's advance there. On 4 July in Petrograd a half-million people gathered to demonstrate under the Bolshevik slogans. Some pro-Bolshevik army units in the capital also joined the protesters. On the eve of the demonstration a group of Bolshevik leaders had argued in favor of the removal of the Provisional Government by force. Lenin, however, advised caution, arguing that the Provisional Government still had sufficient backing of loyal troops, that Russian provinces were not yet ready to support an insurrection, and that a premature rising could provoke a right-wing backlash strong enough to damage irrevocably the party's prospects of ever seizing power. In a heated debate the party leadership had finally decided to scale down the protest to a peaceful rally.

However, the presence of pro-Bolshevik army units among the protesters made violent clashes with the police and progovernment troops almost unavoidable. The rioting continued for two days. As a result of spontaneous exchanges of fire, over four hundred people were killed or wounded. Eventually, the progovernment troops suppressed the insurrection. The Provisional Government resorted to harsh measures to restore order. Marshal law was declared in the capital. Some military units were disarmed and removed from the city. The blame for the uprising was put squarely on the Bolsheviks. Their newspaper *Pravda* was closed, and documents were published claiming that the Bolsheviks were receiving money from the German enemy. Orders were issued to arrest Lenin and a number of other Bolshevik leaders on charges of being German agents. The Bolshevik leader had to leave Petrograd and go underground on the Russian-Finnish border.

In July a Second Coalition Provisional Government was formed with ALEXANDER KERENSKY (1881–1970), a moderate socialist, assuming the position of prime minister to replace Prince Lvov, who resigned. The Socialist-Revolutionary and Menshevik leaders of the Soviets hailed the new coalition cabinet as "a government of the salvation of the revolution" and offered their unconditional support. In a desperate attempt to stem the wave of mass desertions and bolster military discipline, the Provisional Government reintroduced the death penalty at the front, set up military tribunals, and reestablished military censorship. It now took the reins of power firmly in its hands. The period of "dual power" came virtually to an end.

Meanwhile the polarization of class and political forces accelerated. The war went on, the elections to the Constituent Assembly were being postponed, and the industrial dislocation and food crisis deepened. The end of the summer of 1917 was marked by a growing wave of political strikes in the cities, illegal land seizures in the countryside, nationalist unrest on the fringes of the empire, and mass desertions and fraternization with the enemy at the front. In these conditions all attempts of the Provisional Government to steer Russia toward democracy, completely unknown to its people before February 1917, were encountering mounting resistance both from the Left and from the Right.

From the Right, the biggest threat to the Provisional Government came at the end of August when GENERAL LAVR KORNILOV (1870–1918), the new commander-in-chief of the Russian army (appointed to this position in mid-July), attempted to launch a military coup. By that time an increasing number of representatives of the right-wing political forces, including landowners, army officers, and entrepreneurs, were tired of the weakness of the Provisional Government and of its inability to stem the tide of "revolutionary anarchy" both at the front and at home. The extreme Right advocated a strong government with dictatorial powers that would be capable of holding the Russian Empire together and of preventing anarchy by crushing the leftist forces. They found in General Kornilov a willing candidate to impose a military dictatorship. Late in August Kornilov ordered several cavalry units to march on Petrograd, apparently with the aim of crushing the Petrograd Soviet. A counter-revolutionary military dictatorship seemed to be in the offing. But at this moment of crisis the Provisional Government received powerful support from the revolutionary forces led by the Bolsheviks. This stopped Kornilov's troops on their march to Petrograd and scattered them before they could reach the capital.

The Kornilov affair was a crucial event both in strengthening the influence of the Bolsheviks and in crippling Kerensky's government. The embattled Provisional Government had been forced to appeal for Bolshevik support to help defeat Kornilov. It now felt obliged to release imprisoned left-wing socialist leaders and arrest some right-wing politicians. Kerensky found himself and his government trapped in the "no enemies on the Left" syndrome, which tied his hands. By September the Provisional Government had no active support from any large section of society. By trying to satisfy all, it had alienated both its upper-class supporters, whose propertied interests it could no longer protect, and working-class Russians, who had waited in vain for the Provisional Government to resolve such key issues as war, land, the food crisis, and the Constituent Assembly. Nor did it have the firm control over the coercive machinery of state needed to impose its will by force. Delivering the lethal blow proved all too easy.

In the aftermath of the failed military coup Bolshevik popularity soared again, and by early September the Bolsheviks for the first time secured a majority in the Petrograd and Moscow Soviets. Encouraged by the indications of a renewed upsurge of Bolshevik support, Lenin, still in hiding, now revived the slogan "All power to the Soviets." Over the next few weeks he bombarded the party's Central Committee with letters, demanding an immediate insurrection of the armed proletariat, the overthrow of "Kerensky and Company," and the seizure of political power:

> The point is to make the task clear to the Party. The present task must be an armed uprising in Petrograd and Moscow (with its region), the seizing of power and the overthrow of the government.
> History will not forgive us if we do not assume power now.[5]

However, the party's Central Committee was not yet totally convinced by Lenin's arguments about the timing of the insurrection. The lessons of the failed "July uprising," which had led to the suppression of the party and arrests of its activists, were still fresh in the minds of the leading Bolsheviks and now made them more cautious. Moreover, some of the Bolshevik leaders had serious doubts about the European proletariat's readiness to support a socialist breakthrough in Russia by rising in an "international proletarian revolution." Indeed, they were unsure even of their support among Petrograd workers. Two members of the Bolshevik Central Committee in particular, Zinoviev and Kamenev, counseled patience, proposing to wait for elections to the Constituent Assembly, or at least the planned meeting of the Second Congress of Soviets. They argued that by using the elections and by relying on their majority in the Soviets the Bolsheviks could seize power gradually and peacefully without resorting to arms.

Frustrated by these objections, Lenin, on 10 October, returned incognito to the capital to attend a Central Committee meeting that was to consider the issue of the insurrection. His ferocious argumentation succeeded in sweeping aside the hesitations of his comrades and persuading the Bolshevik Central Committee to adopt his line for an immediate armed uprising. However, their decision was not unanimous, as Kamenev and Zinoviev still voted against the decision and publicized this fact in the press. Their behavior showed that, despite his prestige, Lenin's authority was by no means absolute.

By the middle of October, the Bolsheviks had established their firm control over the Petrograd Soviet. Its newly elected chairman was Lev Trotsky, a Bolshevik leader whose standing in the party was by now second only to that of Lenin. A maverick Marxist, Trotsky had finally joined the Bolshevik Party in July. Together with Lenin they made a formidable team — the two most determined and possibly most brilliant of Russia's revolutionary leaders, totally committed to an immediate overthrow of capitalism.

On 12 October 1917 the Petrograd Soviet elected a MILITARY-REVOLUTIONARY COMMITTEE (MRC), nominally to defend Petrograd against counterrevolution and a possible German assault. Its real task, however, was to plan the armed insurrection. The MRC was dominated by Bolsheviks, but it also contained some radical Socialist-Revolutionaries who supported plans to depose the Provisional Government by force. The Mensheviks and the majority of the Socialist-Revolutionaries, however, were strongly against the Bolshevik plan and refused to join. Led by Trotsky, the MRC coordinated the activities of the pro-Bolshevik troops and detachments of the "RED GUARDS" (a part-time militia formed mainly from younger factory workers) on the eve of and during the Bolshevik takeover. It asserted its military control over the capital by appointing commissars, or representatives, to all military units of the Petrograd garrison. These persuaded most units to obey them rather than the Provisional Government. Thus the Provisional Government was effectively deprived of control over its troops.

By the middle of October it was an open secret in Petrograd that the Bolsheviks were getting ready for a coup. The denouement was finally triggered on 24 October by Kerensky, who ordered progovernment soldiers to close down Bolshevik newspapers. At this critical moment, the MRC called upon Red Guards and troops loyal to it to resist the attack and reopen the presses. The government's efforts to reassert its control over the capital were successfully rebuffed. On the evening of the 24th, seizing the initiative from the Provisional Government, the Military-Revolutionary Committee, under Trotsky's command, directed its detachments — formed of workers, revolutionary soldiers, and sailors of the Baltic fleet — to take over the nerve centers of the capital, including the railway stations, the bridges, the central post office, the central telephone exchange, and the electric power stations. There was hardly any resistance as they took control over the capital. That night Lenin himself left his hiding place wearing a disguise and traveled by tram to the MRC headquarters at the building of the former Smolny Institute, where he took charge of the insurrection.

The uprising ended with the virtually bloodless storming of the Winter Palace, where Kerensky and the ministers of the Provisional Government were meeting. Pro-Bolshevik units stormed it during the evening of 25 October. All the ministers of the Provisional Government were arrested except Kerensky, who had managed to escape in a car provided by the United States embassy.

Shortly before the storming of the Winter Palace, a Second All-Russian Congress of Soviets of Workers' and Soldiers' Deputies had assembled in the capital. When news came of the overthrow of Kerensky's cabinet, the minority of moderate socialists at the congress denounced Lenin's seizure of power and walked out. However, the majority, made up predominantly of Bolsheviks with a substantial bloc of radical, left-wing Socialist-Revolutionaries, endorsed the coup and approved the formation of a Bolshevik Government — the COUNCIL OF PEOPLE'S COMMISSARS — empowered to rule Russia until the convocation of the Constituent Assembly. The congress also passed the first two decrees of the new Bolshevik Government: the Decree on Peace, which called on peoples and governments of the belligerent countries to conclude a "democratic peace without annexations and indemnities," and the Decree on Land, which authorized the redistribution of the gentry's land to the peasantry.

The Bolshevik seizure of power set Russian history off on new and uncharted paths. Most of the leaders of the new working-class government came from the radical intelligentsia, yet they claimed to represent the peasants and workers of the Russian Empire. The new ruling elite pledged to build an entirely new type of government, the likes of which had never existed before. It claimed that for the first time in human history a government would serve the interests not of a privileged, exploiting minority, but of the overwhelming working-class majority of society.

Interpretations of the Revolution

Contrary to Lenin's expectations, the victory of the Bolsheviks in Russia failed to ignite the world proletarian revolution. It did, however, produce earthshaking ramifications that have dominated world history ever since. It has also, inevitably, like any other event of such a historic magnitude, given rise to major controversies among historians, politicians, and others about the nature and aims of the Russian Revolution. Much of the discussion turns on the question of the inevitability of Bolshevism. Was the Bolshevik path the only possible way forward for Russia after the collapse of the monarchy in February 1917? Was there any realistic alternative to Bolshevism? What were, for example, the chances for the establishment in Russia of parliamentary democracy on the Western European model? Alternatively, were there inherent factors in the structure of Russian society that ruled out the possibility of its following the capitalist path of development of Western Europe?

This is one set of questions that fuel controversies about the "October Socialist Revolution." The diversity of answers to these questions can be reduced to two diametrically opposed approaches: DETERMINIST versus NONDETERMINIST. The most obvious example of a determinist explanation of the Russian Revolution is the view based on the Marxist interpretation of history that was promulgated by official Soviet historiography until the collapse of the Soviet Union in 1991. In this view, both the "bourgeois-democratic" revolution of February and the "proletarian-socialist" revolution of October were preconditioned by the whole course of Russian, indeed world, history. The Russian people simply had no option, no alternative, to socialist revolution in 1917.

Nondeterminist historians do not accept that the Russian Revolution was inevitable. They tend to stress the small scale of the Bolshevik rising. They do not deny that it was highly significant, but question whether it was truly a mass movement and point to the fact that the Bolshevik government could sustain itself in power only by adopting a policy of state terror. The nondeterminist view is associated with writers such as the American scholar Richard Pipes. In 1992 he expressed his view of the origins of the revolution and its importance in these words:

> The Russian Revolution was made neither by the forces of nature nor by anonymous masses but by identifiable men pursuing their own advantages. Although it had spontaneous aspects, in the main it was [the] result of deliberate action. As such it is very properly subject to value judgement.[6]

Between the poles of this basic "determinist versus nondeterminist" dichotomy there is a wide variety of interpretations spanning the entire ideological, political, and intellectual spectrum. Some of the more influential, or insightful, interpretations and argumentations have been the following.[7]

The Traditional Soviet Interpretation

This view was based on a strictly orthodox Marxist-Leninist-Stalinist approach. According to it, the October Revolution was the product of a clearly discernible, irresistible trend in Russian history. The capture of power had been meticulously planned by the party, acting under the guidance of the omniscient, infallible Lenin. The Bolshevik triumph was the inevitable consequence of Russian domestic conditions and at the same time an integral part of the international struggle of the proletariat against the bourgeoisie, with the Russian comrades acting as a vanguard of the world proletarian forces. The Russian workers were victorious because, under the masterly leadership of Lenin and his Bolshevik Party, they dealt a timely blow to the weakest link in the "chain of capitalism." The "Great October Socialist Revolution" ushered in a new era in history, the era of socialism, which would in turn develop into full communism.

In the former Soviet Union this approach was obligatory in the interpretation of the October Revolution. From the late 1920s until the late 1980s all professional historians, researchers, writers, teachers, and students of the revolution inside the Soviet Union were compelled to operate within this ideological and methodological framework, which condemned all other interpretations as "unscientific." The official view of the revolution thereby played a legitimizing role in the monopoly of political power that the Communist Party of the Soviet Union enjoyed until the late 1980s. It consecrated October 1917 as a once-and-forever transmission of democratic legitimacy from people to a party that would rule for as long as it would take to reach socialism, with no need for any "bourgeois" renewal of mandate. The last Soviet leader, Mikhail Gorbachev, for instance, until the very end, always spoke of "the socialist choice made in October."

The "Liberal" School

A liberal counterorthodoxy to the Bolshevik interpretation became established thanks mainly to the efforts of Russian émigré writers and scholars who fled abroad to escape the revolution. Most of them, naturally, bore a grudge against the Soviet regime both for personal and political reasons. They argued that Imperial Russia had been steadily transforming itself into a modern, democratic, industrial society until it was weakened by the Great War and subverted by the Bolsheviks. They saw the October coup as a rather unfortunate reversal of what was presumed to be Russia's painfully slow evolution toward constitutional democracy.

This line of argument gave rise to the emergence of the liberal school of historians, who concentrated their studies on the activities of leading individuals, such as Nicholas II, Kerensky, and Lenin, or on principal groupings such as the Fourth Duma, the Petrograd Soviet, the Provisional Government, and the Bolshevik Central Committee. Liberal analysts reject the determinist view of the Russian Revolution. Instead, they are inclined to see the Bolshevik coup as a result of circumstances, when the weak Provisional Government, the victim of its own errors, was overthrown by the ruthless, cold-blooded determination of a small group of criminal conspirators. The October coup was a reckless but successful gamble by Lenin and his Bolsheviks who were carried to power by a wave of anarchy that they exploited cynically, without any moral scruples.

The "Revisionists"

A Western revisionist view arose in the mid-twentieth century as a reaction to Western liberal scholarship. The "revisionist" historians were no longer satisfied with the liberal school's analysis of the revolution "from above," focused mainly on the actions of leading personalities and activities of major political groupings. They stressed the importance of undertaking a proper analysis of what the ordinary people of Russia — factory workers, land-hungry peasants, conscript soldiers, radicalized sailors, women in bread lines — were thinking and doing in 1917.

This new generation of Western historians has conducted an impressive amount of research in which the revolution has been investigated using a combination of traditional historiography, economic analysis, sociological enquiry, and the methodology of political science. The result has been a meticulously documented view of the revolution "from below," with the focus of attention not on the political "leadership," but on the activities, aspirations, and motives of "ordinary" Russian workers, peasants, soldiers, and sailors, not only in the capital, but also in the regions. Much of this research demonstrates that after the collapse of autocracy Russian society became increasingly polarized along class lines, with the workers, peasants, and conscript soldiers becoming more and more alienated from the Provisional Government — a government of self-appointed middle- and upper-class conservative politicians that continued to defend the interests of the propertied classes. Lenin's slogan of "All power to the Soviets" simply articulated the feeling of the ordinary people that a government of the Soviets — the elected representatives of the plebeian masses — was the preferred alternative. Ronald Suny, a U.S. historian, has expressed this view as follows:

The Bolsheviks came to power not because they were superior ma-
nipulators or cynical opportunists but because their policies, as
formulated by Lenin in April and shaped by the events of the following months, placed them at the head of a genuinely popular
movement.[8]

The revisionists' conclusions to some extent corroborate the classical
Marxist view that masses and classes are central to the revolutionary
process. They also partially echo the view of another, comparatively
neglected school of thought usually described as "libertarian."

The "Libertarian" School and the Theory of "the Unfinished Revolution"

The "libertarian" school presents an anarchistic view of the revolution,
seeing it as an expression of the elemental will of the people. It con-
tends that the revolution, at least in its early stages, was not the result of
conspiracy or political manipulation, but a spontaneous, uncoordinated
plebeian revolt of the Russian people against the Russian state. Even if
the revolution did later deteriorate into a new and perhaps more dread-
ful form of despotism, it began as a genuinely popular revolution whose
origins were to be found on the factory floor, in the village communes,
and in the military barracks of a disintegrating empire.

This line of thought is close to the theory of "the unfinished revolution" associated particularly with the ideas of those sympathetic to
Trotsky. It argues that a genuine workers' revolution occurred in 1917,
but was later betrayed by Lenin's successors. The initial revolutionary
enthusiasm of the workers was destroyed by the deadening rule of the
bureaucratic and repressive Communist Party of the Soviet Union.

Conspiracy Theories

Controversy over the October Revolution has also given rise to a number of conspiracy theories. The most influential of these — the GERMAN
PLOT theory — was expounded by George Katkov, a Russian émigré
writer. He was convinced that the revolution in Russia was brought
about by the machinations of the German Foreign Office and military
high command, which financially underwrote the subversion of Russia's
war effort as part of their clandestine policy of fomenting social and
economic unrest in the enemy country.[9]

The relationship between the Bolshevik Party and the Kaiser's government during the First World War has long been a puzzle for historians. From time to time sensational pieces of information would surface indicating that the German government, interested in weakening the Russian Empire and taking it out of the war, financed the activity of those socialist parties in Russia that waged a sustained propaganda of defeatism. In the second half of the 1950s certain documents came to light that allowed scholars to probe more deeply into the question of the German money and of the legendary "sealed train" in which the group of Russian Bolsheviks under the leadership of Lenin returned to Russia in early April 1917.[10]

The subversive activities of Germany in relation to Russia were part of Germany's more general strategy aimed at weakening its adversaries. Its so-called "peaceful propaganda" was directed not just at Russia, but also, for example, at Romania, Italy, and France. Tens of millions of German marks were spent just to bribe four French newspapers. In Russia, the only paper that appears to have accepted the German money in 1917 was Lenin's *Pravda*.

It was therefore natural for the German government to see a revolution in Russia as a very desirable outcome of its overall subversive strategy. It had every reason to hope that the revolution would lead to the disintegration of the Russian Empire, its withdrawal from the war, and the conclusion of a separate peace treaty promised by the revolutionaries in the event of their coming to power. By 1917 Germany badly needed peace with Russia, for it could no longer afford to wage war on the two fronts.

Thus, gambling on a revolution in Russia, the German government had chosen to support Lenin's grouping in the days and weeks most critical for the survival of the Provisional Government, and it helped Lenin and other "defeatists" to travel across Germany and Sweden and eventually reach Petrograd. The October uprising did not take the German government by surprise. Rightly or not, it viewed the events in Russia as a result of its own subversive strategy.

However, Germany would never have achieved its objective so easily if the interests of the German government had not dovetailed with the plans of the other interested side, that is, of the Russian revolutionaries-defeatists, among whom Lenin's Bolsheviks represented the most influential faction. The German government and the revolutionaries had certain common goals in the war. Both Germany and Lenin's Bolsheviks wished for the defeat of the Russian government. Both Germany and the Bolsheviks worked for the disintegration of the Russian Empire. The Germans wanted it because their aim was to weaken a postwar Russia; the revolutionaries, among whom there were many representatives of ethnic minorities such as Jews, Poles, Balts, Georgians, and Armenians, regarded the growth of nationalist separatist tendencies as an integral part of the revolutionary movement.

But while converging in some points, the aims of Germany and of the Russian revolutionaries were completely different in others. Germany viewed the revolutionaries merely as a tool of subversion to be used to achieve the withdrawal of Russia from the war. It had no desire to help sustain socialists in power in Russia after the war was over. As for the Russian revolutionaries, they regarded the assistance offered by the German government as a means of achieving a revolution in Russia and even in the whole of Europe, and, in particular, in Germany itself. The German government was aware of the socialists' plan to attempt a revolution in Germany. And the Russian revolutionaries knew that the German government would do everything to prevent German socialists from coming to power in Germany and yet would cynically use Russian revolutionaries to achieve its military objectives. Each side hoped to outplay the other. In the final count, it was Lenin's Bolsheviks who outplayed the rest. As a man totally dedicated to the idea of revolution and the seizure of power in Russia, Lenin was prepared to accept help from any quarters to bring closer the cherished goal of revolution.

The other conspiracy theory, which sees the Russian Revolution as a result of a JEWISH PLOT, originated with the Russian nationalists of the far Right. It feeds on the contemptible anti-Semitic attitudes that had been in evidence at least as far back as the First Russian Revolution of 1905, culminating in pogroms against the Jews.

It must be said that the last two tsars did a lot by their oppressive policies to radicalize Jewish intellectuals. By the start of the First World War, five million Jews — half of the world's Jewish population — lived in Russia. They were forced to live in the Pale of Settlement, a large territory in the western part of the empire, and were subject to numerous special laws against them. Forbidden to reside in major Russian cities, barred from owning land, not allowed to become government bureaucrats or military officers, Russian Jews had developed a natural grudge against the tsarist authorities. Recurrent pogroms after 1881 killed hundreds of Jews and pushed many to emigrate to the United States.

No wonder that Jewish radicals came to play a prominent role in the revolutionary movement in Russia alongside other representatives of national minorities such as Poles, Georgians, and Armenians. Most Jewish radicals were Zionists (those who wished to emigrate to Palestine to create a Jewish state) or Bundists (those who wanted to create a socialist autonomous Jewish entity in Eastern Europe or Russia) or Mensheviks. In particular, it was the fact that some Jews became leaders in the Bolshevik Party (among them Trotsky, Zinoviev, Kamenev, Sverdlov, and Radek) which led to the appearance of the Jewish conspiracy theory.

Post-Soviet Russian Interpretations

The controversy over the origins of the Russian Revolution continues unabated and has acquired a particularly direct and vital relevance after the disintegration of the state, which the October Revolution engendered. During the late 1980s inside Russia itself it became increasingly apparent that the traditional Marxist-Leninist orthodoxy was no longer acceptable. Many Russian analysts and politicians nowadays reject the reductionist "red and white" approach, as well as a rigidly determinist view of the revolution. Some tend to see the period between February and October as being pregnant with a number of different possibilities, including a bourgeois-democratic option (epitomized by Kerensky's ministry), a military dictatorship (under Kornilov's command), an all-socialist coalition government (such as the "homogeneous socialist government" advocated by moderate socialist leaders like Martov), and the radical left alternative associated with Lenin and his Bolsheviks.[11]

It was this last alternative that eventually became the reality. It is hardly possible to single out one decisive factor of the Bolshevik triumph in October 1917. The Bolshevik victory was the result of a combination of factors, including the inability of the Provisional Government to rule decisively at the time of a national crisis, the unwillingness of the propertied classes to satisfy expectations of the working classes, the radicalism of the latter, the support of the Bolsheviks by garrison troops in major cities, confusion in the ranks of the Mensheviks and Socialist-Revolutionaries, and the political skills and determination of the Bolshevik leaders Lenin and Trotsky.

It is possible to analyze the staggering complexity and variety of the contradictions that caused the Russian Revolution by grouping them into categories or presenting them as a hierarchy of layers.[12] The top group of tensions was generated by the need to overcome the country's backwardness and catch up with the group of leading industrialized nations (in such spheres as technological progress, labor productivity, general literacy of the population, and the development of democratic institutions). Russia was again confronted with the historical challenge of making a new revolutionary leap similar in scale to the one it had accomplished in the time of Peter the Great. The pressures of modernization affected Russian society as a whole. They were felt particularly acutely by those social groups within it that were interested in preserving and strengthening a great state, in maintaining its unity and cohesion, and in enhancing its role in the international scene. Striving to accelerate Russia's development along the common vector of world civilization, Russia's progressives belonging to all classes understood that absolutism and the vestiges of feudalism in the countryside and on the empire's fringes were the main obstacles to its successful advance.

The second group of contradictions was represented by internal social antagonisms. The most serious among them were the tensions between peasants and landowners, between workers and capitalist employers, between town and country, between the imperial center and the fringes. The internal schisms were revealed in the struggle of different social forces, between different political parties and programs covering a broad political spectrum, from liberal and democratic agendas to radical blueprints of the extreme Left. As modernizing trends of the early twentieth century began to affect Russia deeper and deeper, the struggle over different visions of the country's future, over different prescriptions for the transformation of its economic and political systems, intensified.

The third group of contradictions was generated by the situation in which the country found itself as a result of the Great War. The mounting economic dislocation, the threat of starvation, the war fatigue, the great human toll of millions of the dead and wounded, and the disaffection with the aims of the war enhanced the rebellious mood of different sections of the population, making a social explosion almost unavoidable.

The cumulative effect of all these diverse tangles of conflicts and contradictions generated a tidal wave of revolution with more and more sections of society openly voicing their protest and actively engaging in the anti-autocratic movement. With the collapse of the monarchy in February, it became increasingly obvious that the unfolding revolution could not be easily defined in terms of any particular social characteristic. It did not conform to any of the usual labels, such as "bourgeois-democratic," "proletarian," or "national-liberation," but revealed the characteristics of many. As the revolutionary process deepened, it became possible to discern within it various strands and currents that were relatively independent and formed "minor revolutions" that made up the great revolution. The currents were rising in the cities (the proletarian current), in the countryside (the peasant current), on the ethnic fringes (the national-liberation movement), and in the army (the antiwar movement). All of them were engendered by their specific social, class, and group interests, but in their entirety they imparted to the events in Russia the scale and the magnitude that justified the name of a "great revolution."

The Russian character of that revolution was revealed in the specific combination of its causes and contradictions, and in the mentality and social behavior of the masses and of the individuals who led them. It was exposed in the way in which the revolution blended together anti-feudal and anti-capitalist aspirations, and general democratic and narrow class interests. It engaged various sections of the population, including the bourgeoisie and the middle and working classes. Different sections of the population joined the revolution at different stages. The revolution was initiated by the liberal bourgeoisie, by groups of the intelligentsia (civil servants, professionals, members of the military), factory workers, and soldiers of the Petrograd garrison. The waves of the revolution spread from the center to the provinces and then to the empire's periphery. Some of the groups participating in the revolution infused it with the spirit of spontaneous, destructive, Pugachev-style insurrection reminiscent of the age-old Russian revolt against the authorities and traditions. Others introduced the element of terrorism and regicide associated with the Narodnik stage of the revolutionary movement. Still others brought with them the experience of class struggle gained during the years of the First Russian Revolution of 1905–7. Each group had its own program of rejuvenating society. Some adhered to the collectivist principles of Russia's traditional society (the peasantry, the Socialist-Revolutionaries); others wished to emulate Western models of capitalism and democracy (the new business classes, the Kadets); still others advanced utopian communist blueprints (some groups of workers, the Bolsheviks). All aspired to the role of leaders of the revolutionary movement.

The bewildering complexity of different strands of the revolution had laid it open to the dangers that threatened it not from without — that is, not from the camp of the counterrevolution (the pro-tsarist forces were crushed relatively quickly and easily) — but from within, from the tensions generated by the infighting and discord among the different currents of the revolution themselves. The main problem was not the resistance of the fragmented supporters of the old regime, but the inability of the main political forces, parties, and leaders to control the tide of the revolution in order to avert the complete disintegration of society. Russian society, which pinned such hopes on revolution, was devoured by the revolution that it had itself produced.

Each of the different interpretations discussed above is important, for each provides a penetrating insight into a particular aspect or dimension of this cataclysmic event and thus helps our better understanding of the revolution. It is unlikely that the controversy over the October Revolution will ever cease or be finally resolved. For some, it will remain a mystery, even a miracle. Yet many of the existing interpretations seem to agree on one point: that it was Lenin who out of all people contributed the most to making this miracle happen. Lenin created the Bolshevik Party in 1903. He held it together during the years of exile. He gave it a political program that gained working-class support. Most importantly, in 1917 he provided decisive leadership at critical moments. He was never tired of repeating to his comrades Marx's words about insurrection, "Insurrection is an art," and this is exactly how he treated and prepared the armed seizure of power in Petrograd.

Finally, and maybe crucially, Lenin gave his followers a new theory that discarded the major Marxist tenet that the proletarian revolution could only take place after an accumulation of the material prerequisites of socialism. Lenin said that the proletariat and his party could take power immediately, without waiting for these "preconditions," and then start the creation of the necessary economic foundations of socialism. The old theory restrained the revolutionary will; the new one completely liberated it. It was his audacity to dismiss "objective prerequisites" and his appeal to his fellow revolutionaries to exercise their active will and thus be the real makers of history that, in the final analysis, made the October Revolution possible.

However, the "revolutionary impatience," which proved so potent in sweeping away the remains of Russia's old regime, was soon to discover its own limits. No amount of revolutionary zeal or political tyranny was enough to build a utopian system that sought to defy basic social, economic, and moral laws of human society.

Conclusion

Paradoxes of the "Fragile Empire"

Tsarist Russia was an empire of great internal contradictions. It was a colossus, which had expanded over one-sixth of the earth's landmass, and yet was ever vulnerable to foreign invasion. It had one of the world's largest populations, yet the majority of its people lived in poverty and discontent. It commanded the world's richest natural resources, yet its productive forces were severely constricted by the remnants of feudalism. It strove to cement its multiethnic population by systematic Russification, but this only stimulated nationalist movements. It tried to portray its political system as "people's autocracy" at a time when the regime was becoming increasingly "detached" from its people. The gigantic empire of the tsars became ever more fragile and vulnerable until it was shattered to pieces in the turmoil of war and revolution. This concluding part brings together the main lines of argument and draws conclusions in the form of paradoxes which are, to paraphrase Shakespeare, such stuff as Russian history is made on.

The Beggarly Empire

In early Russia, in contrast to Western Europe, where flourishing towns and trade links were the cementing force that bound the edifice of national states, the unification of the Russian principalities around Moscow proceeded mainly under the pressure of external political factors. The constant threat of military invasion put heavy demands on the Russian people, which had to strain its limited economic and human resources, scattered over a vast territory, to maintain its sovereignty. National security interests required from this poor, sparsely populated agrarian country the ability to mobilize all available resources at times of military emergency. The solution of how to maintain its military security was found in the creation of a special warrior-class bound by the obligations of military service to the state. As a reward for their ser-

vice and to provide them with an income, the state granted to members
of the military class land and peasants to work it. A system thus took
shape that featured a ruler with sweeping powers, a nobility based on
service to the state, and a peasantry, increasingly tied to land owned by
the nobility.

As the tsarist empire grew, so did the state's expenses. Seeking to secure their income, the state and the ruling military class tightened their
grip over the peasants, and eventually a considerable part of Russian
peasantry became bonded to their squires or the state. The Russian peasants were fully and completely enserfed by the articles of the new legal
code of Tsar Alexis, father of Peter the Great, in 1649, the very year in
which a "bourgeois" revolution occurred in England bringing about the
overthrow of the king. In contrast to the West, where social progress
was achieved through the natural development of economic relations,
the Russian state drew its strength and vitality from the use of non-
economic methods. Force, repression, coercion, and further enserfment
of the mass of the population became the chief means by which Russia
developed its productive forces. The clearest illustration of this is Peter
the Great's era. Under him Russia built up its industry, expanded its military might, and established itself as one of the great powers of Europe.
At the same time the mass of Russia's peasants found itself increasingly
bound by the restrictions of serfdom. The population was treated by
the despotic state merely as building material for the establishment of a
grand empire.

At the turn of the eighteenth century Russia's transformation into a
powerful empire with a leading role in world politics was complete. Its
position as one of the continent's three or four greatest military powers
was universally recognized. Russia had acquired vast new territories;
its economic and human resources had increased considerably. Yet the
main features of Russian life remained the same. The great empire was
a poor, backward country with a predominantly agricultural economy
and rural population. The potential of the traditional system had been
exhausted. Catherine the Great's attempts to infuse it with the liberal
spirit of the Enlightenment failed. With the impact of the French Revolution, Russian absolutism became unenlightened and reactionary. Having
at least to some degree assisted the development of the Russian Empire in the first century of its existence, the autocracy now became a
dead weight on progress in all the major sectors of the national life.
In the economic sphere, serfdom was now clearly the chief obstacle to
the process of modernization of the country. The perpetuation of the
twin institutions of autocracy and serfdom led to the ever widening gap

in levels of development between Russia and the leading countries of Western Europe.

The peasant emancipation of 1861 was a major turning point in Russian history. The Russian peasants were finally given their personal freedom. Yet the government did all it could to compensate the landowners for the loss of their servile labor and make the peasantry shoulder the burden of this compensation. The contradictory nature of the peasant reform aggravated the traits of backwardness in village life and in the final analysis led to a deeper crisis. By conserving some of the elements and relations of the old serfdom system the peasant reform hindered the development of the institution of small- and medium-scale private ownership, particularly the ownership of land. Village communes adhered to archaic production methods that perpetuated the backwardness of the rural economy and the poverty of the peasants. By the end of the century the economic well-being of the peasantry further deteriorated as a result of a vast increase in the size of the population and the growing burden of taxation imposed by the government to finance its ambitious industrialization program. The Great Famine of 1891–92, which struck twenty provinces of Russia, was symptomatic of the severity of problems in the countryside.

In the early twentieth century, although capitalism was making rapid progress in Russia, the agrarian sector continued to dominate the national economy. Although Russia had become a more urbanized society, about four-fifths of the population continued to live in rural communities. The overwhelming majority of the population (73.7 percent according to the 1897 census) was illiterate. Socially segregated from the rest of society, the peasants, many of whom were born under serfdom, remained the "dark people" — a medieval element surviving into the dawning of the modern era. After 1907, the Stolypin plan authorized the destruction of the commune as a way to create a new class of independent, economically viable proprietors in the countryside, who would be attached to the principle of private property. Yet this step, desirable as it was, was far too little and too late. In addition, the reform added new problems to the old by helping to stratify the peasant masses, creating hostility between different groups of peasants. Contrary to the government's expectations, the projected bulwark against an agrarian revolution in the shape of a class of small independent capitalist farmers was never erected.

In towns, the continuing industrialization accelerated the growth of the class of urban wage workers, many of whom were proletarians of the first generation, who had recently arrived from the countryside. So

novel was the class of factory workers to Russia that there was no legal
provision that would have defined its place in Russia's social structure:
in their passports the workers were referred to by the traditional labels as peasants or town-dwellers. Though still a small proportion of
the population, the urban working class assumed an increasingly significant political role due to its high concentration in the two main nerve
centers of the country, St. Petersburg and Moscow. At the beginning
of the twentieth century the Russian working class remained the most
oppressed, impoverished, and discontented in Europe. Much of its dissatisfaction arose from Russia's lack of any proper labor legislation that
would regulate relations between capitalists and workers. There was no
legal provision for the operation of trade unions, for national insurance
covering illness and work-related accidents, or for a system of old-age
pensions. If the government had had the wisdom to give thought to
sponsoring comprehensive labor legislation of this kind, it is possible
that this policy might have diffused an explosive social situation.

In Russia the divide between the working classes of peasantry and the
proletariat and the rest of the population was particularly deep, for here
the remnants of feudal customs and practices coexisted with and were
aggravated by the predatory methods of Russia's capitalism in the early
stages of its development. The absence of civil rights, the economic and
social inequality perpetuated by outmoded social legislation, the government's inability to regulate the relations between different social groups
and to curb the excessive exploitation of wage labor, and the destitution
and poverty exacerbated by social divisions all heightened the rebellious
mood of the people and forced them to adopt a radical, revolutionary
course of struggle for their legitimate demands.

In the early twentieth century, the unprecedented rise of popular discontent erupted into three revolutions in the space of twelve years,
from 1905 to 1917. Popular movements became breeding grounds for
ultra-radical elements that manipulated the public consciousness and the
social behavior of the masses. The middle class was too small to serve
as a balance to radical, extremist slogans. Angered at the regime's age-
long neglect of the peasant problem and frustrated by its inability to
offer legislative protection against abuses by factory owners, Russia's
peasants and workers lent a ready ear to the radicals' call "Expro-
priate the expropriators!" and to the provocative Bolshevik battle cry
"Loot the loot!" In February 1917 the social explosion, ignited by the
protesting women in Petrograd bread lines, culminated in the inglori-
ous collapse of the great empire of the tsars, which had failed to ensure

basic rights and decent standards of living to the mass of its working population.

Polyethnic Monolith

The great social divide between Russia's ruling classes and its people was, arguably, the chief reason for the vulnerability of the tsarist empire. Yet social antagonisms, which were tearing Russian society apart, were further compounded by mounting ethnic tensions. Pre-Petrine Russia was a relatively homogeneous country in terms of its population (predominantly Slavic) and its religion (Orthodox Christianity). Russia's continual territorial expansion, particularly starting from Peter the Great's reign onwards, began to transform a Slavic state into a multi-ethnic empire. Toward the end of the eighteenth century Russia saw a steep rise in its population, which was partly natural and partly the consequence of that imperial drive. The incorporation of Lithuania and White Russia brought in more than 5 million people and that of the Right-Bank Ukraine nearly 3.5 million. The cultural and religious diversity of the population of these newly acquired Baltic and Polish lands was staggering. These areas were inhabited by Poles and Lithuanians, who were Roman Catholics, Ukrainians belonging to the Uniate Church, Estonians and Latvians, who were Lutherans, and Jews. In the nineteenth century, the incorporation of regions as different as Finland and Georgia, Bessarabia and Azerbaidjanian khanates, and Armenia and the Kazakh lands still further increased the extraordinary ethnic, religious, cultural, and linguistic complexity of the empire.

By the start of the twentieth century the political map of the Russian Empire looked like a monolithic unitary state. Yet, in actual fact, it accommodated within its borders very different lands, from territories that were home to ancient civilizations to almost unpopulated areas to the east of the Ural Mountains. According to the 1897 census Russia had a population of 128 million, and in 1914, 178 million. It had one of the most diverse and heterogeneous ethnic mixes in the world, with over a hundred peoples and dozens of distinct ethnic identities with distinctive linguistic, religious, and cultural qualities. Russia's peoples had very different pasts. Some used to have their own centuries-old statehood, while others were at the stage of the disintegration of tribal society. They belonged to different races and linguistic families. They differed in national mentality and held different religions. Russia's Christians were Orthodox, Uniate, Catholic, and Protestant, not to mention adherents of numerous Christian sects. Significant sections of the empire's population adhered to Islam, Judaism, Buddhism, and other religions and creeds.

This multiethnic empire had evolved as a result of a contradictory process of state-building, which cannot be reduced to such simplified definitions as "voluntary reunification" or "forced annexation." Some peoples found themselves incorporated in the empire because of their geographical proximity, common economic interests, or long-standing cultural ties with Russia. To others, engaged in interethnic or religious conflicts with neighbors, Russia's protection offered a chance to survive. Others still had been incorporated as a result of conquest or collusion between Russia and the other great powers.

All this incredible cultural diversity existed within the confines of one unitary state fused together by the autocratic power of Russian rulers. The only national region that was allowed to retain its special legislation, a representative assembly, and its own monetary system was Finland. (However, its autonomy was constantly under threat, and the Russian government's attempt to impose on it harsh Russification, particularly in the period between 1898 and 1905, provoked a violent nationalist backlash.) The internal autonomy of Poland was abolished following the suppression of the national liberation risings of 1830 and 1863. A small number of territories, such as the central Asian khanates of Khiva and Bukhara, were under Russia's protectorate. The remaining ethnic territories on the empire's fringes were incorporated as administrative regions ruled by governors-general appointed from the imperial capital of St. Petersburg.

The singularity of Russia's geographical location meant that the growth of the empire took a direction unfamiliar to Western Europeans. Russia acquired colonies not overseas but along its frontiers, with the result that metropolis and empire became territorially indistinguishable. This type of colonial expansion left Russians with an imperial mentality. For most Russians, and in particular for the Russian political elite, national identity became inextricably linked with the notion of empire. The English and the French had no doubt where they stood in relation to their colonies, for they never identified the colonies with the homeland. By contrast, the Russians, who have always lived among non-Russians, have for centuries equated their national state with an empire. The empire *was* their mother country.

The Russian imperial mentality underpinned the nationalities policy of the ruling circles and of the imperial government, which was built on the principles of great-power chauvinism. The Russian language was made the official language of state, and Orthodoxy claimed the status of the empire's ruling religion. Russian officialdom treated non-Russians patronizingly and contemptuously as "aborigines" and "aliens." The conservative era of Alexander III saw the introduction of a particularly harsh and systematic policy of Russification. Based on the chauvinistic idea of superiority of all things Slavic in general and Russian in particular, the enforced Russification could hardly cement together a multiethnic empire like Russia, where ethnic Russians, at the end of the nineteenth century, made up only 45 percent of the whole population. Jews, Polish Catholics, Baltic Protestants, Central-Asian Muslims — all fell victim in a greater or lesser degree to this ill-conceived policy.

A whole battery of discriminatory legislation was aimed at eradicating various manifestations of non-Russian national identity and un-Orthodox religious practices. The use of the Russian language was imposed in schools, courts of law, and government offices in non-Russian ethnic areas. Centers of minority cultures such as theaters and publishing houses were shut down. Even the East Slavs, Ukrainians, and Belorussians, who were ethnically and culturally most close to Great Russians (i.e., ethnic Russians), were denied their cultural identity and were officially regarded as "Russians," while their language and culture were not recognized as being separate from Russian.

The toughening of the Russification policy at the end of the nineteenth century and early in the twentieth century was also caused by the government's concern over the rise of nationalist movements in regions like the Ukraine, the Caucasus, Poland, the Baltic, and Finland. The authorities were increasingly alarmed at the drive for national rights among millions of non-Russians. Yet the government's policy of systematic Russification not only failed to stem the tide of nationalist unrest, but actually stimulated ever stronger demands for greater cultural and political autonomy. Oppressive Russification generated a vicious circle. On the one hand, the ethnic minorities whose national feelings were offended developed a natural grudge against the tsarist authorities and were forced to protest against the discrimination. The ever-growing number of representatives of national minorities such as Poles, Balts, Georgians, Armenians, and Jews joined Russian radicals and played a prominent role in the revolutionary movement in Russia. On the other hand, the active involvement of ethnic minorities in the activities of the radicals scared the government into adopting even sterner discriminatory measures.

Despite the authorities' preoccupation with maintaining a privileged status for Russians, the nationalities policy had no beneficial effect on the economic well-being of the ethnic Russian population. The standards of living in the Russian heartlands were often lower than on the ethnic periphery. In addition, the incorporation of territories that lagged behind in socioeconomic development or were culturally different conflicted with the country's historic goal of catching up with the leading nations of the West. Only by straining all its economic, demographic, and military resources could it sustain the status of a great power capable of playing an influential role in the international arena and controlling the numerous nationalities that populated its huge territory. In a paradoxical way, the territorial expansion provided Russia with increases in population and an impressive amount of materials, enough to give Russia the status of a great power on the world stage. Yet the growth of the empire was achieved at a crippling social cost, caused mounting ethnic problems, and, in the final analysis, was a factor that did more to constrain, rather than advance, the economic and sociopolitical development of Russia.

The great state, which accommodated the traditions and ways of life of so many different peoples, found it more and more difficult to cope with the pressures of ethnic assimilation and nationalism. It was becoming increasingly vulnerable to the danger of being torn apart by the incompatibility of the diverse cultures brought together into one empire over the course of many centuries. With the collapse of the autocracy in February 1917, followed by the Bolshevik takeover in October, the seemingly monolithic structure of the Russian Empire rapidly unravelled. Fanned by the Bolshevik slogan of the right of nations to self-determination up to the point of secession, aided by the chaos of war and revolution, the national liberation movements on the fringes of the decomposing state spontaneously and instantly destroyed the tsarist colossus from within, splitting it into a multitude of large and small entities (the Russian Soviet Federated Socialist Republic, the Ukraine, Belorussia, Finland, the Baltic states, the newly created republics in Transcaucasia, the North Caucasus, the Volga region, Kazakhstan, and central Asia). Some lands, like Poland and Finland, gained full independence and became sovereign states. Most, however, would succumb to the recentralizing drive of the new communist authorities in Moscow, which would reincorporate them into the Union of Soviet Socialist Republics in the name of "the proletarian internationalist interests." They would finally escape from the tight grip of communist authoritarianism seven decades later, when in 1991 the tsarist empire's successor would itself collapse.

Unlimited Power Limited

Ultimately, it was the power of autocracy that bound together different social strata and various ethnic groups of a gigantic empire. Russian autocracy was a form of absolutist government that derived its sanctity and legitimacy from the concept of the traditional "God-given" power of the Russian tsar and from the claim of the right of succession to the great empires of antiquity. An absolute monarch was the central element in the Russian political system. The Russian autocrat was a towering figure at the pinnacle of the pyramid of state, exercising total power in the country. There were no recognized formal limits on his political authority and no rule of law to curb his arbitrary will. The entire business of government was under his command, and individual liberties of his subjects existed only inasmuch as they were granted by the tsar. In Western Europe, even in the age of absolutism, monarchs had to reckon with the interests of powerful social groups such as the nobility and the bourgeoisie, and they often faced opposition in the form of a parliament, or municipal councils, or self-governing religious bodies. By contrast, the absolute rule of the Russian tsars met with no opposition from society.

A state like the Russian autocracy, which completely dominates society and treats its subjects as its property, stifles the freedom of private and public life, inhibits the development of mature civic consciousness in its subjects, and prevents the emergence of organized associations and self-governing bodies that would represent interests of different sections of society. In short, it suppresses all those things that characterize modern forms of the political life of the state. Modern predemocratic structures began to evolve in Western Europe in the eighteenth century, and by the end of the nineteenth century parliamentary democracies and constitutional monarchies had been established throughout almost all of Europe. Yet Russia, practically right to the very end of tsarism in 1917, remained firmly in the grip of autocracy.

Most of the tsars of the Romanov dynasty were personally well-educated and civilized men and women. Many of them recognized the historical inevitability of political change and came close to the realization of the need to transform Russia into a constitutional monarchy. Thus, Catherine the Great regarded highly Montesquieu's political ideas, including his concept of the separation of powers, and strove to transform Russia's tyrannical government into an enlightened one. Her grandson, Alexander I, entrusted his liberal-minded minister Speransky to draw up plans for a complete reform of the Russian political system. The plans envisaged a separation of powers, local self-government, civil rights for all sections of the population, and a national legislative assembly. Alexander I's nephew, Alexander II, was even seriously considering the introduction of a constitution (Loris-Melikov's plan) when his life was tragically cut short by a terrorist bomb. The great social upheaval of the Revolution of 1905–7 finally compelled his grandson, Nicholas II, to institutionalize the principle of the separation of powers (even then in a very truncated form) and to introduce basic civil freedoms. However, this change was too little and too irresolute to bring Russia's political system up to the standards of the European civilization of the twentieth century. Despite the Petrine Europeanization, Catherine's "enlightened absolutism," Alexander I's liberal aspirations, the liberal reforms under Alexander II, and the constitutional experiment under Nicholas II, the essential features of Russia's political system were still practically unchanged in the early twentieth century from what they had been in the seventeenth century.

In spite of their worthy upbringing and European education (and, one may also add, sometimes non-Russian lineage), the Romanovs remained essentially a very Russian dynasty, whose mentality was deeply rooted in the conditions of life in Russia and whose ability to effect change was severely constricted by Russian realities, such as the special status of the nobility, the country's industrial backwardness, and the conservatism of many sections of the population. Russian absolutism has often been portrayed as the unchallenged authority of the supreme ruler resting on the support of the ruling class of the nobility, or on the balance of power between groups of the nobility and the bourgeoisie, or even on the popular support of the peasantry. However, such characterizations of the three-hundred-year rule of the Romanovs often lose sight of the very significant personal aspect. Each of the Romanovs, despite the seemingly unlimited nature of his or her power, was not absolutely free to do what he or she liked and was often vulnerable and insecure both as a ruler and as a human being.[1] Few of the Romanovs lived to die peacefully. Some of them were murdered as a result of a coup d'état or an assassination (Peter III, Paul I, Alexander II); others were deposed and imprisoned and later killed, like Nicholas II. Others still passed away in rather mysterious circumstances (Peter I, Alexander I, Nicholas I). Only the earliest tsars of the dynasty and also Catherine the Great and Alexander III did not meet their end in some tragic way. Yet even Catherine had to risk her life in the struggle for the throne, while Alexander III, after the murder of his father, made himself a voluntary prisoner at his suburban palace of Gatchina in fear of regicidally inclined revolutionaries.

Even more insecure and dependent on the fortunes and will of the ruler was the position of the tsars' ministers and favorites, such as Speransky, Witte, and Stolypin. These able statesmen had to use all their political skills to preserve the balance between the interests of the ruling elite and the country's national interests, for these often were not the same. Reform-minded officials usually had to elaborate their reform plans in the deep secrecy of government privy committees and were always in danger of incurring the disfavor of their royal patron (Witte), or falling into disgrace and being sent into exile (Speransky), or being assassinated (Stolypin).

By the start of the twentieth century it became manifestly obvious that Russian absolutism was no longer capable of providing effective and competent political leadership for the country in a modern age. Under the Russian system of government the emperor was expected to rule as well as reign. As chairperson of the Russian government, he had to coordinate and manage it effectively, and he bore ultimate responsibility for everything. The Russian administration was a large and quite sophisticated organization carrying out various complicated tasks. By the early twentieth century no human being could have acted as chief executive of the Russian government throughout his or her adult life. The strain of the job was crushing.[2] It is not at all surprising that Nicholas II showed increasing signs of physical and emotional exhaustion. However, brought up to believe fully in the divine origin of autocratic power, Nicholas was probably even psychologically unable to contemplate the possibility of sharing his "God-given" duty of safeguarding his country's destiny with anybody else. The emperor loved his country and served it loyally to the best of his abilities. Yet he was a hostage to the system of government he inherited. His refusal to allow any dilution of his autocratic prerogatives, and his rejection of calls for a Western-style government and a ministry responsible to a majority in the Duma, precipitated a constitutional crisis that cost him his crown and his empire.

Ironically, it was the government-sponsored modernization that brought into stark relief the serious limitations of the autocratic form of government. The tsarist empire's ability to accelerate socioeconomic progress was not matched by the desire to modernize the antiquated political system. As a result of rapid industrialization, Russia's educated society had increased enormously, its composition augmented by the rapid growth of new professional and business groups. And yet the country remained in essence, as before, an autocratic monarchy with no place for either a constitution or parliament. The government's policy of suppressing every current of opposition thought and its refusal to engage in any meaningful political interaction with educated society led to a deepening sociopolitical crisis. There was an urgent need for an institutional framework that would allow the educated and increasingly articulate intelligentsia, landowners, and professionals to express legally their grievances and aspirations. Democratic institutions would have gradually associated these classes with the undertakings of the government, would have given them a sense of participation, and thus would have provided a school of civic activities. In the absence of such a system, a large mass of educated, progressive people was pushed into the ranks of the revolutionary movement. By refusing to grant to its subjects *political* emancipation, by denying the main sections of the population a role in government at an all-Russian level, the autocracy absolved them from civic and political responsibility and delayed the "coming of age" of Russian society. The Imperial Duma, conceded under pressure in 1905, came too late and failed to alter radically the political structure of tsarism. By its very nature, the autocracy proved to be incompatible with modern forms of the political life of the state, for its basic instincts compelled it to suppress and stifle any moves toward a democratic system of government. The most dangerous aspect of the government's position was its naive belief in the loyalty of the masses of the peasants and the conviction that popular discontent was deliberately provoked by the irresponsible agitation of the intelligentsia. The truth of the matter, however, was that the working classes felt increasingly alienated from the regime and were becoming consumed by anti-government attitudes. The mass of rural and urban working people felt oppressed by the state, which imposed heavy economic and fiscal burdens on it, yet was unable to resolve its long-standing problems and respond to its elemental hopes and aspirations. The shooting of the peaceful demonstrators on 9 January 1905 killed Russia's age-old popular trust in the tsar as the people's protector. "Bloody Sunday" thus struck the final nail in the coffin of the patrimonial state. Yet the Russian Empire became neither a nation nor a bourgeois society. The alienation of the Russian population from the tsarist administration — the weakening of a sense of national identity and belonging, which unites the government with society — was at the root of the crisis that crippled Imperial Russia. The incompetent and unpopular regime grew increasingly isolated, its base of support eroding fast from under its feet, until it became completely "detached" from its people. The political bankruptcy of tsarism was starkly and disastrously revealed with the onset of the Great War. The war provided the last mighty push to bring the whole rotten structure tumbling down.

Leaps in Circles

Many contradictions of the modern age are attributable to the fact that peoples and countries had entered it at different levels of development. There was a "top league" of the industrialized nations of Europe and North America, which used their great industrial muscle to spread their political and economic domination over a considerable part of the globe. At the other end, there were colonial countries, for which the contact with Western civilization brought a plundering of their natural resources and exploitation of their populations. There was also a third group of states, in Asia as well as in Europe, which had their own centuries-old history, yet had emerged as actors on the international scene relatively recently. Some countries of that group were in the position of semi-colonies, while others were themselves colonial empires. Yet all of them had one thing in common: they were confronted with the historical challenge of closing the gap with the developed nations.

The countries in that middle group had fallen behind in rates of development for various reasons: Spain, because it had come to depend too much on the exploitation of its vast colonies in Latin America; Japan, due to its self-imposed isolation; Italy, because of political fragmentation; and so on.[3] The main reason, however, was that these states had been slow to modernize the traditional socioeconomic system inherited from the medieval era and had preserved many of its characteristics. They now faced the task of overcoming their backwardness by taking the path of capitalist modernization and following the lead of the advanced industrialized nations. Russia was one of these modernizing, developing states.

From the times of Peter the Great, Russia has made several modernization attempts, seeking a radical restructuring and rejuvenation of all essential spheres of the country's life, from its economy to its political system. However, the problem with all of Russia's modernizing efforts was that reforms were launched too late, when the country was already in the grip of a social and political crisis and when the government was under intense direct pressure either from "below" in the form of mass social discontent or from an external threat or as a consequence of a military defeat. In such exceptional circumstances and under such great pressure the reforming government was compelled to act quickly and in great haste, often without enough time to think through its new policies and their consequences. As a result, the periodically undertaken reforms were never carried out in a comprehensive and consistent manner. Each generation of reformers inherited unresolved problems from previous reform efforts and passed on its own unresolved problems to the next. Not only did every new generation of reformers have to deal with a backlog of accumulated past problems, but it had to draw up a new reform plan for an empire that had grown in the size of its territory and population and that consequently required a restructuring on a bigger scale and of greater complexity than before.

The series of modernization attempts, inaugurated by the "Great Reforms" of the 1860s and 1870s until the Revolution of 1917, are a clear illustration of this pattern. The "Great Reforms" were an attempt on the part of the government of Alexander II to overcome the weakness that had been so patently revealed by the Crimean War. The reform impulse came from the liberally minded aristocratic intellectuals who had debated the main parameters of the reform during the preceding decade. The preparation and implementation of the reform were entrusted to a group of progressively thinking members of the government bureaucracy. The "Great Reforms" abolished serfdom and opened the way for "bourgeois" transformations in the economy and in the judicial system. However, Alexander II's reforms were incomplete. Russia remained a country with an autocratic form of government; no genuinely representative institutions were set up; and no unified government along Western lines was established (the ministers did not work jointly, as a cabinet, but reported individually to the tsar). The traditional system of social estates was preserved, as was communal landholding, which hindered the modernization of agriculture. Moreover, within the government bureaucracy itself the opponents of the reform process gained the upper hand over its supporters with the result that the reforms were not only stopped but to some extent even reversed by the counterreforms of the 1880s and 1890s. The triumph of the conservatives was epitomized in the propagation of the official doctrine of "people's autocracy," which extolled Russia's political system as the most perfect in the world. The political system based on autocracy, the agricultural economy based on the vestiges of serfdom, and the rigid regulation of the economic and social life, which constrained the freedom of the individual, could hardly result in the type of economic modernization and social transformation that Russia needed in order to close the gap with Western Europe.

The terrible famine that struck the Russian countryside in 1891–92 compelled the government to reassess the situation and to embark on a new series of reforms in the second half of the 1890s. The new reform had been masterminded by the minister of finance Sergei Witte, who was in favor of the government's active involvement in directing the industrialization process and who regarded the concentration of unlimited power in the hands of the state as Russia's great advantage and as a way to help the government accomplish the reform. Witte promised that in a decade Russia would catch up with the leading European countries in the level of its economic development. Indeed, Witte's policies (such the establishment of a gold standard and the encouragement of foreign investment) accelerated the economic development of the country. However, the impact of the world economic crisis, the unsuccessful Russo-Japanese War, and the Revolution of 1905–7 forced the government to curtail its experiment of speedy industrialization.

With the start of the twentieth century the reforms in Russia had already to be carried out in conditions of revolution and under the pressures of civil discontent. Witte and Stolypin were the two key reform figures associated with that period. Russia was finally granted a representative assembly in the shape of the State Duma and received a modern-style cabinet of ministers (although responsible to the tsar and not to the Duma). Important agrarian reform got under way. In actual fact, this new spurt of reforms was only a belated attempt to finish the process of transformation begun by the reforms of the 1860s and 1870s. The new reform cycle had one serious limitation, however, which was typical of all previous modernization attempts in Russia: despite the establishment of the Duma, the reforms did not infringe on the autocratic foundations of power. The new policies were not enough to save Russia from another revolutionary crisis. In the conditions of a devastating world war, revolution swiftly overtook reform.

In 1917, the question that Russia faced at critical junctures in its history — reform or revolution? — was decided in favor of revolution. However, in Russia's case this question in itself contains a paradox, for government reforms there have often been equated with revolutions. The unlimited power at the disposal of the autocratic government and the enforced and often brutal manner in which it thrust its reforms upon society generated the perception of them as revolutions from above. They were reforms-revolutions that punctuated Russian history with cyclic regularity. A period of stagnation in the economic and social life, induced by the government's reluctance to pursue change, suddenly gave way in times of crisis to changes so radical that they were perceived as revolutionary by contemporaries and, later, by historians.

The coercive and brutal nature of these transformations meant that Russia's modernization attempts often defeated their main purpose: that of creating conditions for unfettered modern social and economic development.[4] Thus, for example, having abolished serfdom, the government intentionally hindered the destruction of the peasant commune instead of helping create the conditions in which the peasants themselves could choose whether to stay in the commune or leave it. Having conserved the communal relations for half a century after the abolition of serfdom, the government then suddenly decided to eradicate them by imposing on the countryside Stolypin's policy of the forced destruction of the communes.

The perception of government reforms as brutal disruptions of revolutionary magnitude was further enhanced by the fact that reformism induced by the pressure of circumstances produced ill-conceived policies that had not been properly prepared or explained clearly to the population. Thus, for instance, the problem of setting up a representative assembly in Russia was first formulated in the blueprint of government reforms prepared by Speransky as early as at the start of the nineteenth century and then shelved in secret governmental archives and forgotten. After the revolutionary crisis of the early 1880s, the government of Alexander III imposed a virtual ban on any airing in public of the issue of a national representative institution. Even on the eve of the Revolution of 1905 and shortly before the tragic January events of that year, the government flatly rejected proposals for the introduction of some form of parliamentary system in Russia. And then suddenly, just a few months later, the government was compelled to reexamine Speransky's plan, which had been gathering dust for nearly a century, and announce the convocation of a consultative State Duma. Some weeks later still, it was pushed into changing its mind again and promised a legislative State Duma. Thus, a representative parliamentary institution was introduced, as it were, overnight, and political parties were allowed to form in a country that had never had any parliamentary traditions or legal political parties before. Such precipitate reform could not but affect the composition of the Duma and its relations with the government. The political system that emerged after October 1905 was the result of a half-hearted and incomplete reform. It only partially satisfied the demands of society, while it was regarded by the government merely as a forced and temporary concession. The reform "under duress" failed to deliver a workable constitutional system.

The government's policies — based on the elevation of the concept of the so-called people's autocracy, as opposed to Western-type parliamentarianism, and in favor of the government-sponsored industrialization based on rigid state control of industry and finance, as opposed to a "bourgeois" economic modernization — did not enable Russia to catch up with the economically advanced countries or meet the expectations of the business and liberal groups of Russian society. The inability of the authorities to implement vitally needed change opened the way for the advocates of revolution. Russia's progress toward a law-based state, launched by the reforms of the 1860s and 1870s, continued by the political reforms of 1905–7, and then by the February Revolution of 1917, remained incomplete and was aborted in October 1917. The Provisional Government was handed over a tangle of delayed reforms begun soon after the Crimean War and not completed even by the outbreak of the Great War. Yet time was running out for the new government; it was already unable to stop the revolution and keep Russia on the track of liberal transformations. The hardships inflicted by the drawn-out war and the anger stirred up by the humiliation of military defeats produced a tidal wave of discontent that the reformism of the liberal kind could no longer assuage. However, the Bolshevik takeover, which swept away the Provisional Government, was only the dawn of yet another reform-revolution that would propel communist Russia into the position of a world superpower, only to reveal, some decades later, that the reconstituted "Red Empire" was as frail and rotten as its tsarist predecessor.

The inconclusive and contradictory nature of Russia's reform cycles demonstrates the limits of bureaucratic-style modernization and of the pattern of revolution from above as the chief response of backward Russia to the challenge of the West. Even with unlimited human and material resources at its command, the bureaucratic-authoritarian state cannot evoke organized support and popular initiative from the oppressed and fragmented civil society and is compelled to rely on force and coercion in implementing long-overdue reforms. Its belated attempt to prevent or localize the crisis usually just manages to avert a social explosion, after which the reform attempt is abandoned. Yet with every new reform cycle, the unresolved problems multiply and the tangle of contradictions grows. Then comes the moment when all of them burst to the surface, causing a social eruption of an enormous destructive force that sweeps away the fragile fruits of modernization only to reveal abiding traits of Russia's backwardness. Each time backward Russia strives to catch up with and overtake the West, its own backwardness catches up with and overtakes its incipient modernization.

Tables and Statistics

TABLE 1. THE HOUSE OF ROMANOV

Mikhail
1613–45

Alexis
1645–76

Fyodor
1676–82

Peter I
1682–1725
(co-ruled with Ivan V: 1682–89)

EMPERORS OF RUSSIA

Peter I the Great
1721–25

Catherine I
1725–27

Peter II (grandson of Peter I)
1727–30

Anna (daughter of Ivan V)
1730–40

Ivan VI
1740–41

Elizabeth (daughter of Peter I)
1741–61

Peter III (grandson of Peter I)
1761–62

Catherine II the Great
1762–96

Paul I
1796–1801

Alexander I
1801–25

Nicholas I (brother of Alexander I)
1825–55

Alexander II
1855–81

Alexander III
1881–94

Nicholas II
1894–1917

TABLE 2. GROWTH OF THE POPULATION OF THE RUSSIAN EMPIRE[1]

Year	*1500*	*1700*	*1800*	*1897*	*1914*
Population size	6 million	13 million	37 million	128 million	178 million

TABLE 3. PERCENTAGE OF URBAN AND RURAL POPULATIONS IN THE EUROPEAN PART OF THE RUSSIAN EMPIRE[2]

	1800	*1897*
Urban population	5%	13%
Rural population	95%	87%

TABLE 4. THE SEVEN BIGGEST CITIES IN THE EUROPEAN PART OF THE RUSSIAN EMPIRE IN 1897 (IN MILLIONS OF INHABITANTS)[3]

St. Petersburg	1.26
Moscow	1.04
Warsaw	0.68
Odessa	0.40
Lodz	0.31
Riga	0.28
Kiev	0.25

TABLE 5. THE TEN LARGEST NATIONALITIES IN THE EUROPEAN PART OF THE RUSSIAN EMPIRE IN 1897 (IN MILLIONS)[4]

	Size of population
Russians	55.4
Ukrainians	22.0
Poles	7.9
Belorussians	5.8
Jews	3.8
Tartars	3.8
Germans	1.8
Bashkirs	1.4
Latvians	1.4
Lithuanians	1.3

TABLE 6. PRINCIPAL LANGUAGES AND RELIGIONS
OF THE RUSSIAN EMPIRE IN 1897[5]

Language*	Entire population — 100%
Russian	47%
Ukrainian	19%
Belorussian	5%
Other	29%

*That is, the language given by the respondents of the 1897 census as their mother tongue.

Religion	Entire population — 100%
Orthodox	70.8%
Catholics	8.9%
Muslims	8.7%
Other	11.6%

TABLE 7. SOCIAL STRUCTURE OF THE RUSSIAN EMPIRE IN 1897
AS DEFINED BY OFFICIAL CATEGORIES[6]

Official categories	%
Hereditary nobles	1.0
Nonhereditary nobles and nonnoble bureaucrats	0.5
Christian priests	0.5
Hereditary and nonhereditary "honored citizens"	0.3
Merchants	0.2
Petty commercial classes	10.6
Peasants in rural areas	70.1
Peasants in towns	7.0
Cossacks	2.3
Settlers	6.6
Foreigners	0.5
Others (unclassifiable)	0.4

TABLE 8. SOCIAL STRUCTURE OF THE RUSSIAN EMPIRE IN 1897
AS DEFINED BY CLASS[7]

Classes of population	%
Ruling class (tsar, court, and government)	0.5
Upper class (nobility, higher clergy, military officers)	12.0
Commercial class (merchants, factory owners, financiers)	1.5
Working class (factory workers and small traders)	4.0
Peasants (land dwellers and agricultural workers)	82.0

TABLE 9. GROWTH INDICES OF SOME INDUSTRIES IN RUSSIA
IN 1890–1900 AND IN 1905–13[8]

	1890	1900	1905	1913
Pig iron	100	314	100	169
Coal	100	269	100	193
Steel	100	586	100	213
Petroleum	100	275	100	122
Sugar consumption	100	197	100	144
Cotton consumption	100	193	100	155
Tobacco	100	119	100	147

TABLE 10. INDUSTRIAL OUTPUT IN THE RUSSIAN EMPIRE
(BASE UNIT OF 100 IN 1900)[9]

1900	1904	1905	1906	1909	1911	1912	1913
100	109.5	98.2	111.7	122.5	149.7	153.2	163.6

TABLE 11. DEVELOPMENT OF PUBLIC EDUCATION IN RUSSIA
IN 1894–1914 (MILLIONS OF PUPILS/STUDENTS)[10]

	1894	1914
Primary schools	3.275	6.416
Secondary schools	0.224	0.733
Higher educational institutions	0.014	0.089

TABLE 12. RUSSIAN GOVERNMENT IN 1725[11]

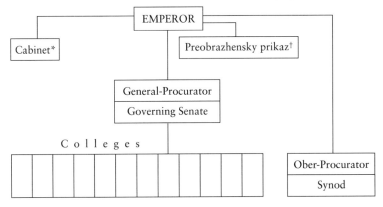

*"Cabinet" was initially Peter I's personal chancellery.
†Preobrazhensky prikaz was in charge of investigating political crimes.

TABLE 13. RUSSIAN GOVERNMENT IN THE NINETEENTH CENTURY[12]

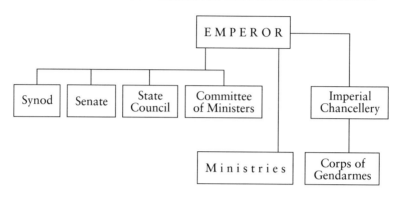

TABLE 14. RUSSIAN GOVERNMENT IN 1906–17[13]

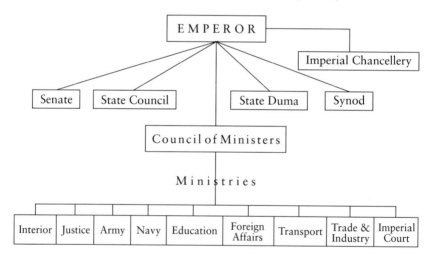

Notes

Introduction

1. Martin Malia, *The Soviet Tragedy: A History of Socialism in Russia, 1917–1991* (New York: Free Press, 1994), 58.

2. Cited in Mikhail Iroshnikov and others, *The Sunset of the Romanov Dynasty* (Moscow: TERRA, 1992), 10.

3. See M. M. Gorinov and L. M. Liashenko, *Istoria Rossii, chast' I: Ot drevney Rusi k imperatorskoy Rossii* (A History of Russia, part 1: From ancient Rus to Imperial Russia) (Moscow: Obshchestvo "Znanie" Rossii, 1994), 18.

4. On the concept of Russian patrimonialism, see Richard Pipes, *Russia under the Old Regime* (London: Penguin, 1990).

1. Peter the Great

1. Stephen Lee, *Peter the Great* (London: Routledge, 1993), 68.

2. See S. V. Kuleshov and others, *Nashe Otechestvo, chast' I* (Our Motherland, part 1) (Moscow: TERRA, 1991), 56.

3. Vladimir I. Lenin, *Polnoe sobranie sochineniy* (Complete works) (Moscow, 1958–65), 36:301.

4. Vasili Klyuchevsky, *Peter the Great* (London: Macmillan; New York: St. Martin's Press, 1969), 271.

5. Tibor Szamuely, *The Russian Tradition* (London: Secker & Warburg, 1974), 108.

6. *Obshchestvennye dvizhenia v Rossii v pervuiu polovinu XIX veka* (Social movements in Russia in the first half of the nineteenth century) (St. Petersburg, 1905), 1:109, 112–13.

7. Cited in Mikhail Iroshnikov and others, *The Sunset of the Romanov Dynasty* (Moscow: TERRA, 1992), 12.

8. Klyuchevsky, *Peter the Great,* 263.

9. Cited in Szamuely, *The Russian Tradition,* 110.

10. Cited in A. A. Kara-Murza and L. V. Poliakov, *Reformator: Russkie o Petre I* (The Reformer: Russians on Peter I) (Ivanovo: Fora, 1994), 103.

11. Peter Chaadaev, "Apology of a Madman," in *The Mind of Modern Russia: Historical and Political Thought of Russia's Great Age,* ed. Hans Kohn (New York: Harper & Row, 1962), 53.

12. Cited in Marc Raeff, ed., *Peter the Great: Reformer or Revolutionary?* (Boston: n.p., 1963), 82.

13. Cited in David Christian, *Imperial and Soviet Russia* (London: Macmillan, 1997), 66.

14. Cited in Kara-Murza and Poliakov, *Reformator,* 153.

15. Ivan Kireevsky, "Letter to Count E. E. Komarovskii," in *Russian Intellectual History: An Anthology,* ed. Marc Raeff (New York: Harcourt, Brace & World, 1966), 176.

16. Cited in Kara-Murza and Poliakov, *Reformator,* 172.

17. Nicholas A. Berdyaev, *Istoki i smysl russkogo kommunizma* (The origin of Russian communism) (Moscow: Nauka, 1990), 12.

18. Maximilian Voloshin, "Rossia" (Russia), *Yunost* 10 (1988): 78.

19. I. A. Il'in, *Nashi zadachi* (Our tasks) (Moscow, 1992), 1:286–87.

20. Cited in Kara-Murza and Poliakov, *Reformator,* 165.

21. Cited in Raeff, *Peter the Great,* 88.

22. Cited in Kara-Murza and Poliakov, *Reformator,* 61.

23. Klyuchevsky, *Peter the Great,* 270.

2. Catherine the Great

1. Vasili Klyuchevsky, *Peter the Great* (London: Macmillan; New York: St. Martin's Press, 1969), 249.

2. Cited in A. A. Kara-Murza and L. V. Poliakov, *Reformator: Russkie o Petre I* (The Reformer: Russians on Peter I) (Ivanovo: Fora, 1994), 32.

3. Cited in S. V. Kuleshov and others, *Politicheskaia istoria: Rossia–SSSR–Rossiiskaia Federatsia* (A political history: Russia–USSR–Russian Federation) (Moscow: TERRA, 1996), 1:145.

4. Tibor Szamuely, *The Russian Tradition* (London: Secker & Warburg, 1974), 113–14.

5. Richard D. Charques, *A Short History of Russia* (n.p.: Phoenix House, 1956), 117.

6. Cited in Sheila Jones, *A Student's History of Russia* (Oxford: Pergamon, 1966), 73.

7. Isabel de Madariaga, *Russia in the Age of Catherine the Great* (London: Weidenfeld and Nicolson, 1981), 587.

8. M. M. Bogoslovsky, *Byt i nravy russkago dvorianstva v pervoy polovine XVIII veka* (Life and customs of the Russian gentry in the first half of the eighteenth century) (Moscow, 1904), 37–38.

3. Alexander I

1. Cited in Tibor Szamuely, *The Russian Tradition* (London: Secker & Warburg, 1974), 130.

2. Ibid., 131.

3. Based on Y. S. Pivovarov, "M. M. Speransky: Sud'ba reformatora v Rossii" (M. M. Speransky: A reformer's lot in Russia), in *Iz istorii reformatorstva v Rossii* (On the history of reforms in Russia), ed. A. A. Kara-Murza (Moscow: Ross. Otkr. Univ., 1991), 50.

4. Alexander Pushkin, "To Chaadayev," trans. Babette Deutsch, in *The*

Works of Alexander Pushkin, ed. Avrahm Yarmolinsky (New York: Random House, 1936), 51–52.

5. Alexander Pushkin, "Message to Siberia," trans. Alan Myers, in *An Age Ago: A Selection of Nineteenth-Century Russian Poetry* (New York: Penguin Books, 1989), 36.

4. Nicholas I

1. Cited in S. V. Kuleshov and others, *Politicheskaia istoria: Rossia–SSSR–Rossiiskaia Federatsia* (A political history: Russia–USSR–Russian Federation) (Moscow: TERRA, 1996), 1:176.

2. Cited in Tibor Szamuely, *The Russian Tradition* (London: Secker & Warburg, 1974), 135.

3. The term "bureaucratic dictatorship" to refer to the tsarist regime is used by David Christian, *Imperial and Soviet Russia* (London: Macmillan, 1997), 36.

4. *Istoria Rossii v XIX veke* (The history of Russia in the nineteenth century) (St. Petersburg: Izdatel'stvo bratiev Granat, 1907), 1:443.

5. See, in particular, Konstantin Aksakov, "On the Internal State of Russia," in *Russian Intellectual History: An Anthology,* ed. Marc Raeff (New York: Harcourt, Brace & World, 1966), 231–51.

6. See, in particular, Hans Kohn, ed., *The Mind of Modern Russia: Historical and Political Thought of Russia's Great Age* (New York· Harper & Row, 1962), 116–37.

7. Cited in Szamuely, *The Russian Tradition,* 204.

8. Ibid., 48.

9. Cited in Mikhail Iroshnikov and others, *The Sunset of the Romanov Dynasty* (Moscow: TERRA, 1992), 56.

10. Cited in Szamuely, *The Russian Tradition,* 205.

5. Alexander II

1. Dominic Lieven, *Nicholas II: Emperor of All the Russias* (London: Pimlico, 1994), 253–54.

2. Cited in Mikhail Iroshnikov and others, *The Sunset of the Romanov Dynasty* (Moscow: TERRA, 1992), 53–55.

3. Cited in David Christian, *Imperial and Soviet Russia* (London: Macmillan, 1997), 80.

4. Nicholas A. Berdyaev, *Istoki i smysl russkogo kommunizma* (The origin of Russian communism) (Moscow: Nauka, 1990), 51.

6. The Revolutionary Movement

1. S. N. Bulgakov, "Geroism i podvizhnichestvo" (Heroism and selfless devotion), in *Vekhi: Sbornik statey o russkoy intelligentsii* (Milestones: Collected essays on Russian intelligentsia) (1909; reprint, Moscow: Novosti, 1990), 34.

2. S. L. Frank, "Etika nigilisma" (The ethics of nihilism), in *Vekhi,* 175.

3. A. S. Izgoev, "Sotsialism, kul'tura i bolshevism" (Socialism, culture, and Bolshevism), in *Iz glubiny: Sbornik statey o russkoy revoliutsii* (Out of the depths: Collected essays on the Russian revolution) (Moscow: Moscow University Press, 1990), 157.

4. *Vekhi,* 177.

5. Nicholas Chernyshevsky, extracts from *What Is to Be Done? The Mind of Modern Russia: Historical and Political Thought of Russia's Great Age,* ed. Hans Kohn (New York: Harper & Row, 1962), 151.

6. Tibor Szamuely, *The Russian Tradition* (London: Secker & Warburg, 1974), 216.

7. Nikolay Valentinov (N. V. Volsky), *Encounters with Lenin* (London: Oxford University Press, 1968), 63–64.

8. Sergei Nechaev, "The Catechism of the Revolutionary," in *Imperial Russia: A Sourcebook: 1700–1917,* ed. Basil Dmytryshyn (Hinsdale, Ill.: Dryden Press, 1974), 303–4.

7. Appearance of Marxism

1. Karl Marx, *Selected Works* (London: Lawrence and Wishart, 1942), 1:16.

2. Karl Marx and Friedrich Engels, *The Communist Manifesto* (London: Penguin, 1985), 85.

3. Ibid., 85–86.

4. Ibid., 56.

8. The Last Romanovs

1. Alan Wood, *The Origins of the Russian Revolution 1861–1917* (London: Routledge, 1991), 25.

2. Vlas Doroshevich, cited in Mikhail Iroshnikov and others, *The Sunset of the Romanov Dynasty* (Moscow: TERRA, 1992), 115.

3. Nicholas II, cited in Iroshnikov, *Sunset,* 116.

4. P. Shostakovsky, cited in Iroshnikov, *Sunset,* 31.

5. Ibid., 33.

6. R. W. Goldsmith, "The Economic Growth of Tsarist Russia," *Economic Development and Cultural Change* 9 (1960–61): 442.

9. The Birth of Bolshevism

1. Vladimir I. Lenin, "The Proletarian Revolution and the Renegade Kautsky," in *The Lenin Anthology,* ed. Robert C. Tucker (New York: Norton, 1975), 466.

2. Nicholas A. Berdyaev, *Istoki i smysl russkogo kommunizma* (The origin of Russian communism) (Moscow: Nauka, 1990), 102.

3. Vladimir I. Lenin, *What Is to Be Done?* in *Imperial Russia: A Sourcebook: 1700–1917,* ed. Basil Dmytryshyn (Hinsdale, Ill.: Dryden Press, 1974), 371.

4. Ibid., 376.

5. Berdyaev, *Istoki,* 99.

10. The Revolution of 1905–7

1. In contrast to underground revolutionaries, "legal Marxists" questioned classical Marxist sociological and economic doctrines, rejecting revolution in favor of evolution. Most went on to become liberals and, eventually, conservative nationalists and believers in Orthodox Christianity.

2. S. V. Kuleshov and others, *Politicheskaia istoria: Rossia–SSSR–Rossiiskaia Federatsia* (A political history: Russia–USSR–Russian Federation) (Moscow: TERRA, 1996), 1:614.

3. Father Gapon, "Petition to Nicholas II," in *Imperial Russia: A Sourcebook: 1700–1917,* ed. Basil Dmytryshyn (Hinsdale, Ill.: Dryden Press, 1974), 380–81.

4. Kuleshov, *Politicheskaia istoria,* 1:621–22.

5. Ibid., 623.

6. Ibid., 628.

7. Ibid., 633.

11. Russia between Revolutions

1. B. V. Anan'ich, ed., *Vlast'i reformy: Ot samoderzhavnoy k sovetskoy Rossii* (Power and reforms: From autocratic to Soviet Russia) (St. Petersburg: Dmitri Bulanin, 1996), 550.

2. Y. A. Pevzner, *Ekonomicheskoe uchenie Karla Marksa pered sudom dvadthsatogo stoletia* (The twentieth century's verdict on Karl Marx's economic teaching) (Moscow: IMEMO, 1996), 18.

3. D. Shturman, *O vozhdiakh rossiiskogo kommunizma* (The leaders of Russian communism) (Paris: YMCA-PRESS, 1993), 2:212; a *pood* is a Russian weight, about thirty-six pounds avoirdupois.

4. See, for example, G. R. Urban, ed., *Stalinism: Its Impact on Russia and the World* (Aldershot, England: Wildwood House, 1985), 142.

5. "Program of the Socialist Revolutionary Party," in *Imperial Russia: A Sourcebook: 1700–1917,* ed. Basil Dmytryshyn (Hinsdale, Ill.: Dryden Press, 1974), 404.

6. David Christian, *Imperial and Soviet Russia* (London: Macmillan, 1997), 158.

7. "Respublika ili monarkhia" (Republic or monarchy), in *Krest'anskaia Rossia* (Prague, 1923), 54.

8. Max Weber introduced the term "pseudo-constitutionalism" to describe the tsarist political system after October 1905. See his essay "Russia's Transition to Pseudo-constitutionalism," in *The Russian Revolutions* (Cambridge: Polity Press, 1995), 148–240.

9. The idea of the Great War acting as a catalyst for the overthrow of tsarism was powerfully expressed by Lenin in an article written immediately after the fall of tsarism and published in the Bolshevik party newspaper *Pravda* in March 1917: "Apart from an extraordinary acceleration of world history, it was also necessary that history make particularly abrupt turns, in order that at one such turn the filthy and blood-stained cart of the Romanov monarchy should be overturned at *one stroke.* This all-powerful 'stage manager,' this mighty accel-

erator was the imperialist world war." In Vladimir I. Lenin, *Selected Works in Three Volumes* (Moscow: Progress Publishers, 1970), 2:32.

10. Christian, *Imperial and Soviet Russia*, 166.

11. Nicholas V. Riasanovsky, *A History of Russia*, 3d ed. (New York: Oxford University Press, 1977), 505.

12. February and October Revolutions

1. David Christian, *Imperial and Soviet Russia* (London: Macmillan, 1997), 182.

2. Vladimir I. Lenin, "The Military Program of the Proletarian Revolution," in *Selected Works in Three Volumes* (Moscow: Progress Publishers, 1970), 1:770–71.

3. Vladimir I. Lenin, "On the Slogan for a United States of Europe," in *Selected Works,* 1:664–65.

4. Vladimir I. Lenin, "April Theses," cited in Martin McCauley, *Octobrists to Bolsheviks: Imperial Russia 1905–1917* (London: Arnold, 1984), 105–6.

5. Vladimir I. Lenin, "The Bolsheviks Must Assume Power: A Letter to the Central Committee of the RSDLP (Bolsheviks)," in *Selected Works,* 2:378.

6. Richard Pipes, *The Russian Revolution, 1899–1919* (London: Fontana, 1992), xxiv.

7. For a detailed exposition of the Soviet, "liberal," "libertarian," and "revisionist" interpretations, see Edward Acton, *Rethinking the Russian Revolution* (London: Arnold, 1992).

8. Ronald Suny, "Toward a Social History of the October Revolution," *American Historical Review* 88 (1983): 52.

9. George Katkov, *Russia 1917: The February Revolution* (London: Longmans, 1967), 422–23.

10. See B. I. Nikolaevskiy, *Tainye stranitsy istorii* (Secret pages of history) (Moscow: Izd. Guman. Lit., 1995).

11. See, for example, S. V. Kuleshov and others, *Nashe Otechestvo, chast' I* (Our Motherland, part 1) (Moscow: TERRA, 1991), 389.

12. This view is expounded in M. M. Gorinov, A. A. Danilov, and V. P. Dmitrenko, *Istoria Rossii, chast' III: XX vek: Vybor modeley obshchestvennogo razvitia* (A history of Russia, part 3: The twentieth century: Choosing the models of social development) (Moscow: Obshchestvo "Znanie" Rossii, 1994), 21–24.

Conclusion

1. See A. N. Sakharov, "Dinastia Romanovykh kak istoricheskiy fenomen" (The Romanov dynasty as a historical phenomenon), *Nezavisimaia gazeta* (31 December 1997): 14–15.

2. Dominic Lieven, *Nicholas II: Emperor of All the Russias* (London: Pimlico, 1994), 260.

3. S. V. Kuleshov and others, *Nashe Otechestvo, chast' I* (Our Motherland, part 1) (Moscow: TERRA, 1991), 202.

4. B. V. Anan'ich, ed., *Vlast' i reformy: Ot samoderzhavnoy k sovetskoy Rossii* (Power and reforms: From autocratic to Soviet Russia) (St. Petersburg: Dmitri Bulanin, 1996), 8.

Tables and Statistics

1. Based on S. P. Tolstov, ed., *Narody mira* (Peoples of the world) (Moscow: Nauka, 1964), 17; S. V. Kuleshov and others, *Politicheskaia istoria: Rossia–SSSR–Rossiiskaia Federatsia* (A political history: Russia–USSR–Russian Federation) (Moscow: TERRA, 1996), 1:39.

2. Based on V. A. Aleksandrov and others, *Narody yevropeiskoy chasti SSSR* (Peoples of the European part of the USSR) (Moscow: Nauka, 1964), 1:20.

3. Based on ibid., 1:20–21; and J. N. Westwood, *Endurance and Endeavor: Russian History 1812–1986,* 3d ed. (Oxford: Oxford University Press, 1987), 531.

4. Based on Aleksandrov, *Narody yevropeiskoy chasti SSSR,* 1:23; Westwood, *Endurance and Endeavor,* 530.

5. Based on Kuleshov, *Politicheskaia istoria,* 1:39.

6. Adapted from Westwood, *Endurance and Endeavor,* 531.

7. Adapted from Michael Lynch, *Reaction and Revolutions: Russia 1881–1924* (London: Hodder & Stoughton, 1992), 10.

8. Adapted from John Laver, *Russia 1914–1941* (London: Hodder & Stoughton, 1991), 2.

9. Adapted from Lynch, *Reaction and Revolutions,* 23.

10. Based on D. Shturman, *O vozhdiakh rossiiskogo kommunizma* (The leaders of Russian communism) (Paris: YMCA-PRESS, 1993), 2:212.

11. Based on M. M. Shumilov, ed., *Istoria Rossii IX–XX vv.* (The history of Russia from the ninth to the twentieth century), 3d ed. (St. Petersburg: Obrazovanie-Kul'tura, 1995), 342.

12. Based on L. B. Yakover, *Posobie po istorii otechestva* (Russian history textbook) (Moscow: Mosk. Pedag. Gos. Univ., 1995), 71.

13. Based on ibid., 99.

Chronology

9th century	Emergence of Kievan Rus
988	Kievan Rus adopts Christianity as its state religion
1237	Mongol invasion
1480	End of Mongol yoke
1497	Law Code for the first time limits the peasant's freedom of movement from one squire to another
1598–1613	"Time of Troubles": period of dynastic crisis
1613	Romanov dynasty established
1649	Tsar Alexis's Law Code marks culmination of the process of enserfment of the peasant
1682–1725	Reign of Peter I
1695–96	Azov military campaign against the Crimean Tartars and the Turks
1697–98	Peter's grand tour of the West
1700–21	Northern War against Sweden
1711	Governing Senate established
1714	Peter I's decree confers hereditary status on manors of service nobility
1721	Peter assumes title of emperor
1722	Table of Ranks introduced
1762	Compulsory service for the nobility abolished
1762–96	Reign of Catherine the Great
1767	Convocation of Legislative Commission
1773	Pugachev revolt
1785	Charter of the Nobility codifies exclusive privileges of landowning gentry
1790	Publication of A. Radishchev's *Journey from St. Petersburg to Moscow*

1878–81	Wave of assassinations staged by terrorist-revolutionaries
1881	Assassination of Alexander II by members of the "People's Will"
	Loris-Melikov's plan of constitutional reform withdrawn
1881–94	Reign of Alexander III
1883	"Emancipation of Labor," first Russian Marxist group, led by G. Plekhanov, set up in Switzerland
1887	Alexander Ulianov, Lenin's elder brother, is executed for his part in attempt on the life of Alexander III
1891–92	Mass hunger
1892–1903	Sergei Witte minister of finance
1894–1917	Reign of Nicholas II
1895	Marxist groups of St. Petersburg unite into "League of Struggle for the Emancipation of the Working Class" under leadership of Lenin and Martov
1896	Khodynka tragedy mars Nicholas II's coronation celebrations
1898	Russian Social-Democratic Labor Party holds its first congress in Minsk
1901	New illegal neo-Narodnik organization, Socialist-Revolutionary Party, established
1902	Lenin produces work on party organization *What Is to Be Done?*
1903	Russian Social-Democratic Labor Party splits into Bolshevik and Menshevik wings
	Left-wing liberals set up their illegal organization, "Union of Liberation"
	Right-wing liberals set up "Union of Zemstvo Constitutionalists"
1904–5	Russo-Japanese War
1905–7	First Russian Revolution
1905	9 January: Bloody Sunday
	May: first Soviet of Workers' Deputies set up in Ivanovo-Voznesensk to coordinate strike action in the town
	October: general strike led by St. Petersburg Soviet
	17 October: Tsar's October Manifesto grants basic civil and political rights and elected legislative assembly
	October: Left-wing liberals set up the Party of Constitutional Democrats (Kadets)

	December: right-wing liberals set up their party, "Union of 17 October"
	Moscow workers' uprising suppressed
1906–11	Peter Stolypin chairman of Council of Ministers
1906	April: constitutional experiment begins with elections to First Duma
	November: Stolypin introduces land reform by decree
1911	Assassination of Stolypin
1912	Shooting of striking miners at Lena goldfields in eastern Siberia
1914	July: Russia enters the First World War
	Russia's capital renamed Petrograd
1915	Nicholas II assumes command of the army
	"Progressive Bloc" of liberal and moderate conservative groupings is formed in Fourth Duma
1916	Assassination of Grigory Rasputin
1917	February Revolution leads to abdication of Nicholas II and collapse of autocracy. Provisional Government assumes official power in Russia. Simultaneously, Petrograd Soviet of Workers' and Soldiers' Deputies is established by socialist intellectuals
	April: Lenin arrives in Russia from exile and unveils his plan of proletarian revolution in the April Theses
	June: first All-Russian Congress of Soviets in Petrograd
	4 July: unsuccessful Bolshevik uprising in Petrograd. Provisional Government brings charges against Lenin and other Bolshevik leaders
	August: General Kornilov launches an unsuccessful military coup
	September: Bolsheviks gain majority in Petrograd Soviet
	25–26 October: Bolshevik forces stage a coup in Petrograd and arrest ministers of Provisional Government
	26 October: Second All-Russian Congress of Soviets of Workers' and Soldiers' Deputies approves formation of a Bolshevik government
1918	March: Russian Social-Democratic Labor Party (Bolsheviks) renamed Russian Communist Party
	July: Nicholas II with other members of royal family murdered at Ekaterinburg in Urals on Bolshevik orders

Index

absolute government, 46. *See also* absolutism
absolutism: Catherine the Great and, 36–37, 45, 46; defined, 23; enlightened, 37; the French Revolution's undercutting of, 202; the paradoxes of the empire and, 209–12; the Petrine Reform and, 23–27
Academy of Sciences, the, 26
administration: pre-Petrine systems of, 11–12; reforms of, under Alexander II, 78–79. *See also* bureaucracy
agriculture: during Catherine's reign, 41–42; comparison of pre-Petrine Russian and Western European, 4–5; early twentieth-century capitalism and, 120–21; during the First World War, 167; reforms in, prior to the First World War, 158
Aksakov, Konstantin, 32, 61
Alexander I: death of, 210; the Decembrists and, 53–57; the defeat of Napoleon and, 71; early years of, 49–53; emancipation of the Baltic serfs by, 60; limitations of reforms by, 209, 210; modernization and, xii; Radishchev and, 49; Speransky and, 50–51; weakness of rule of, 57
Alexander II: administrative reform of, 78–79; and competition with the West, 71–72; death of, 98, 210; educational reforms and, 80; the Great Debate and, 64; the judiciary and, 161; legal reform and, 79–80; limitations of reforms of, 210; Loris-Melikov's scheme and, 83; military reforms and, 80; modernization and, xii; Nicholas II and, 113; overall assessment of reforms of, 83, 214; peasant emancipation and, 73–78; the People's Will group and, 97–98; and the policies of his successors, 109; on reform from above, 27; relaxation of censorship under, 81
Alexander III: characteristics of the reign of, 109–11; industrialization and, 114–16; the judiciary and, 161; Russification and, 207; "self-imprisonment" of, 210
Alexandra, Empress, 168, 171
Alexei (son of Nicholas II), 168
Alexis (Tsar), 3, 21, 34
All-Russian Congress of Soviets of Workers' and Soldiers' Deputies, 177, 185, 190
All-Russian Union of Zemstvos and Cities, 166, 173
All-Russian Union of Zemstvos for the Relief of the Sick and Wounded, 166

All-Union Communist Party, 132. *See also* Bolshevik Party; Bolshevism; Communist Party
anarchism, 87, 93
anti-bourgeois mentality of the intelligentsia, 87
anti-religiousness, 88
anti-Semitism, 111, 147, 155–56, 196
April Theses (Lenin), 183–85
arbitrary government, 46
Article 87, 153, 154
Assembly of Russian Factory Workers of St. Petersburg, 143
Assembly of the Land, 62
atheism, 88
autocracy: the Great Debate on, 63–64; Nicholas I and, 61; Nicholas II's retention of, after the Revolution of 1905–7, 153; opposition to, on the eve of the Revolution of 1905–7, 135–39; the paradoxes of the empire and, 202–3, 209–12; in pre-Petrine Russia, 14; Slavophiles on, 62; Speransky on, 50–52; the theory of the people's, 110
Azov campaign, 18

Bakunin, Michael, 92, 93, 95, 96
banks, 118
barshchina, 42
Basil III, 10
Batu (grandson of Genghis Khan), 2
Belinsky, Vissarion, 32, 36, 63
The Bell (newspaper), 65
Berdyaev, Nicholas, 32, 33, 77–78, 104, 125, 129
Black Hundreds, 156
Black Repartition group, 96, 103
Bloody Sunday massacre, 142–43, 148, 212
Bobrikov, Nikolay, 111
Bogoslovsky, Michael, 46
Bolsheviks: debates about the inevitability of the takeover by, 190–200; defeatism and, 172, 173; the First World War and, 167, 172, 195–96; Jews and, 197; Lenin's centrality for, 200; Lenin's ideas on the formation of the party of, 127–29; liberal school of interpretation and, 192–93; Menshevism and, 130–32; Nechaev and, 95; Peter the Great and, 33; the Petrograd Soviet and, 176; reasons for takeover by, 178–90, 197; the Revolution of 1905–7 and, 135–36; Tkachev and, 94; on a "Union of Unions," 138
borders, natural, 6–7

Soviets of Workers' Deputies, 146, 184
The Spark (newspaper), 122
Speransky, Michael, 50–53, 57, 211, 209, 216
The Spirit of the Laws (Montesquieu), 38
Stalin, Joseph: and the great-power status of the Soviet Union, 72; industrialization and, 157, 158; on "Marxism-Leninism," 134; Nicholas II's abdication and, 180; peasants' traditions of collectivization and, 5; the Provisional Government and, 181
State Council, the, 52, 82–83, 153
Stolypin, Peter, 215; the communes and, 203, 216; optimistic view of work of, 164; precariousness of the position of, 211; reforms of, 159–62; the Revolution of 1905–7 and, 152
strikes, 141, 145–49, 162–63
Struve, Peter, 104, 137
Sverdlov, Yakov, 197
syndicates, 117
Szamuely, Tibor, 29, 41, 68, 91

Table of Ranks, 25–26, 27, 59, 85
"The Tasks of the Proletariat in the Present Revolution," 183
taxation, 21, 42, 116
technology, 29–30
temporary dictatorship, 55
territorial expansion of the empire, 3–4
terrorism, 89, 96–99, 199
Third Section of the Imperial Chancellery, 58, 81
"Time of Troubles," 3
Tkachev, Peter, 92, 93–94, 127
trade unionism, 127, 138–39
Trans-Siberian Railway, 115, 157
Treaty of Nystadt, 19
Trotsky, Lev: the Jewish conspiracy theory and, 197; Lenin and, 189; after the Revolution of 1905–7, 151; the St. Petersburg Soviet and, 146; skills of, 197; theory of the unfinished revolution and, 194
Trubestkoy, Nicholas, 32–33
Trudovik (Labor) Group, 153, 172
tsarism: Orthodox Christianity and, 8; pre-Petrine power of, 14–15; reasons for the collapse of, 209–12. *See also* absolutism; autocracy; *and the names of specific tsars*

Ulianov, Vladimir. *See* Lenin, Vladimir
unfinished revolution theory, 194
Union of Liberation, 138, 139

Union of Salvation, 54–56
Union of 17 October. *See* Octobrists
Union of the Russian People, 155–56
Union of Unions, 138–39
Union of Zemstvo Constitutionalists, 138
utilitarian morality, 89
Utopianism, 20

vanguard of the proletariat, 128
village communes: agricultural methods and, 203; Chernyshevsky on, 90; early twentieth-century capitalism and, 120; Herzen and, 66–69; industrialization and, 116; Marx and Engels on, 107; the Narodniks on, 92; paradoxes of the government's policies toward, 215–16; powers of, following the emancipation, 76; pre-Petrine peasants and, 5; Stolypin and, 160–62, 203
Voloshin, Maximilian, 33
Voltaire, 37

War Industries Committee, 166, 173
Weber, Max, 229n.9
West, the. *See* Europeanization; Westernization
Westernization: early Marxists on, 106; the Great Debate and, 60–64; Herzen on, 65. *See also* industrialization; modernization; Reform, the Petrine
Westernizers, the, 31–32, 33, 62–63, 64
What Is to Be Done (Chernyshevsky), 90–92
What Is to Be Done (Lenin), 127, 129, 130
Witte, Sergei: background of, 115; economic modernization and, 116; limitations on reforms proposed by, 214–15; the October Strike and, 147; precariousness of the position of, 211; Revolution of 1905–7 and, 152; Russo-Japanese War and, 141
working class. *See* proletariat
World War I. *See* First World War

Yusupov, Felix, 169

Zarudny, S., 75
zemsky sobor, 62
zemstvos: administrative reform and, 78–79; Alexander III and, 109; First World War and, 166; Nicholas II and, 113; Stolypin's reforms and, 161. *See also* gentry (or *zemstvo*) liberalism
Zhukovsky, Vasili, 73
Zimmerwald conference, 172
Zinoviev, Grigori, 180, 188, 197
Zionism, 111